Viable populations for conservation

VIABLE POPULATIONS

FOR CONSERVATION

EDITED BY MICHAEL E. SOULÉ

School of Natural Resources, University of Michigan

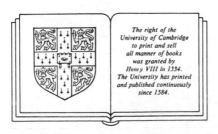

The right of the
University of Cambridge
to print and sell
all manner of books
was granted by
Henry VIII in 1534.
The University has printed
and published continuously
since 1584.

CAMBRIDGE UNIVERSITY PRESS

Cambridge

New York   Port Chester   Melbourne   Sydney

Published by the Press Syndicate of the University of Cambridge
The Pitt Building, Trumpington Street, Cambridge CB2 1RP
40 West 20th Street, New York, NY 10011, USA
10 Stamford Road, Oakleigh, Melbourne 3166, Australia

First published 1987
Reprinted 1988, 1989, 1990

Printed in Great Britain at the University Press, Cambridge

British Library cataloguing in publication data
Viable populations for conservation.
1. Nature conservation
I. Soulé, Michael E.
639.9   QH75

Library of Congress cataloguing in publication data
Viable populations for conservation.
Includes index.
1. Population biology.   2. Wildlife conservation.
3. Extinction (Biology)   I. Soulé, Michael E.
QH352.V53 1987   574.5'248   86-33438

ISBN 0 521 33390 3 hardback
ISBN 0 521 33657 0 paperback

For Paul R. Ehrlich, pioneer and prophet

Contents

Contents

Contributors

Richard Baker
Department of Environmental Studies
Wickson Hall
University of California at Davis
Davis, CA 95616

George F. Barrowclough
Department of Ornithology
American Museum of Natural History
New York, NY 10024

Gary E. Belovsky
School of Natural Resources
Dana Building
University of Michigan
Ann Arbor, MI 48109-1115

P. J. Brockwell
Department of Statistics
Colorado State University
Fort Collins, CO 80521

Peter F. Brussard
Department of Biology
Montana State University
Bozeman, MT 59717

Warren J. Ewens
Department of Biology
University of Pennsylvania
Philadelphia, PA 19104

J. M. Gani
Department of Statistics
University of Kentucky
Lexington, KT 40506

Michael E. Gilpin
Department of Biology (C-016)
University of California at San Diego
La Jolla, CA 92093

Daniel Goodman
Department of Biology
Montana State University
Bozeman, MT 59717

Russell Lande
Department of Biology
University of Chicago
Chicago, IL 60637

Lynn A. Maguire
School of Forestry and Environmental Studies
Duke University
Durham, NC 27706

S. I. Resnick
Department of Statistics
Colorado State University
Fort Collins, CO 80521

Hal Salwasser
USDA Forest Service
P.O. Box 2417
Washington, DC 20013

Christine Schonewald-Cox
Department of Environmental Studies
Wickson Hall
University of California at Davis
Davis, CA 95616

Ulysses S. Seal
VA Medical Center
54th St and 48th Ave South
Minneapolis, MN 55417

Mark Shaffer
1937A Villa Ridge Drive
Reston, VA 22090

Michael E. Soulé
School of Natural Resources
University of Michigan
Ann Arbor, MI 48109-1115

Preface

As the biosphere retreats in the face of physically superior forces, some conservation biologists are tempted to employ emotive rhetoric in the defense of ecological and species diversity, believing that such utterances will inspire others to join in their cause. Such a tactic may not be appropriate in a volume directed at managers and scholars, so let me only say that the subject of this book is central to conservation and conservation biology. It is also distinguished by its intellectual challenge.

The 'viable population problem' is very young. As documented in Chapter 1, it is only in the last decade or so that its importance has become recognized and its complexity appreciated. Herein we describe the significant advances that have already occurred. Our purpose is to spur increased interest in this aspect of conservation biology.

The logic of this volume is accretionary. Chapter 1 describes the viable population issue, examines its history, and warns of its complexity. In Chapter 2, Daniel Goodman provides the first of several major elements – a theory of persistence based on population dynamics, especially the interaction of environmental variability and the rate of population growth. He shows how it is possible to directly estimate the likelihood of persistence. Some of his conclusions support earlier work of Roughgarden (1979) and Leigh (1981) (references in Chapter 3). In Chapter 2, Gary Belovsky tests the power of Goodman's model with actual data. He also uses established allometric relations to predict the sizes of viable populations for ecological and body size categories of mammals, producing some startling predictions.

In Chapter 3, Ewens, Brockwell, Gani, and Resnick examine the effect of some catastrophe models on the loss of genetic variation and on the probability of persistence. Following this, Shaffer (Chapter 4) synthesizes the results of Goodman, Belovsky, and Ewens, *et al.*, and writes about the relative importance of three different kinds of chance events: demographic, environmental, and catastrophic.

In Chapter 6, Lande and Barrowclough review the genetic components of viability analysis and discuss the factors that enter into the calculation of effective population size. Gilpin (Chapter 7) elaborates on the issue of effective population size at the level of the metapopulation. He also explains the behavior of a metapopulation model that can produce interesting aggregations of patch populations.

What are our options when extinction in nature appears inevitable, or when there is insufficient space available *in situ* for a self-sustaining viable population? In Chapter 8, Maguire, Seal, and Brussard show how decision analysis can be used to compare potential management interventions, using the Sumatran rhinoceros as an example.

In many situations, success depends on cooperation among different governmental and non-governmental agencies and organizations. In Chapter 9, Salwasser, Schonewald-Cox and Baker review this issue and illustrate it with case histories and scenarios.

The final chapter is both retrospective and prospective. A synthesis is attempted, several caveats and qualifications are noted, and the possibility of a general, integrated theory of viability analysis is discussed, and directions for further research are suggested.

The book is in part the result of a workshop held at the University of Michigan in October 1984. The chapters were written in 1985 and 1986. Sponsors of the workshop included the United States Department of Agriculture Forest Service, the United States Department of Interior Fish and Wildlife Service, the New York Zoological Society, the Griffin Foundation, and the National Wildlife Federation.

I wish to personally thank my fellow authors, and my colleagues and students at the University of Michigan, especially Kathy Rude for her organizational assistance. This book would have been impossible without the encouragement and collaboration of David Hales and the support of James Crowfoot. In addition, Bill Conway, Tom Lovejoy, Hal Salwasser, and Chris Servheen have provided moral support and assistance in funding. Bruce Wilcox, Jim Brown, and Egburt Leigh III contributed freely of their editorial assistance and advice. Julie Wick contributed her word-processing skills.

1

Introduction

MICHAEL E. SOULÉ
School of Natural Resources, University of Michigan, Ann Arbor, MI 48109-1115

And of every living thing of all flesh, two of every sort shalt thou bring into the ark. Genesis

Definition: How much is enough?

Given biblical precedence, it is not surprising that for millennia, a pair (male and female) has been deemed sufficient to initiate, if not perpetuate, a population. In fact, there is more than scriptural authority behind this myth. With luck, two can indeed be a sufficient number of founders.

What is luck? Without going into theories of randomness and probability, luck implies a fortunate or unusual circumstance leading to a good result. The result of interest in this book is the survival of a population in a state that maintains its vigor and its potential for evolutionary adaptation. Such a population is a viable population. Legend does not question Noah's success with each of his multitudinous experiments. He must have been very lucky indeed. He also had some advantages over us, not the least of which was a fresh, well-watered planet.

The problem that we address in this book is 'How much is enough?'. Put more concretely, it is: What are the minimum* conditions for the long-term† persistence and adaptation of a species or population in a given place? This is one of the most difficult and challenging intellectual problems in conservation biology. Arguably, it is the quintessential issue

---

* See the following section for a discussion of the 'minimum' issue.

† We are not concerned here with short-term survival criteria or rules such as 'the rule of 50' discussed in Frankel and Soulé (1981, Chapter 6). Such short-term guidelines apply only to captive breeding and similar 'holding operations,' although they have often been misapplied to populations in nature. For example, the short-term rule of 50 does not protect the population against the loss of most of its genetic variation (Franklin, 1980; Soulé, 1980).

in population biology, because it requires a prediction based on a synthesis of all the biotic and abiotic factors in the spatial-temporal continuum.

Returning to the definition, we must define 'long-term persistence,' and 'adaptation.' The former phrase means the capacity of the group to maintain itself without significant demographic or genetic manipulation for the foreseeable ecological future (usually centuries) with a certain, agreed on, degree of certitude, say 95%. The probabilistic qualification is necessary (Shaffer, Chapter 5), because it would be impossible to guarantee absolutely the survival of a group. The qualifying phrase 'without significant demographic or genetic manipulation' is meant to imply that we are concerned with the ability of populations to maintain themselves in nature, given sufficient habitat and other elements of benign neglect, including freedom from excessive harvesting.

The term 'adaptation' implies that the group maintains a normal level of immediate fitness (individual vigor, fertility, fecundity), and has sufficient genetic variation to adapt by natural selection to changing environmental conditions within the predicted range of frequency and amplitude of disturbance and change.

If the entire history of our planet were condensed into one hour, it is only in the last few fractions of a second that mankind and its technology has spread across the globe – with devastating results for other species. For this reason, viability is now a *cause célèbre*. The last time a similar degree of disturbance occurred (during the Pleistocene glaciations), the pace of change was slow enough for vegetation belts to be compressed towards the equator or to shift in accordance with the changing distribution of rainfall. Such shifts are now impossible because of the geographic distribution of anthropogenic habitat destruction, and because the rate of change and destruction today is measured in years and decades rather than in centuries and millennia. Therefore, termination rates are now expected to be much greater.

Major extinctions have occurred before, and many species did go extinct in the Pleistocene. The difference is that now it is our species that is responsible, and countermeasures are therefore feasible. Presumably, glacial and interglacial humans could have prevented the Pleistocene extinctions if they had had our values, our knowledge of genetics, ecology, biogeography, and our level of technology.

History of the viable population concept
The following sketch of the history of the population viability idea is incomplete and assuredly biased. I must leave it to others to correct the account. My personal view is that the subject of population viability

has a very short history, although its roots attenuate to a distant past. As described below, I distinguish *population* viability from *system* viability, although the two subjects are interdependent in most cases.

Conservationists (including preservationists) wish to maintain the health and diversity of natural systems – ecosystems, communities, habitats, as well as species. Until recently, however, most of the emphasis has been on the protection of whole systems. The favored technique, since the early decades of this century, has been the setting aside of areas for this purpose. The management of such 'set asides' is becoming increasingly difficult and sophisticated, in part because of the growing numbers of humans.

These difficulties (see Soulé, 1986a for reviews) have led biologists to ask 'What are the (minimum) conditions for the viability of natural systems?' The quest for answers has generally followed two somewhat independent tracks. First, community ecologists have focused on minimum areas (e.g., Moore, 1962; Lovejoy, 1980) for system viability, with seminal contributions from island biogeography (Diamond, 1975; Terborgh, 1975; see Wilcox, 1980). Population biologists have focused on the minimum population sizes (e.g., Franklin, 1980; Frankel and Soulé, 1981; Shaffer, 1981) or densities (e.g., Hubbell and Foster, 1986) for target species. These two tracks are now coming together because of the realization that often the most pragmatic way to define system viability is to do so in terms of the viability of critical or keystone species within the system (Frankel and Soulé, 1981; Shaffer, 1981; Wilcox and Murphy, 1985; Soulé and Simberloff, 1986). This is not to say that other, more holistic criteria, such as preserving entire watersheds, are not equally or more important in some circumstances.

During the last few decades, there has been an exponential increase in the estimates of population sizes that ensure viability. One reason for this is the changing interpretation of the term 'viability.' In the early days it meant short-term persistence in a constant environment, or resilience. In other words, the time scale of concern (Frankel and Soulé, 1981) was short. Since 1980, the time scale has increased because biologists started to consider threats such as epidemics, catastrophes, and genetic drift.

The first systematic attacks on the problem considered only *population dynamics*, or, more strictly, the birth-and-death branching process (Feller, 1939, MacArthur, 1972; MacArthur and Wilson, 1967; Richter-Dyn and Goel, 1972). As more factors have been introduced into the analysis, the estimates have increased. These factors are *environmental variation* (randomness, stochasticity) (Leigh, 1981; Ginzburg, *et al.*, 1982; Shaffer, 1983; Goodman, Chapter 2; Belovsky, Chapter 3), *genetics* (Frankel, 1974; Franklin, 1980; Soulé, 1980; Frankel and Soulé, 1981; Lande and

Barrowclough, Chapter 6), *catastrophe* (Shaffer, 1981; Ewens *et al.*, Chapter 4), and *metapopulation structure* and *fragmentation* (Shaffer, 1985; Gilpin, Chapter 7).

The preceding paragraph might give the impression that these factors interact in a simple, additive fashion, an impression laid to rest by Shaffer (1981) who encouraged an overall systems approach to the problem, emphasizing the interaction of factors, and the probabilistic nature of viability estimates. This theme was picked up by Schonewald-Cox (1983), who tabulated degrees of risk associated with different population levels. More recently Gilpin and Soulé (1986) portray perturbed populations as a system of interacting extinction vortices that can exacerbate themselves and each other by positive feedback loops.

The moral of this tale is that the closer we approach reality, the more complex the problem appears. This should come as no surprise.

Minimum viable populations

Until now, I have avoided using the term 'minimum viable population' or MVP, even though the term and acronym are in common use in conservation biology. Indeed, many of the chapters in this book use the term. Nonetheless, it is controversial. Some conservationists argue that the term is tactically self-defeating and ethically offensive. Their reasoning is that the job of conservation biologists should be to recommend or provide for more than just the minimum number or distribution of a species. Just as a compassionate physician ought to prescribe the optimum conditions for health, they would say, a conservation biologist should avoid a garrison mentality. They should prescribe to managers and policy makers the conditions for robust and bountiful populations.

The dilemma is that such recommendations would be swept aside as impossibly idealistic. For example, say that each nation has a national policy to maintain viable populations of all native vertebrate predators. Now consider the timber wolf (*Canis lupus*). Some would say that an optimum population of the wolf might be its pre-human or pre-agricultural density and range, including the places where Moscow, Oslo, and Chicago now exist. This definition of 'optimum' would obviously expose conservationists to ridicule. Any other definition of 'optimum' would be arbitrary.

But the underlying point is important. It is that MVP estimates should include built-in margins of safety. That is, MVPs should, in a sense, be 'bountiful.' This is already inherent in the definition of MVP in the preceding section – one simply adjusts the level of risk (probability of persistence) to suit society's requirements, including one's definition of bountiful. For example, certain groups in society might be content with a 50% probability of persistence for 100 years, while other groups would settle for nothing less than a 99% probability of persistence for 1000 years.

Some people have suggested that we retain the term MVP, but change its meaning from 'minimum viable population' to 'managing for viable populations.' Although no one can dictate such conventions, my preference is to retain the original, more precise meaning.

As discussed elsewhere (Gilpin and Soulé, 1986) an MVP can be thought of as a set of estimates that are the product of a systematic process for estimating species-, location-, and time-specific criteria for persistence; the process itself is referred to as population vulnerability (or viability) analysis, PVA. But whatever jargon we choose to adopt, the point is that *there is no single value or 'magic number' that has universal validity*. Not only is each situation unique, but the acceptable level of risk determines the numbers, densities, and distribution in space of the MVP (Schonewald-Cox, 1983).

On the other hand, there are some components of viability analysis that establish relatively fixed floors below which MVPs should not drop. Genetic criteria, particularly, may yield such thresholds (Franklin, 1980; Soulé, 1980; Lande and Barrowclough, Chapter 6). It is a grave mistake, however, to substitute such relatively 'hard' components of viability analysis for the MVP itself. This is discussed further in Chapter 10.

Issues of scale and dimensionality

The viable population problem involves several kinds of scale, and it is essential to consider the kinds and degrees of scalar phenomena that affect a particular viability analysis. These scale phenomena include the range (areal extent) of the species, and the patchiness/uniformity of its distribution in space. A related issue is the temporal dynamics (rate of turnover) of the patchiness. These issues come to light when examining the meaning of 'population,' because scale phenomena are related to population structure and dynamics.

'Population' means different things to different people. To the non-biologist it means the people in a certain place or in the whole world. Biologists usually use the term to mean the individuals of a particular species in a particular group or in a definable place. Thus we may speak of the world's population of sperm whales (*Physeter catodon*), or a particular patch of *Delphinium barbeyi* in a particular meadow in the Rocky Mountains. Michael Gilpin (Chapter 7) illustrates this diversity of population structure in his discussion of patchiness and metapopulations.

In the case of certain endangered species, one patch may comprise the entire species, and the extinction of such a patch is then the extinction of the species. In most cases, however, managers will not be dealing with the last remaining patch or subpopulation, but rather with one of several populations or with a group that is thinly dispersed over a large area (such as many predators).

Therefore, a population may be a very real, functional group of individuals (as with a herd of ungulates, a nesting colony of geese, or a pack of wolves), or it may be a completely arbitrary designation (motivated by administrative regulations), such as the peregrine falcons (*Falco peregrinus*) that reside in a particular national park, or the sperm whales that happen to be within 200 miles of the coast of Argentina on January 17.

The biologist/manager must be mindful of these distinctions throughout the course of a viability analysis. One of the pitfalls of viability analysis is confusion about the population size of a particular group being managed, and the ultimate viability of the 'population' to which it belongs. For example, the wolves in the Appennini Mountains of Italy, and grizzly bears (*Ursus arctos horribilis*) in and around Yellowstone National Park, may never be viable if considered in isolation from conspecific groups in other places. On the other hand, such isolated groups may be important for the viability of the species as a whole. But even if they are not essential for the health of the species, they may still be 'viable,' if they are managed as part of the species as a whole, assuming that natural or assisted movement of individuals between groups (and other management interventions) is possible.

The consideration of this kind of viability, that of component groups, raises other questions. For example, some component populations are more critical than others. The Canadian grizzly population, which numbers in the thousands, is more critical, for example, than is the US population, which numbers in the low hundreds (Gilpin, Chapter 7). On the other hand, the viability of a species may sometimes depend on the viability of a relatively small subgroup that occupies a transitional isthmus. This may be the situation with some of the Appalachian groups of black bear (*Ursus americanus*); if one of the linking populations disappears, the entire population could be at risk.

Managers are often faced with the situation of managing a component population of a large vertebrate or a migratory species. In such cases viability may depend on joint, cooperative actions of two or more jurisdictions (Salwasser *et al.*, Chapter 9): no single jurisdiction can contain a population that is large enough to be viable in the sense defined above. At the same time, each subpopulation must be managed so as to benefit the entire population, and so as not to cause problems for the other jurisdictions.

Another related issue is the rate of turnover (extinction and recoloniz-ation) of populations in patches of habitat. This is because the turnover rate determines whether one is going to analyze and manage single populations, with unbroken genetic and temporal continuity, or whether one is dealing with a dynamic metapopulation structure in which the individual subpopulations (patch populations) come and go in ecological time (decades or less). Where persistence times are relatively long, the genetics and dynamics of the target population are the paramount concern, along with, perhaps, the possible interchange of individuals and genetic material between these relatively stable entities.

In the latter (turnover) case, however, it would be folly to bet heavily on the viability of individual patch populations, because each of these has a high probability of extinction. Rather, one's focus shifts upward in the spatial-temporal hierarchy to the metapopulation – the paramount con-cern is the persistence of the unit or set of populations, which depends on the rates of extinction and colonization of patches (Ewens *et al.*, Chap-ter 4, and Gilpin, Chapter 7).

There are some obvious, if rough, indicators of a species' position on this turnover continuum. These indicators are morphological or life history traits that correlate with persistence in absolute time (Belovsky, Chapter 3). Among them are body size, age at first reproduction, birth interval (Andy Dobson, pers. comm.), and susceptibility to catastrophe. At the high turnover end of the spectrum are small, short-lived or annual species. At the low turnover end are large-bodied, long-lived species. Subpopulations of the latter kind of species, e.g., redwoods (*Sequoia*), probably have a natural turnover rate that is geological in temporal scale.

Viability is not the only issue

Just because we have put together a whole book on the subject of population viability should not lead anyone to the conclusion that we believe that viability analysis is the beginning and end of conservation and conservation biology. By analogy, a book on electro-magnetism admits the existence of other forces. There are other issues and problems in conservation biology that are just as challenging and important (Soulé, 1986b).

In most cases, population viability will be seen in a larger ecological context. Viability, in the strict sense, will be impossible for some popu-lations in certain situations, but wise management may still be able to insure the persistence of a relatively 'natural' community or system. Probably the majority of nature reserves in the world are too small to contain more than a few family groups of primates or herds of large ungulates. Such tiny groups in vest pocket reserves may contribute virtually nothing to the viability of the species as a whole, but their survival may be important , nonetheless, for ecological and social reasons, including the maintenance of certain successional habitats, and the educational experiences that such animals afford visitors. When such groups die out, therefore, they should simply be replaced from whatever source is available.

Purists might object that this kind of management is 'unnatural,' but this argument lacks force in today's world. (An implied norm behind this criticism is the existence of a natural law that forbids the artificial maintenance of community and ecological structure where anthropogenic factors have led to the imminent extinction of some species within the system.) The subject of such difficult or 'hopeless' situations is dealt with in Chapters 8 and 10.

Candidates for viability analysis

Earlier in this chapter I mentioned that viability analysis of critical or keystone species may be an efficient way to begin to cope with the issue of whole system viability (Soulé and Simberloff, 1985). This may appear to be an overly naive approach to the problem of defining the minimum viable size of nature reserves, but it may be the most practical. We cannot ignore the simple fact that no methodology has been proposed that permits us to determine the minimum areas of reserves with reference only to ecological or system processes. Other guidelines, such as 'protect entire watersheds' are too vague to be of much use in areas with too little or too much topographic relief.

As ecologists, we may be reluctant to place the responsibility for the viability of hundreds or thousands of species – an entire ecosystem – on the shoulders of just a handful of 'indicator' or keystone species. It seems too simple, too non-ecological. But there do not appear to be good alternatives.

On the other hand, one of the oldest ecological principles is Liebig's Law of the Minimum – the limiting factor for system viability is the one in shortest supply. In a very real sense, keystone species are often the critical limiting factors in systems (Gilbert, 1980; Terborgh, 1986). Therefore, the MVP approach to system viability is more 'ecological' than it may appear at first sight. At the very least it is a convenient, identifiable handle to a problem that has been intractable for too long.

Implicit in much of the preceding discussion are some of the rules for choosing the candidates for viability analysis. I shall end this chapter by listing some of the obvious ones:

(1) species whose activities create critical habitat for several other species;
(2) mutualist species whose behaviors enhance the fitness (e.g., reproduction, dispersal) of other species;
(3) predatory or parasitic species that regulate the populations of other species, and whose absence would ultimately lead to a decrease in species diversity;
(4) species that have spiritual, aesthetic, recreational, or economic value to humans;
(5) rare or endangered species.

Note that the origins of these rules are diverse. All of them rest on the normative axiom that diversity is good (Soulé, 1985), although the first three rules depend on conventional ecological knowledge. The basis of the fourth rule is at least partly instrumentalist – nature is a valuable source of commodities and experiences, although spiritual and aesthetic uses of nature are often non-consumptive and unselfish. The last rule is fundamentally ethical, because it implies that other species have intrinsic value.

References

Diamond, J. 1975. The island dilemma: Lessons of modern biogeographic studies for the design of natural reserves. *Biol. Conserv.* **7**: 129–46.

Feller, W. 1939. Die Grundlagen der Volterraschen Theorie des Kampfes ums dasein in wahrscheinlichkeitstheoretischer Behandlung. *Acta Biotheoretica* **5**: 11–40.

Frankel, O. H. 1974. Genetic conservation: our evolutionary responsibility. *Genetics* **78**: 53–65.

Frankel, O. H. and Soulé, M. E. 1981. *Conservation and Evolution*. Cambridge University Press, Cambridge.

Franklin, I. A. 1980. Evolutionary change in small populations. Pp. 135–49 *in* M. E. Soulé and B. A. Wilcox (eds.) *Conservation Biology: An Evolutionary-Ecological Perspective*. Sinauer Associates, Sunderland, Mass.

Gilbert, L. E. 1980. Food web organization and the conservation of Neotropical diversity. Pp. 11–13 *in* M. E. Soulé and B. A. Wilcox (eds.) *Conservation Biology: An Evolutionary-Ecological Perspective*. Sinauer Associates, Sunderland, Mass.

Gilpin, M. E. and Soulé, M. E. 1986. Minimum Viable Populations: the processes of species extinctions. Pp. 13–34 *in* M. E. Soulé (ed.) *Conservation Biology: The Science of Scarcity and Diversity*. Sinauer Associates, Sunderland, Mass.

Ginzburg, L., Slobodkin, L. B., Johnson, K., and Bindman, A. G. 1982. Quasiextinction probabilities as a measure of impact on population growth. *Risk Analysis* **2**: 171–81.

Hubbell, S. P. and Foster, R. B. 1986. Commonness and rarity in a Neotropical forest. Pp. 205–32 *in* M. E. Soulé (ed.) *Conservation Biology: Science of Scarcity and Diversity*. Sinauer Associates, Sunderland, Mass.

Leigh, E. G. 1981. The average lifetime of a population in a varying environment. *J. Theor. Biol.* **90**: 213–39.

Lovejoy, T. E. 1980. Discontinuous wilderness: minimum areas for conservation. *Parks* **5**(2): 13–15.

MacArthur, R. H. 1972. *Geographical Ecology*. Harper and Row, New York.

MacArthur, R. H. and Wilson, E. O. 1967. *The Theory of Island Biogeography*. Princeton University Press, Princeton, New Jersey.

Moore, N. W. 1962. The heaths of Dorset and their conservation. *J. Ecology* **50**: 369–91.

Richter-Dyn, N. and Goel, N. S. 1972. On the extinction of a colonizing species. *Theor. Pop. Biol.* **3**: 406–23.

Schonewald-Cox, C. M. 1983. Guidelines to management: A beginning attempt. Pp. 414–45 *in* C. M. Schonewald-Cox, S. M. Chambers, B. MacBryde, and L. Thomas (eds.) Genetics and Conservation. Benjamin Cummings, Menlo Park, Calif.

Shaffer, M. L. 1981. Minimum population sizes for species conservation. *Bioscience* **31**: 131–4.

Shaffer, M. L. 1983. Determining minimum viable population sizes for the grizzly bear. *Int. Conf. Bear Res. Manage.* **5**: 133–9.

Shaffer, M. L. 1985. The metapopulation and species conservation: The special case of the Northern Spotted Owl. Pp. 86–99 *in* R. J. Gutierrez and A. B. Carey (eds.) *Ecological and Management of the Spotted Owl in the Pacific Northwest*. Gen. Tech. Rep. PNW-185. Portland, Or: USDA, Forest Service, Pacific Northwest Forest and Range, Expt. Stn.

Soulé, M. E. 1980. Thresholds for survival: maintaining fitness and evolutionary potential. Pp. 151–69 *in* M. E. Soulé and B. A. Wilcox (eds.) *Conservation Biology: An Evolutionary-Ecological Perspective*. Sinauer Associates, Sunderland, Mass.

Soulé, M. E. 1985. What is conservation biology? *Bioscience* **35**: 727–34.

Soulé, M. E. 1986a. *Conservation Biology: Science of Scarcity and Diversity*. Sinauer Associates, Sunderland, Mass.

Soulé, M. E. 1986b. Conservation biology and the 'real world.' Pp. 1–12 *in* M. E. Soulé (ed.) *Conservation Biology: Science of Scarcity and Diversity*. Sinauer Associates, Sunderland, Mass.

Soulé, M. E. and Simberloff, D. 1986. What do genetics and ecology tell us about the design of nature reserves? *Biol. Conserv.* **35**: 19–40.

Terborgh, J. 1975. Faunal equilibria and the design of wildlife preserves. Pp. 369–80 *in* F. Golley and E. Medina (eds.) *Trends in Terrestrial and Aquatic Research*. Springer, New York.

Terborgh, J. 1986. Keystone plant resources in the tropical forest. Pp. 330–44 *in* M. E. Soulé (ed.) *Conservation Biology: Science of Scarcity and Diversity*. Sinauer Associates, Sunderland, Mass.

Wilcox, B. A. 1980. Insular ecology and conservation. Pp. 95–117 *in* M. E. Soulé and B. A. Wilcox (eds.) *Conservation Biology: An Evolutionary-Ecological Perspective*. Sinauer Associates, Sunderland, Mass.

Wilcox, B. A. and Murphy, D. D. 1985. Conservation strategy: the effects of fragmentation on extinction. *Amer. Natur.* **125**: 879–87.

2

The demography of chance extinction

DANIEL GOODMAN
Department of Biology, Montana State University, Bozeman, MT 59717

With many sorts of habitats and some entire ecosystems dwindling in extent, the extinctions of many species are imminent. Attempts at saving some of these species as ecologically functioning members of more or less natural communities, rather than zoo populations, involve the establishment of reserves whose extent is very modest in comparison to the original range of the species, and which, for that reason, can only maintain comparatively small relict populations. We wish, therefore, to estimate the viabilities of these small populations, and to learn what management measures and reserve-design features will enhance their viabilities. Furthermore, since there is inevitably pressure, in a crowded world, to encroach upon reserves, we should like to estimate the minimum extent of a reserve that will suffice to confer upon a population an expected time of extinction that is, by some criterion, acceptably remote. We shall scale this measure of reserve extent in units of population size. This is the minimum viable population problem.

At the most elementary level, the minimum viable population problem can be framed in demographic terms; but the magnitudes of the demographic variables will depend on a variety of factors, such as habitat quality, environmental variation, and genetic composition of the population (Shaffer, 1981; Soulé, 1980).

In this chapter, we will use a simple model to examine the relation between the expected survival time of a population and its associated demographic variables, the values of which are determined by the life history and by environmental variation. In the discussion, we will relate the results of these analyses of properties of population models to considerations of population management, habitat management, and reserve design.

Chance extinction

Self evidently, a population goes extinct when its last member dies. This death may be due to various causes, and among those causes will be many where 'chance' plays a role. Similarly, the population is reduced to its last member when its second to last member dies, and this death too may be due to chance, etc. In this perspective then, we might conclude that, aside from extremely thorough catastrophes, populations become extinct, at least proximately, because of bad luck.

Ultimately, of course, we would want to inquire into the circumstances that exposed the population to this luck. If we were compiling an historical narrative, we would doubtless call these circumstances the 'cause' of the extinction. Yet it is informative to pursue the idea that luck dealt the final blow, for this motivates a search for the mathematical connection between what we are loosely calling the 'circumstances' of the population and the 'life expectancy' of that population in a somewhat unpredictable world.

If we were concerned with a particular population, about which much was known, we might construct a detailed model relating the dynamics of reproduction, maturation, and mortality to environmental variables; and then we could set a computer to sampling environmental states and demographic events according to distributions which we had already decided were realistic. In this manner, we could, in successive trials, generate a distribution of the times to extinction under the model, and arrive at summary statistics applicable to that population under the given circumstances. This approach is illustrated by Shaffer's (1983) analysis of the dynamics of a small population of grizzly bears.

For a more general picture of the determinants of expected persistence time, we would necessarily paint with a much broader brush, reducing the dimensionality of the determinants to the barest minimum, in the hopes of revealing the most important factors. We will adopt this impressionistic strategy for the present analysis.

A mathematical model for demography of small populations

We are concerned to construct a generalized model of population dynamics, which will accept as input a minimal description of the population's essential demographic statistics, and which will generate as output a calculated expected time to extinction. The mathematical model called a *birth-and-death process* offers several advantages in this application. This model was first developed almost half a century ago (Feller, 1939), and it has been used extensively.

The classical formulation of the birth-and-death process model describes a population in terms of the number of individuals, the mean birth rate, and the mean death rate; and it leads to a direct algebraic solution for the expected time to extinction. For a population with N individuals at some arbitrary starting time, the average time remaining until extinction, in this model, is

$$T_{(N)} = \sum_{x=1}^{N} \sum_{y=x}^{N_m} \frac{1}{yd_{(y)}} \prod_{z=x}^{y-1} \frac{b_{(z)}}{d_{(z)}} \qquad (1)$$

(Richter-Dyn and Goel, 1972), where $b_{(z)}$ is the mean per capita birth rate when the population size is z individuals, $d_{(z)}$ is the mean per capita death rate when the population size is z individuals, and N_m is the maximum population size, which we call the population ceiling.

When the per capita birth and death rates are treated as constant, except at the population ceiling where of course $b_{(N_m)} = 0$, the model of equation (1) exhibits an extremely rapid increase in the expected population persistence time as the size of N_m is increased: the persistence time $T_{(N_m)}$ increases approximately as the power of N_m (MacArthur, 1972). As a consequence, this model, and others like it, predict enormous persistence times even for some populations with very modest ceilings.

Unfortunately, the model of equation (1) is not realistic when applied literally to a population in a random environment. The crucial discrepancy arises because the mean birth and death rates as defined in the model are not identical to what we actually measure as demographic birth and death rates in a real biological population (Goodman, 1986). The solution to this problem is to redefine the elements of the model in such a way that the input is framed in terms of elements that do correspond directly to quantities that are measurable in real populations.

Two measurable quantities that are sufficient to redefine the elements of the model are the mean population growth rate and the variance in that growth rate (Leigh, 1981; Goodman, 1986). The resulting expression for the persistence time of a population initiated at N individuals is

$$T_{(N)} = \sum_{x=1}^{N} \sum_{y=x}^{N_m} \frac{2}{y[yV_{(y)} - r_{(z)}]} \prod_{z=x}^{y-1} \frac{V_{(z)}z + r_{(z)}}{V_{(z)}z - r_{(z)}} \qquad (2)$$

where $r_{(z)}$ is the mean per capita population growth rate when the population size is z individuals, and $V_{(z)}$ is the variance in the per capita growth rate when the population size is z individuals.

When the mean per capita growth rate and its variance are treated as constant, except at the population ceiling where of course no further growth is possible, the model of equation (2) exhibits a relatively slow increase in the expected population persistence time as the size of N_m is increased: the persistence time $T_{(N_m)}$ increases much less than linearly with N_m – actually it increases less than the square of the logarithm of N_m (Goodman, 1987). As a consequence, this model, in agreement with an alternate diffusion model (Goodman, 1987), but unlike the classical birth-and-death process formulation, predicts disconcertingly short persistence times for some populations with modest ceilings.

The mathematics of this revised formulation of the birth-and-death process model, for application to the minimum viable population problem, will not be discussed further in this chapter, as they are dealt with at length elsewhere (Goodman, 1987). Here, we will consider, instead, some numerical explorations of the behavior of the revised model as it might apply in various situations, and we will examine some computer simulations to support the claim that the revised model does generate adequate predictions from the kinds of data that would be obtained in actual practice.

Parameter estimation and interpretation

The state description of the population, at time t, in the birth-and-death process model is simply the current population size, $N_{(t)}$, in units of individuals. The population ceiling, N_m, specifies the maximum number of individuals that the population can contain. This is not exactly the same as what we usually designate by carrying capacity, K, for the latter is itself an average which might be exceeded at times; whereas the ceiling N_m refers to the highest value which can be reached. Thus it is quite possible that the population in question will almost always be considerably less numerous than its ceiling, N_m.

For purposes of mathematical analysis, we may, at times, wish to construct hypothetical models where the population often is near its ceiling N_m; but that may or may not correspond to the biological reality. We will consider, in a moment, the circumstances under which we may, without serious loss of accuracy, truncate the model of a particular population, treating N_m as the greatest usual value of population size, rather than as the highest possible value (for, of course, it may be difficult in practice to obtain a good estimate of the greatest possible population size).

The two dynamical parameters in our revised version of the birth-and-death process model are the set of values for population-size specific mean per capita population growth rates $r_{(N)}$, and the set of values for population-size specific variance in the per capita population growth rates $V_{(N)}$. These patterns in mean growth rate and variance in growth rate, have, in principle, a distinct value of the respective mean and variance at each value of population size, N. If the population ceiling is N_m, then there are N_m values in the list of values for r, and N_m values in the list of values for V. Obviously, the burden of obtaining separate, reliable estimates for r and V at each possible population size in a real population is unmanageable. For this reason, we must look for some pattern in the sets of values, so that we can proceed more simply by obtaining estimates for some parameters of the pattern.

For the mean per capita population growth rates, the patterns we can consider are those which arise under our usual formulations for density dependent population growth. One obvious example is simple density independent growth with a ceiling, where the mean per capita growth rate is the same for all population sizes up to the ceiling N_m. Another obvious example is logistic density dependence, where the mean per capita growth rate declines linearly with population size in the range of N between 1 and N_m. For the logistic pattern, we might consider setting the population ceiling (N_m) just above the greatest population for which the mean growth rate is non-negative (that is, at the carrying capacity, K).

We will find, in the next section, that there is little practical difference between these density independent and logistic patterns of mean growth rate, from the standpoint of the calculated persistence times they confer. Therefore, a practical starting point for estimating N_m and the pattern of r is simply to take N_m to be the highest population value that is commonly reached, and to take the mean r to be a constant value that is estimated from the observed average per capita growth rate when the population size is in its usual range.

Of course, when more data are available to support a more detailed model of density dependence of growth rate in a particular population, these data may be used to construct a more detailed set of values for r. In particular, if we have empirical information on the actual pattern of density dependence of the growth rate in the range of very low population sizes, incorporating this information into the estimated pattern of r will add appreciably to the accuracy of the prediction of the mean persistence time. We should note, however, that data are seldom available for real populations at densities much below their usual range. Simply extrapolating values from other smaller populations is not necessarily sound, since these other smaller populations might have different demography than would the populations in question when they reach these low levels, owing especially to effects of habitat quality and habitat heterogeneity.

We have less guidance from familiar models, or from familiar data, to help us formulate reasonable patterns for the variances in the per capita growth rate with respect to population size. In the abstract, we can describe two theoretical patterns. We will call these patterns 'individual' and 'environmental.'

The 'individual' pattern arises where all the variance in birth and death rates is owing to events which occur absolutely independently among individuals, but where the probabilities of these events are the same at all times for all individuals in the population. The resulting theoretical pattern of variance in r, as a function of N, is

$$V_{(N)} = \frac{V_1}{N} \tag{3}$$

where V_1 is the average variance in r that would be exhibited under these circumstances in a population consisting of one individual. We see that the variance in r, in this pattern, declines rapidly with growth in population size in small populations. Consequently, it is no surprise to learn that this pattern, by itself, would allow quite generous persistence times under reasonable values for parameters in very modest sized populations. Incidentally, it is this pattern that is implicitly assumed in using the model of equation (1), with constant values of b and d, as in some of the prior literature.

Unfortunately, the individual pattern of variance in r does not capture the bulk of the actual variance in population growth that occurs in real populations, for it omits environmental driving of the variation. The few examples of demographic events that more or less conform to the individual type of pattern are determination of sex at birth (actually at fertilization) and chance causes of death in a constant environment. There are some chance elements of reproduction that conform to this pattern, such as the probability of encountering a mate, and differences in reproduction between individuals that would be manifested even in a constant environment, but these are quite difficult to disentangle from environmental driving, and, further, they make up only a small fraction of the actual variance in a population that is at least of modest size.

A pure 'environmental' pattern of variance in per capita growth rates arises where all the variance in birth and death rates is owing to changing environmental conditions to which the entire population is exposed. The resulting theoretical pattern of variance in r, as a function of N, where environmental variation is the only source of variance, is simply

$$V_{(N)} = V_e \tag{4}$$

where V_e is a constant value representing the environmental variation, scaled in units of its effects on r. Since, under this pattern, the variance in the population's growth rate does not decrease as population size increases, the effects of variance on the probability of chance population decline are not escaped through population growth. Consequently, environmental variation poses a far more serious challenge to population persistence than does individual variation, except in extremely small populations.

We may combine the two patterns of equations (3) and (4) into a more generalized representation, where

$$V_{(N)} = V_e + \frac{V_1}{N}. \tag{5}$$

In practice, when we observe the variation in population growth in a population consisting of more than a handful of individuals, the component owing to V_e will swamp the V_1/N term, so that we obtain estimates only for the parameter V_e. Therefore, it will usually be necessary to use less direct (and probably less reliable) methods to obtain estimates for the parameter V_1, drawing on observed differences between individuals in the same environment at the same time.

It is important to understand that $V_{(N)}$ refers to the variance in the growth rate exhibited by the entire population. Estimates obtained from demographic studies on a subsample of the population may be very misleading, since some environmental variation will be independent across the spectrum of occupied local habitats, so that the variance seen in any one habitat will be substantially larger than that of the entire population which, of course, averages over these habitats. For related reasons, we see how the rough pattern of equation (5) might be an oversimplification, if the population, as it increases and decreases in size, expands and contracts into more, or less, favorable habitats, giving rise to a more complicated relation of variance in r as N changes.

A practical starting point for estimating the set of values of V is to obtain an estimate for the variance in r when the population is in its usual range of densities, for which, presumably, $V_{(N)}$ is dominated by the constant V_e. The observed variance may be taken as an estimate of V_e to be used in equation (5). Care must be taken to ensure that the value obtained is not inflated owing to incorporation of measurement error and sampling error in the variance estimate. An estimate of V_1 may be obtained by summing estimates of the amount of variance in birth and death rates that is uncorrelated among individuals, measured in a habitat that is thought to be the preferred habitat (the habitat to which the population would retreat when it was at its lowest densities). For this calculation, the observations would be grouped into blocks of time, between which the temporal variation (owing presumably to environmental driving) is mathematically removed before calculating the between-

individual variation on the pooled set. When more information is available concerning the pattern relating variance in r to population size, this
information of course could profitably be incorporated into our estimate
of the set of values for V.

In brief, the parameters we have called the mean per capita population
growth rate and the variance in the per capita population growth rate, in
the revised formulation of the birth-and-death process model, correspond
exactly to usual definitions of mean and variance for the observable
quantity defined as the per capita population growth rate. That is, these
parameters pose no theoretical or interpretational difficulties; and in
principle they could readily be estimated simply by accumulating extensive data on the population growth rate over the spectrum of accessible
population sizes.

In practice, however, customarily sketchy demographic data sets for
natural populations will pose formidable obstacles to the estimation of
secure parameters for the persistence time calculation. The mean growth
rate values (associated with different population sizes) can be obtained
from usual sorts of demographic analysis (which often come up against
data insufficiencies). The estimation of the variance in growth rate (and
its pattern) will involve a number of considerations which go beyond
traditional analysis of wildlife demography. Dealing correctly with these
considerations will require a high level of statistical and demographic
expertise.

Given the ready availability of computing power nowadays, the calculation of expected persistence time, from equation (2), once the parameter estimates for the sets of values for r and V are in hand, will be a
simple matter.

Numerical results

Influence of maximum population size on mean persistence time
Our discussion of the revised formulation of the general birth-
and-death process model resolved three factors which will determine the
expected time to extinction. These are the population ceiling, the set of
mean growth rates at each population size, and the set of variances in the
growth rate at each population size. The sets of growth rate mean and
variance values may themselves be represented as simplified functions
specified by two parameters each.

Here we begin an exploration of the computed persistence time in the
parameter space defined by these few factors. In Figure 2.1 we show the
response to mean growth rate (r) and population ceiling (N_m), where the
growth model is density independent (up to population size N_m), the

variance in growth rate conforms to the individual pattern where all the variance is due to independent differences between individuals, and this variation is constant (density independent) at a value of 1. That is, we are representing a situation where for equation (5) V_e equals zero and V_1 equals 1. To recapitulate the interpretation of the variance V_1: it represents the variance we would expect to observe between individuals if we made simultaneous measurements of the growth contributions of many individuals over a very short time interval in a superficially constant and uniform environment. If, hypothetically, the distribution were normal, a variance of 1.0 would correspond to a distribution where 95% of the observed instantaneous rates of individuals would be less than $r + 2.0$ and greater than $r - 2.0$.

The contours representing persistence times in Figure 2.1 are labeled at intervals corresponding to powers of 10. That these contours are relatively evenly spaced in the horizontal indicates that the expected persistence

Figure 2.1. Plot of mean population persistence time (contours), as a function of the population ceiling (N_m) and mean population growth rate (r), in a model with no density dependence, no environmental variance, and with the between-individual variance in r being unity expressed on the basis of a single individual (V_1).

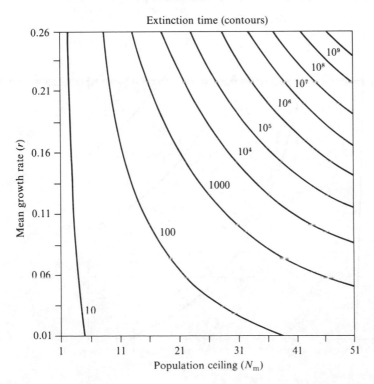

time is related more or less to the power of population size – as has previously been deduced (MacArthur, 1972) from mathematical analysis of approximate versions of equation (1). We see that the dependence on r is slight for the very smallest population sizes, but that at modest magnitudes (or larger) for the population ceiling, there is an appreciable effect of r, especially in the range of small r.

Further, we note that, with this assumption of only individual sources of variance, the expected time to extinction becomes very large at quite modest population sizes, provided the mean growth rate is reasonably large. However, at mean growth rates of just a few % per year (as might be the case for many large mammals), an expected time to extinction of say 1000 years will require a fairly substantial maximum population size (i.e., more than 50), when the variance is of the magnitude in this example.

Figure 2.2 represents a similar contour plot of expected time to

Figure 2.2. Plot of mean population persistence time (contours), as a function of the population ceiling (N_m) and mean population growth rate of a vanishingly sparse population ($r_{(0)}$), in a model with linear density dependence of the mean growth rate at each density, no environmental variance, and with the between-individual variance in r being unity expressed on the basis of a single individual (V_1).

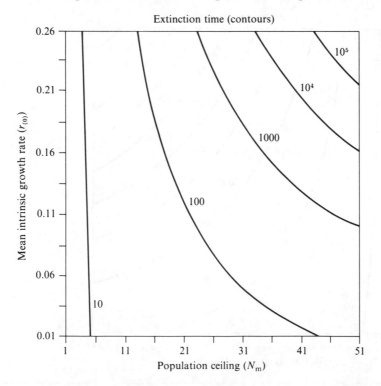

extinction as a function of a mean growth parameter and population ceiling, for individual variation only, with variance equal 1.0, only here the model is density dependent, with linear (logistic) decline in the realized mean growth rate with population size. The axis representing the mean growth rate parameter in this plot refers to the maximum rate, realized at the lowest population size, whereas in the plot of Figure 2.1 it referred to the realized value of r at any population size (except N_m). Regardless of the introduction of density dependence, we again find a power function form to the response surface, but the magnitudes of the persistence times are greatly reduced.

On reflection, it may not be reasonable to maintain a constant variance attributable to individual variation whilst the mean growth rate is declining linearly to zero. For example, if the reduction in growth rate is brought about by a decline in birth rate, we might expect the variance between individuals to decline also (but not necessarily to zero). For example, if V_1 declines linearly to half its zero density value at $N - N_m$, with the model otherwise identical to that of Figure 2.2, we obtain the plot of Figure 2.3. The expected persistence times, with density dependence, in Figure 2.3, are very close to those with density independence in Figure 2.1. We conclude that density dependence may not be terribly important to our calculation of time to extinction in small populations, provided the variance in the growth rate declines in a manner that is more or less commensurate with the decline in mean growth rate, as density increases.

In Figure 2.4 we show the response of persistence time to mean growth rate (r) and population ceiling (N_m), where the growth model is density independent, as in Figure 2.1, but with all the variation in growth modeled as environmental variance, and this variance is constant at a value 1. That is, we are representing a situation where for equation (5) V_e equals 1 and V_1 equals zero. Thus at a population size of 1, the realized variance in r for the population modeled in Figure 2.4 is identical to that of the population in Figure 2.1; but at any larger population size, the realized variance is smaller for the model of Figure 2.1 than for that of Figure 2.4. To recapitulate the interpretation of the variance V_e: it represents the variance we would expect to observe between sample determinations of the growth rate, taken at different times in a fluctuating environment, where each sample spanned a very short time interval, but with each sample including sufficient individuals that the contribution of independent variation between individuals would be negligible.

Comparing the contour plot of Figure 2.4 with Figure 2.1, we find that, with environmental variance, the time to extinction is much shorter and it is much less responsive to the maximum population size. This reflects the important role of the decline of variance with *N* in the model of Figure 2.1. Whereas the contours in Figure 2.1 were labeled at intervals corresponding to powers of 10, in Figure 2.4 they are labeled at arithmetic intervals. We see that, with environmental variance, the expected extinction time, far from increasing exponentially with N_m, increases somewhat less than linearly with N_m – as has previously been deduced (Goodman, 1986) from an approximate version of equation (2). We see that a truly massive population ceiling would be required to achieve a reasonably long time to extinction when the environmental variances were of the magnitude in this example.

We conclude, from our initial exploration, that the variance in the

Figure 2.3. Plot of mean population persistence time (contours), as a function of the population ceiling (N_m) and mean population growth rate of a vanishingly sparse population ($r_{(0)}$), in a model with linear density dependence of the mean growth rate at each density, no environmental variance, and with the between-individual variance in *r* being unity in a vanishingly sparse population (expressed on the basis of a single individual) and declining linearly with density, to a value of one half at the population ceiling.

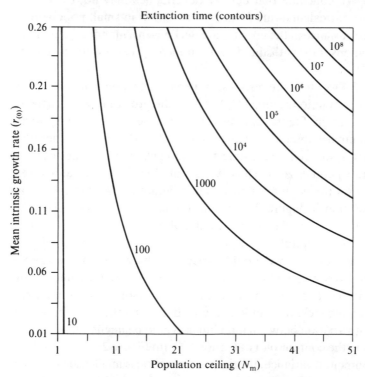

population growth rate, and especially that component of variance owing to environmental variation, will probably prove to be the critical element in determining the mean extinction time for a given small population whose mean growth rate is positive. Further, to the extent that the variance is dominated by environmental variance, the response of persistence time to the size of the population ceiling will be very gradual, rather than exhibiting the appearance of a dramatic threshold. These results concur with mathematical deductions based on approximations of the birth-and-death process model (Leigh, 1981; Goodman, 1987).

The distribution of persistence times

The machinery described in the preceding sections conveniently calculates a mean time to extinction. This does not tell us how representative the mean might be. To explore this latter question, we undertake a

Figure 2.4. Plot of mean population persistence time (contours), as a function of the population ceiling (N_m) and mean population growth rate (r), in a model with no density dependence, no between-individual variance in r, and with the environmental variance in r being unity.

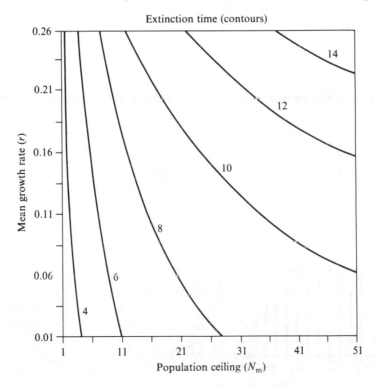

Extinction time (contours)

much less convenient course of simulation (for which, incidentally, the birth-and-death process is rather awkward).

The central algorithm of the simulation begins by first sampling an exponential distribution, the parameter of which is $V_{(N)}N^2$, to obtain the time to the next demographic event. This is followed by sampling a binomial, the parameter of which is $[V_{(N)}N + r_{(N)}]/[2V_{(N)}N]$, to determine whether the event is a birth or a death. Accordingly the population increases or decreases, and the elapsed time is accumulated until the population reaches zero. Each simulation is initialized with a population at its ceiling.

Figure 2.5 shows a histogram of extinction times for 1000 such trials of a population model where: the population ceiling is 20; the mean growth

Figure 2.5. Histogram of time to extinction in 1000 trials of a simulated birth-and-death process, in a model with no density dependence, where the population ceiling (N_m) was 20, the mean growth rate (r) was 0.05, the variance component in r owing to the environmental variation corresponded to a standard deviation of 0.5, and the variance component in r owing to between-individual variation corresponded to a standard deviation of 0.5 expressed on the basis of a single individual ($\sqrt{V_1}$).

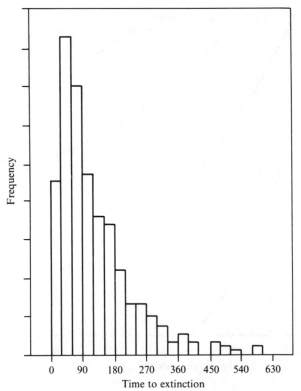

rate is 0.05, with no density dependence; the environmental component of the variation in growth rate is 0.25, expressed as a standard deviation (i.e., the square root of V_e of equation (5)); and the individual component of variation, expressed as a standard deviation in a population of 1 in a constant environment (i.e., the square root of V_1 of equation (5)), is 0.5. The mean persistence time in this simulated sample was 122.6, compared to the calculated theoretical expectation of 121.4 from equation (2).

The distribution is strongly skewed to the right. This, in concert with the observation that the standard deviation (103.4) is rather near to the value of the mean, suggests an exponential distribution. Transforming the values by raising e to the negative power of the observed value divided by the mean would, for a true exponential distribution, result in a uniform distribution in the range 0 to 1. This transformation, performed on the sample from the simulation, resulted in the histogram of Figure 2.6, which

Figure 2.6. Histogram of times to extinction from the simulation shown in Figure 2.5, where the times have been transformed in a manner that would transform an exponentially distributed variable to a uniformly distributed variable on the interval (0, 1) as explained in the text.

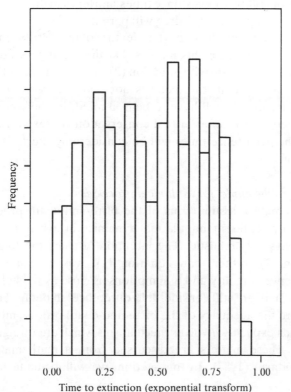

is rather like a uniform distribution, except for the slight deficiency of the smallest values. This confirms that the distribution of persistence times in the simulation is rather like an exponential, except for a slight deficiency of shortest persistence times.

It makes sense that the distribution of persistence times should be like an exponential. If the probability of extinction in the next time interval were constant from one interval to the next, the process would be exactly exponential. In our model there is a slight difference from one interval to the next, owing to the effect of current population size: at low population size, extinction in the next interval is more likely than at high population size, owing to the amount of time that is likely to be involved in declining from the high density, if extinction is to take place. If, however, we think in terms of longer intervals, the effect of current population density weakens, since the longer interval allows sufficient time for the decline regardless of what the population size was when the interval began. Figuratively, the model has a short 'memory' of what the population size was. Alternatively we might think of this as a demographic 'drag' on the otherwise random dynamics. The slight deficiency of shortest persistence times revealed in the distribution graphed in Figure 2.6 is accounted for by the relative improbability of persistence times shorter than the memory of the model (or more rapid than the drag will permit).

From a practical standpoint, the important feature of the distribution is the strong skew to the right, for this implies that the mean persistence time – which is what we calculate with equation (2) – is rather greater than the mode. In this sense, then, the mean is not really representative, though it is a true mean. We will have to bear in mind, in applying the calculated mean persistence times in real conservation contexts, that a large fraction of the persistence times will be considerably shorter than the calculated mean.

Adequacy of the model for biological processes

The mathematical assumptions of the birth-and-death process model do not really represent population dynamics in a way that is biologically and physically realistic. The intention of using the formulation of equation (2), rather than equation (1), was to make the correspondence between reality and assumptions as close as possible in some regards, but there are still considerable differences in detail. Here we begin to explore the adequacy of the birth-and-death process model for a situation which explicitly involves mechanisms which are foreign to the mathematics. These matters are discussed from a mathematical standpoint in Goodman (1987). In this section, we will evaluate their implications for our use of the model by examining the adequacy of equation (2) for predicting mean persistence times of simulations which explicitly violate the assumptions of the model.

In the first such test, we introduce 'genetic' differences between individuals determined at birth, 'environmental' variation, which affects all individuals simultaneously, and age structure, which gives rise to time lag effects that are expressed as serial correlation in the growth rates, where probabilities of reproduction and survival are functions of age.

The structure of the simulation model is as follows. There are eight age classes, with dynamics governed by a stochastic Leslie matrix. There are constant underlying schedules of age-specific fecundity and mortality. At birth an individual is assigned a 'genotype' by sampling a uniform distribution to obtain a value which is applied multiplicatively to the 'underlying' schedules of fecundity and mortality yielding genotypic schedules which will be associated with that individual for the rest of its life. At each time step in the simulation, the 'environment' is allowed to vary, by sampling another uniform distribution to obtain a value that is applied in multiplication to the genotypic schedules of fecundity for every individual in the population in that time interval, and it is applied as a divisor to the genotypic schedules of mortality for every individual in the population in that time interval. Then, at each time step, for each individual independently, the modified schedules of fecundity and mortality (modified once at birth, independently for each individual to represent 'genotype' effects, and modified each time step, for all individuals in concert to represent 'environment' effects) are used as parameters of binomial distributions which are sampled independently for each individual in the population to determine 'birth events' and 'death events'. The population ceiling in the simulation was set at 20 individuals; it was enforced by truncating the number of births to replacement, whenever they exceeded it, at this density.

In Table 2.1 we show the summary statistics of the simulated population's mean per capita growth rate, $r_{(N)}$, and variance in that growth rate, $V_{(N)}$, at each population density, where the simulation was allowed to run until 200 extinctions had been recorded. The combination of individual and environmental variance gave rise to a pattern in variance values which resembles that described by equation (5). The predominant serial correlations in the realized sequence of per capita growth rates were negative, despite the influence of age structure which necessarily contributes positive serial correlation at a lag corresponding to the generation time. The positive correlation at that lag was 0.004. The dominant correlation, which was at lag 1, was negative, -0.11, arising presumably

Table 2.1. *Summary statistics of the observed growth rates in a simulation of a population with age structure (eight age classes), genotypic variation (uniform random variable sampled at birth), individual variation in vital rates (binomial random variables for reproduction and survival events, sampled independently for each individual in each time step), and environmental driving of dynamics (uniform random variable, sampled once each time step, and applied to all individuals).*

Population size (N)	Mean value of growth rate ($r_{(N)}$)	Variance of growth rate ($V_{(N)}$)
1	0.078	0.386
2	0.036	0.171
3	0.054	0.126
4	0.052	0.107
5	0.032	0.082
6	0.036	0.072
7	0.036	0.068
8	0.045	0.064
9	0.048	0.057
10	0.046	0.058
11	0.046	0.053
12	0.043	0.049
13	0.046	0.047
14	0.046	0.048
15	0.035	0.044
16	0.031	0.044
17	0.037	0.041
18	0.025	0.039
19	0.020	0.037
20	−0.065	0.010

through the effective density dependence enforced by the frequent population fluctuations just at the population ceiling.

The actual mean time to extinction observed in the simulations was 261.0 time steps. The calculated mean time to extinction, obtained by using the observed sets of values for r and V from Table 2.1 in equation (2) was 260.6, which is remarkably close. Note, however, that the values of r and V used in the theoretical calculation were based on the same sequence of realizations from which the empirical observation of the mean persistent time was taken, so this study does not address the question of sampling properties.

Influence of strong serial correlation on adequacy of the model

Real environments exhibit considerable serial correlation in measures of their favorability for population growth. Some of this is owing to serial correlation in the physical (e.g., meteorological) variables that contribute to driving the system, some is owing to the dynamics of biological components, such as vegetation, parasites, and predators, which also contribute to determining the favorableness of the environment. As a consequence, in real systems, there will be a substantial degree of serial correlation in population growth rates, with episodes of greater than average growth, and episodes of less than average growth. The duration of these episodes will be greater than is consistent with the assumptions made in the mathematical development of the birth-and-death process model.

Often, the most marked serial correlation will appear as positive correlations at short lags, decaying to near zero at longer lags. Cyclic phenomena will show positive correlations at short lags, crossing to negative correlations at lags corresponding to half a cycle, returning to positive at one cycle, etc., decaying eventually to zero as the phase of the cycle drifts under noise.

Here we explore whether strong serial correlation, which of course departs from the assumptions of the birth-and-death process, will seriously compromise the practical applicability of the model for computing mean persistence times. Intuitively, we must expect that the serial correlations will cause equation (2) to overestimate persistence times if the variance estimates used for $V_{(N)}$ are not corrected accordingly. This is because the serial correlation in the realized growth rates will lead to a substantial excess of 'runs' of consecutive decreases (and increases) in population size, which make it more likely that a particular downward run will result in extinction. Our concern here is to see how great the discrepancy from using the uncorrected variances might be for an example with a plausibly strong degree of serial correlation.

The structure of the simulation model is as follows. There is no age structure, and no independent variation among individuals. The dynamics are governed by an underlying set of density dependent growth rates, to which an environmental disturbance term is added at each time step. The environmental disturbance term is generated from a second order autoregressive model, driven by a pure random Gaussian variable. The autoregressive model results in a strong serial correlation structure in the environmental disturbance term, which causes serial correlation in the realized growth rates of the simulated population. The population ceiling for the simulation was set at 40 individuals, with the deterministic equilibrium of the underlying linear density dependent dynamics being 20.

In Table 2.2, we show the summary statistics of the simulated population's mean per capita growth rate, $r_{(N)}$, and variance in that growth

Table 2.2. *Summary statistics of a simulated population, with a population ceiling of 40, driven by an autocorrelated random environmental variable (created by sampling a Gaussian random variable each time step, and using this in a second order autoregressive process to generate the environmental variable) affecting the vital rates of all individuals simultaneously, and where the underlying mean growth rate (at each population size) follows a logistic function.*

Population size (N)	Mean value of growth rate $(r_{(N)})$	Variance of growth rate $(V_{(N)})$
1	0.015	0.095
2	0.002	0.049
3	0.000	0.031
4	0.001	0.024
5	0.003	0.020
6	0.001	0.017
7	0.004	0.016
8	0.002	0.014
9	0.002	0.014
10	0.003	0.012
11	0.004	0.012
12	0.003	0.012
13	0.000	0.012
14	0.004	0.011
15	0.002	0.011
16	0.001	0.010
17	0.001	0.010
18	0.000	0.010
19	0.001	0.010
20	0.002	0.009
21	−0.003	0.009
22	−0.001	0.009
23	−0.004	0.009
24	−0.001	0.008
25	−0.000	0.008
26	−0.005	0.007
27	−0.004	0.008
28	−0.003	0.007
29	−0.007	0.007
30	−0.001	0.007
31	−0.004	0.007
32	−0.004	0.006
33	−0.006	0.006
34	−0.002	0.006
35	−0.008	0.006
36	−0.011	0.005
37	−0.012	0.004
38	−0.014	0.004
39	−0.018	0.002
40	−0.038	0.002

rate, $V_{(N)}$, for each population size, where the simulation was allowed to run until 200 extinctions had been recorded. The growth rates, for the most part, were slightly positive below a density of 20, slightly negative from 21 to 39, and more markedly negative at 40, reflecting the operation of the population ceiling and the underlying logistic dynamics in the model. Owing to the discrete-time representation of the dynamics, the variance in r decreased as population size increased, despite representation of the variation as environmental only.

Figure 2.7 shows the pattern of strong positive autocorrelation in the growth rates at short lags, owing to the second order autoregressive process used to generate the environmental driving. In 200 extinctions, the actual mean persistence time was 545 time steps (standard deviation 544). The calculated mean time to extinction, obtained by using the observed sets of values for r and V, from the same sequence of realizations, in equation (2) was 586 time steps, which is in the right ball park, despite the strong autocorrelation. As expected for this situation,

Figure 2.7. Time series analysis of the per capita growth rates realized in a simulation of a population with a ceiling of 40, driven by an autocorrelated random environmental variable (created by sampling a Gaussian random variable each time step, and using this in a second order autoregressive process to generate the environmental variable) affecting the vital rates of all individuals simultaneously, and where the underlying mean growth rate (at each population size), follows a logistic function.

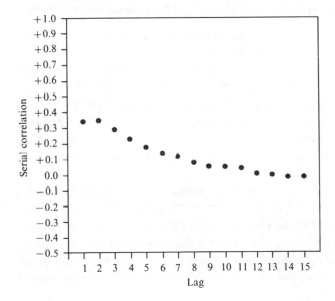

equation (2) does err in the direction of overestimation. Again, this simulation does not address the question of sampling properties.

Discussion and conclusions

The classical birth-and-death process model represents the random variation in population vital rates as due entirely to chance differences experienced by individuals, in an environment where the probabilities of birth and death events are constant over space and time. Obviously, this representation does not capture variation owing to random environmental fluctuations which may affect many individuals simultaneously. In this chapter, we have reviewed a mathematical means for representing the effects of random environmental fluctuations in a birth-and-death process model that predicts the expected persistence time of a population.

We found that incorporation of environmental fluctuations leads to predicted persistence times which are vastly different from those predicted by the classical model, which only considered random differences between individuals. In a simplified form of the classical model, the population persistence time increases approximately as a quantity raised to the power of the maximum population size, so very long persistence times are possible with quite modest population sizes. In a similarly simplified form of the model incorporating environmental fluctuations, the persistence time increases much less than linearly with the maximum population size; so, extremely large population sizes may be necessary to confer reasonably long expected persistence times.

We have explored some numerical solutions for persistence time, showing the relation to such parameters as the mean population growth rate, the maximum population size, and the variance in the population growth rate. We noted in particular that the persistence time depends strongly on the magnitude of the variance in population growth rate. The dependence on the average population growth rate was slight enough, by comparison, that for the same variance in population growth rate, linear density dependence in the mean growth rate makes little practical difference in the estimated time to extinction, compared to a calculation with density independent growth.

Further, we have considered some simulations of populations with dynamics more complex than those of the birth-and-death process model, in order to confirm that the model provides a reasonable approximation for the expected persistence times even in these more realistic simulations which do not exactly conform to the assumptions of the birth-and-death process. We observe that the simple birth-and-death process model provides an adequate approximation despite such complications as age structure, and serial correlation in environmental fluctuations.

These results lead us to conclude that the modified birth-and-death process model provides a convenient mathematical formulation for estimating persistence times of populations under various scenarios. These estimates in themselves may serve usefully for evaluating the prospects for a population, and perhaps more importantly they may serve as a comparative means for evaluating management programs and reserve designs.

We may be discomfited at having to abandon as unrealistic the reassuring predictions, from the classical birth-and-death process model, that quite modest population sizes are sufficient for conferring extremely long persistence times. With the modified, and more realistic model, which we have reviewed in this chapter, the persistence times predicted for populations subject to substantial environmental variation can be distressingly short, and these persistence times are not dramatically increased by modest increases in the maximum population size. These results argue that for some sorts of populations which are sensitive to environmental fluctuations, (1) the minimum reserve size necessary to achieve a reasonably long persistence time is extremely large, on demographic grounds alone, and (2) in the absence of immense reserves, specific programs of management intervention directed to reducing the effective variance in population growth rate might offer the only practical prospects for achieving acceptable persistence times.

We found that the distribution of population persistence times under a simulated example of the birth-and-death process model looks rather like an exponential. The slight departure from an exponential distribution is explicable in terms of a demographic drag. The fact of approximately exponential distribution of persistence times suggests that the establishment and extinction processes of local populations have stochastic dynamics which to an extent meet the assumptions of a birth-and-death process in which the local population, rather than the individual, is the basic unit. This allows convenient modeling of metapopulations in a birth-and-death process framework (Goodman, 1987). Such an approach may be used to analyse the relative merits of several small reserves versus a single large one of equivalent total area. The conclusion of this analysis is that multiple reserves are preferable to the single large reserve, provided the environmental variation in the separate multiple reserves is at least partially independent, and provided there is at least a small rate of natural or managed recolonization of reserves which experience local extinction (Goodman, 1987). This result differs qualitatively from the conclusions of Wright and Hubbell (1983), who, however, omitted environmental fluctuations from their model.

Inasmuch as incorporation of effects of environmental variation leads to qualitative, as well as enormous quantitative differences, in the predictions of stochastic population models bearing on the central questions of conservation biology, we conclude that: (1) practical models must take environmental variation into account, (2) serious attention must be given to field programs of estimation of the relevant parameters of environmental variation – most especially, the magnitude of the variance that environmental variation causes in realized population growth rates, and the degree of correlation in that variation over space and time – and (3) strategies for population management and reserve design must be re-evaluated in light of the results of models which incorporate environmentally driven variation.

References

Feller, W. 1939. Die Grundlagen der Volterraschen Theorie des Kampfes ums dasein in wahrscheinlichkeitstheoretischer Behandlung. *Acta Biotheoretica* **5**: 11–40.

Goodman, D. 1987. Considerations of stochastic demography in the design and management of biological reserves. *Nat. Res. Model.* In press.

Leigh, E. G. 1981. The average lifetime of a population in a varying environment. *J. Theor. Biol.* **90**: 213–39.

MacArthur, R. H. 1972. *Geographical Ecology*. Harper and Row, New York.

Richter-Dyn, N. and Goel, N. S. 1972. On the extinction of a colonizing species. *Theor. Pop. Biol.* **3**: 406–33.

Shaffer, M. L. 1981. Minimum population sizes for species conservation. *Bioscience* **31**: 131–4.

Shaffer, M. L. 1983. Determining minimum viable population sizes for the grizzly bear. *Int. Conf. Bear Res. Manage.* **5**: 133–9.

Soulé, M. E. 1980. Thresholds for survival: maintaining fitness and evolutionary potential. Pp. 151–70 *in* M. E. Soulé and B. A. Wilcox (eds.) *Conservation Biology: An Evolutionary-Ecological Perspective*. Sinauer Associates, Sunderland, Mass.

Wright, J. S. and Hubbell, S. P. 1983. Stochastic extinction and reserve size: a focal species approach. *Oikos* **41**: 466–76.

3

Extinction models and mammalian persistence

GARY E. BELOVSKY
School of Natural Resources, University of Michigan, Ann Arbor, MI 48109-1115

A population, regardless of its size, faces some real probability of becoming extinct by a 'random walk' through a series of inopportune events; this idea is not a new one (Goodman, Chapter 2). A number of mathematical models have been constructed to depict this probability of extinction over time. Most of the models have been based upon the intrinsic variation in the reproductive output and deaths of individuals in a species population (MacArthur and Wilson, 1967; MacArthur, 1972; Richter-Dyn and Goel, 1972; Hubbell, 1979; Feller, 1939). The intrinsic variation referred to in the models arises from random changes in birth and death rates and differences in these values that are inherent to individuals (genotypes) composing the population. Solutions to these models demonstrate small probabilities of population extinction for all but very small populations. More recently, it has been demonstrated that populations are much more susceptible to extinction if the environment (Leigh, 1975; 1981; Wright and Hubbell, 1983; Goodman, Chapter 2; Ginzburg *et al.*, 1982; Roughgarden, 1979), including competitors (MacArthur, 1972), contributes to variations in birth and/or death rates.

Another type of extinction model does not rely on variations in birth and death rates. Rather, such models employ a reduction ('catastrophe') in population size that occurs at random intervals and perhaps intensities (Strebel, 1985; Hanson and Tuckwell, 1978; Ewens *et al.*, Chapter 4). These 'catastrophic' models will not be examined in this chapter; however, Strebel's (1985) model begins to bring the 'catastrophe' models and models based on variation in birth and death rates together.

Although mathematical expressions for a population's probability of extinction or expected persistence over time have heuristic value, their realism or applicability to the ecological realm has not been demonstrated. To make a first attempt at applying these models, several questions must be addressed.

(1) What is the minimal data set needed to solve an extinction model?
(2) If the extinction models can be solved for different populations of species, are there general verifiable patterns which emerge for the probability of extinction (e.g., can the probability of extinction be related to body size)?
(3) Do the extinction probabilities for specific populations agree with extinction probabilities reported in the literature?

To address the first question, an extinction model must be chosen and its variables must be defined in terms of measurable biological values. The second question can be addressed using data sets that generalize the necessary parameters for a group of species. The third question can be addressed using an historical review of biogeographic data and comparing the data with the predictions found from answering the second question.

Question 1: An extinction model and its parameters

Several extinction models based upon environmental variability have been developed (Leigh, 1975; 1981; Wright and Hubbell, 1983; Goodman, Chapter 2; Ginzburg *et al.*, 1982), where environmental variation acts upon the growth rate of a population. These models have similarities and, given common assumptions, they provide similar predictions. A model developed by Goodman (Chapter 2) was chosen for the analysis presented here because its parameters are better defined biologically than some of the other models. More importantly, the model has been presented in terms of an expected persistence time, the time expected for a population of a given size to become extinct, and the probability distribution of this expected time.

Goodman's model (Chapter 2) can be written as:

$$T = \sum_{x=1}^{N_m} \sum_{y=x}^{N_m} \left(\frac{2}{y(yV - r)} \right) \prod_{z-y}^{y-1} \left(\frac{zV + r}{zV - r} \right) \tag{1}$$

where T is expected persistence time, r is the population's average growth rate, V is the variance of r attributed to environmental fluctuations, and N_m is the population's maximum size. In this formulation, density dependence is ignored since it does not substantially modify the results from the analytically simpler density independent formulation (Goodman, Chapter 2).

The extinction model (equation (1)) can be simplified, using several assumptions. Using stochastic calculus, Roughgarden (1979) argues that the extinctions of populations are only possible if $V > 2r$, otherwise, populations tend towards their carrying capacity. Assuming $V > 2r$ and that V is much greater relative to r, T can be found to be proportional to a function varying between $(2/V - r) \ln N_m$ and $2N_m/V - r$ (Goodman, Chapter 2; Leigh, pers. comm.). These simplified forms provide T values that vary over a wide range, given a set of V, r and N_m values. Therefore, although simplification of an equation is usually a good first step toward understanding its behavior, the simplified functions for T in this case have little value for making quantitative predictions.

To remedy this problem, the extinction model (equation (1)) can be rewritten in its recursive form and, with a few approximations, a function that is easily solved on a personal computer can be written:

$$T \simeq [(N_m - 1)V - r] \left[\left(\frac{V + r}{V - r} \right) \left(\frac{1}{r(V - r)} \right) \left(\sum_{y=1}^{N_m} \frac{1}{y^2} \right) \right.$$
$$- \frac{1}{r} \left(\sum_{y=1}^{N_m} \frac{1}{y(yV - r)} \right)$$
$$\left. - \frac{2V}{V - r} \left(\sum_{y=1}^{N_m} \frac{1}{y^2} \right) \left(\sum_{y=2}^{N_m} \frac{1}{[(y - 1)V - r](yV - r)} \right) \right] \quad (2)$$

(Goodman, unpubl. ms.). The computer program written to solve equation (2) is provided in the Appendix to this chapter, and used in the calculations presented here.

The extinction model presented here provides an expected or average persistence time; however, this value is distributed as a negative exponential (Goodman, Chapter 2). This means that, although a population of a given size may have a large expected persistence time, a majority of populations of that size will persist for far less time and a few will persist for far more time. Therefore, to achieve a given persistence time with a high degree of certainty, the expected or average persistence time will have to be much greater.

Finally for a given maximum population size, N_m, the expected persistence time is dependent on r and V, the environmentally-induced variation in r. Although in this model, V is attributed to r, it may not be an easy task to ascertain whether variations should be imposed on r, N_m or both.

Environmental changes in r or N_m might arise from weather, food abundance, competition, predation, and/or disease. As intraspecific competition is reduced, population members often respond to this change in N_m by varying their reproductive output and survival. Therefore, it may be more elegant to assess environmental variation on r since it is composed of birth and death rates. For example, if the food available to a population increases, we might expect birth rates to increase and death rates to decline and N_m to increase. While a predator might decrease N_m, the reduced intraspecific competition for food might increase birth rates and decrease death rates because of more food per capita.

Assessing environmental variation only on N_m, small animals appear to be less vulnerable to extinction than large species because smaller species generally possess higher population growth rates (see below; Diamond, 1984a; b) permitting rapid recovery from low population sizes. On the other hand, assessing environmental variation on r, large animals appear to be buffered from declines because of their smaller variation in r values, which reflects their higher survival and longer generation time. In other words, the variance in r may be as important as the magnitude of r. One way of proceeding, therefore, is to ask what life history traits are correlated with the variance in r.

Question 2: Generalities about extinction probabilities

To solve an extinction model such as equation (1), long term demographic data might be required from a population or even from experimental studies. Regardless, we must ask if some generalizations about extinction can be made given the limited existing data in the literature. An obvious avenue for generalization is the differences between r values for large and small animals.

Three parameters, r, N_m, and V, must be known to solve the extinction model. To estimate these parameters, each can be broken down into its constituent elements and estimated from ecological principles.

r is the difference between birth and death rates. A considerable literature exists on the evolution of life history strategies that produces 'optimal' net reproductive rates (maximum r values) for individuals inhabiting a given environment (Calow, 1981; Schaffer and Gadgil, 1975; Stearns, 1976; Horn and Rubenstein, 1984). Although observed r values are determined by complex selective pressures operating on births and deaths, simple body mass dependent relationships exist for the maximum r values (r_m) for species ranging from unicellular animals to mammals (Fenchel, 1974; Smith, 1954; Pianka, 1970; Peters, 1983; Calder, 1984; McNab, 1980; 1984; Hayssen, 1984; Hennemann, 1984; Caughley and Krebs, 1983; Millar and Zammuto, 1983; Blueweiss *et al.*, 1978; Tuomi, 1980; Western, 1979; Western and Ssemakula, 1982; Schmitz and Lavigne, 1984). These body mass dependent relationships are of the form:

$$r_m = \alpha W^\beta \tag{3}$$

where α and β are constants and W is the animal's body mass. These relationships explain 70% to over 90% of the observed variance in r_m, not in $\ln r_m$. The body mass dependent relationships are presented in Box I for different mammal species. r_m can be used as a first approximation for r for different mammals in the extinction model.

To estimate N_m and V, we might make one basic assumption: animal populations are ultimately limited by energy. The amount of energy input to the biosphere is set by solar radiation and its conversion into organic matter by photosynthesis (Colinvaux, 1978; Odum, 1971; Ricklefs, 1973). Therefore, the upper limit of population size is set by available energy levels. If C is the amount of food energy per unit area that can be consumed by a species in the environment, then the maximum density of the species ($1/A$) can be written as:

$$\frac{1}{A} = \frac{C - S}{M} \tag{4}$$

where M is the energy metabolism for an individual of the species, S is its energetic cost for foraging (moving) over a unit area, and A is the minimum area required by an individual to satisfy its energy demands. Therefore, given an area, R, to be inhabited by a population, the carrying capacity, K, is:

$$K = R\left(\frac{C - S}{M}\right) \tag{5}$$

and K is assumed to be equal to N_m.

Both S and M are functions that are dependent on body mass (Peters, 1983; Calder, 1984); therefore, R, C, and the animal species' body mass, W, are the data required to estimate K using equation (5). R is set by the size of the region inhabited by the population. Initially, we might estimate C, the density of usable food, as a function of primary production in the environment. A first approximation of the conversion of primary production into C might be accomplished by employing commonly-used average trophic transfer values; e.g., 10% conversion of plant energy into herbivore energy (Slobodkin, 1960; 1962; 1972; Odum, 1971). Estimates of C based on primary production might be generalized for terrestrial environments since terrestrial primary production is often a function of evapotranspiration or rainfall (Rosenzweig, 1968).

Estimating C by whatever methods, direct or indirect, poses problems in computing N_m. First, direct measurement of C is often difficult and time consuming in the field. Second, neither direct measurement or an estimated measurement of C includes reductions in C due to competitors or in N_m due to predators and/or disease. Although these difficulties can be overcome by careful, detailed field studies, how do we obtain estimates of N_m for the examination of general extinction trends or the potential for extinction of endangered species that are difficult to study?

Fortunately, there are body mass relationships observed for the population densities of many taxa (Peters, 1983; Calder, 1984; Peters and Raelson, 1984; Damuth, 1981; Peters and Wassenberg, 1983), explaining 30% to over 80% of the variance in a species' population density. These observed densities should reflect the effects of competitors and predators on population density. The empirical functions for population density obscure differences in food density at different locations except those arising from the most striking environmental differences (e.g., tropical *versus* temperate but not grassland *versus* forest). These body mass dependent relationships for mammals appear in Box I and can be used as first approximations of N_m in the extinction model. Although the exact relationships between body mass and population density may be biased due to sampling procedures (J. H. Brown, pers. comm.), there is no reason to question the general trend expressed.

Measuring V (variance in r) due to environmental changes poses the same problems as measuring K as an estimate for N_m. If we employ the assumption that K is determined by available food energy, we might expect r to vary (V) with changes in food availability in the environment. This is easier to conceptualize for herbivores and their food plants, since primary production is often a function of rainfall in terrestrial environments. Therefore, environmental variation in K or r for herbivores might be related to the variation in rainfall.

However, computing V is not straightforward. One cannot simply measure some variation in an environmental measure, such as rainfall, and call this the variation in r, since the variance must be scaled to r. The ratio of the variance in an environmental measure to its mean might be multiplied by r to estimate V; but this is inappropriate since r has an inherent variability even in the absence of environmental fluctuations due to genetic and random differences between individuals. Perhaps the best way to approximate V, given some environmental fluctuation, is to scale the inherent variability in r by the environmental fluctuations and call the increase in variance, V. Therefore, to estimate V we need to know the inherent variability in r.

Goodman (1986; Chapter 2) points out that, without environmental variance, the variance in r equals the sum of birth (b) and death (d) rates or $2b - r$, because r is distributed in a Poisson fashion. Since b is a function of body mass for mammals (Calder, 1984; Western, 1979), we can compute the ratio of the variance in r to the mean r as $(2b/r) - 1$ in the absence of environmental variation. Using the body mass functions for a mammal's b and r values, this ratio is found to be approximately 4.28. Multiplying this value by the square of the coefficient of variation for the environmental parameter, we obtain an estimate of the ratio between r's variance due to environmental fluctuations and a mean r. To do this, a set of environmental measures is required.

The environmental changes can be computed using rainfall, stream flow, lake level or tree ring width data (see Box I for the range of values for 10 environments). For each data set, the positive and negative deviations from the overall mean value (e.g., rainfall) were averaged separately and a coefficient of variation was computed for each. Using these values in the above defined procedure, V was estimated to range between $1.43r$ and $7.32r$ (see Box I), near Goodman's (Chapter 2) assumption that $V > 2r$.

With the data in Box I, the extinction model can be solved for mammals of different body masses. This was accomplished by choosing an expected persistence time, T, and solving for the necessary population size that permits this persistence, N_m. By solving for N_m rather than T, we have the advantage of employing neither the estimate nor the empirically determined body mass relationship for K as a substitute for N_m. Using this approach, we find the following relationship for N_m with W, given T (see Box I):

$$N_m = \gamma W^\theta \tag{6}$$

where γ and θ are constants.

Question 3: Is the extinction model supported by empirical observations?

The predictions made using the model in Box I are extremely crude. We know that two mammals of the same body mass can have different population growth rates and densities, in the same environment. We also know that many adaptations of animals serve to reduce the impact of environmental fluctuations. Nonetheless, a general solution to the extinction model based on body mass and environmental variability should provide insights into the types of organisms and environments that are most prone to the potential of extinction. Obviously, detailed data on each species is ideal, but this luxury is seldom afforded ecologists or conservationists.

Two data sets for mammals appear appropriate for testing the predictions for persistence time from the model. Brown (1971) and Patterson (1984) report the distribution of boreal forest mammals of different body masses on mountaintops in the Great Basin desert and the Southern Rocky Mountains of North America. Presumably, a complete boreal fauna existed throughout these two areas until approximately 8000 years ago when a warming and drying trend restricted the forests to mountain-tops above 2300 meters. After this time, extinction of species presumably took place without replacement by recolonization since the mountaintop populations of boreal mammals were too widely separated. This process is called faunal collapse (Soulé, Wilcox, and Holtby, 1979). With this information on the boreal mammal populations and the body masses of the different species, the extinction model can be tested.

Brown (1971) surveyed the presence of 13 species of boreal mammals on 17 mountaintops and Patterson (1984) examined 26 species on 28 mountaintops. The carnivorous species were dropped from my analysis (three species: Brown, 1971; nine species: Patterson, 1984) because they do not span a large range of body masses and because the measures of environmental variation are more applicable to herbivores (see above). The remaining herbivore species can be lumped into four classes of r_m values based upon body mass and three different mountaintop-area classes. These categories and their respective sample sizes are presented in Table 3.1.

Pooling the data from these two studies into the above classes effec-tively increases the number of replicate populations that might have gone extinct over the past 8000 years. Goodman (1986; Chapter 2) indicates that the persistence times for a given species' population size should be distributed as a negative exponential (mean equals standard deviation). Mountaintop area can be converted into N_m for each r_m-class using the body mass function for temperate herbivore population densities in Box I and the r_m-class's average body mass. An expected persistence time for populations (T) of a given r_m and mountaintop-area class can be com-puted, using the proportion of populations which persisted for at least 8000 years and a negative exponential probability distribution. With estimates of N_m, T, and the W for each r_m/mountaintop-area category, a multiple regression relating these variables can be constructed. Trans-forming N_m, T, and W using logarithms, a rather good fit is obtained by a multiple regression:

$$N_m = 186.2T^{1.14}W_g^{-0.44} \qquad (7)$$

($r^2 = 0.83$, $N_m = 24$, $p < 0.001$).

The power value for W in equation (7) is an estimate of θ in equation (6). On the basis of θ's sign and absolute value, the extinction model, equation (3), cannot be rejected and the congruence ($\theta = -0.36$ to -0.40) is quite good.

Table 3.1. *The categories of data constructed from Brown's (1971) and Patterson's (1984) studies of boreal mammal distributions on mountaintops in the southwestern US. In the sample size columns, the first value is for Brown's study and the second for Patterson's.*

r_m category (young/yr)	Sample size (no.)	Mountaintop-area category (km² above 2300 m)	Sample size (no.)
1–<2	2/3	<140	6/13
2–<3	3/4	>140–<595	6/6
3–<4	2/3	>595	5/9
4–5+	3/7		

How good is the model and what does it tell us

We need to address how predictive the extinction model is and what it tells us about extinction. This can be accomplished by comparing the predicted persistence times for different r_m/mountaintop-area classes with the observed values (see above). We might expect boreal mountaintops distributed in arid environments to have a high variance in annual rainfall. Therefore, the maximum observed V was employed along with the body mass dependent estimates of N_m to predict persistence time, T, using the extinction model. Because T is exponentially distributed, the probability that a population will persist for 8000 years can be easily computed since we know that T's standard deviation is simply its mean value. Using the probability density function for the negative exponential, the probability of a population with a given T persisting 8000 years can be computed. This predicted probability can be compared with the observed proportion of mountaintops in an area class that still contains the populations composing an r_m-class (Brown, 1971; Patterson, 1984). This comparison (Figure 3.1) indicates a close agreement between the predictions from the model and the observed persistence (Brown, 1971: $r^2 = 0.75$, $N_m = 12$, $p < 0.01$).

Both data sets provide very similar regression equations comparing predicted and observed persistence probabilities. The predicted persistence, however, for large N_m values (large mountaintops) is consistently greater than observed. This might be due to the approximations used for the model's parameters which may oversimplify species differences in r which lead to this bias. This may be the case since many of the species found only on the largest mountaintops have the most restrictive habitat requirements and consequently lower densities (J. H. Brown, pers. comm.). More importantly, the body mass dependent estimates gloss over differences in habitat suitability and the presence of greater densities of predators or competitors on large mountaintops that could reduce N_m and persistence time.

Even with the above-mentioned difficulties, the model appears to capture the dynamics of the extinction process and may be a useful first approximation for the probability of extinction. The population sizes necessary for a 95% probability of persistence for 100 years ($T = 2000$ years) and 1000 years ($T = 20\,000$ years) are presented in Figure 3.2a for mammals of different body masses given the highest and lowest observed environmentally-induced variances (V, Box I).

The predicted minimum N_m values necessary to provide an expected persistence time of 100 or 1000 years (Figure 3.2a) may appear to be prohibitively large for the management of species preserves. It should be kept in mind that these N_m values reflect a 95% chance of a population's successful persistence for a chosen time period. This probabilistic approach requires a 20-fold increase above the desired time to guarantee a 95% chance of success. This large increase is due to persistence time

Figure 3.1. The persistence of populations of boreal herbivorous mammals that possess similar *r* values and inhabit mountaintops of different areas (different *K* values) are predicted using the extinction model and compared with the observed persistence on mountaintops in the Great Basin (a) and Southern Rocky Mountains (b) over the past 8000 years. The greatest observed *V* value was employed (Box I).

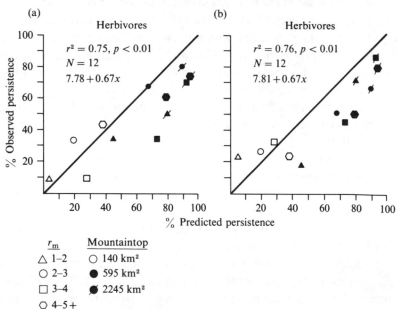

being exponentially distributed. Therefore, a manager's willingness to reduce the probability of success can drastically decrease the necessary population size needed to provide a sought-after persistence time.

Using the body mass dependent functions to estimate N_m (Box I), we can convert the predicted population sizes for a given 95% probability of persistence into the necessary habitat area required to sustain the population (Figure 3.2b, c). Comparing the population size necessary for persistence with habitat area provides two important bits of knowledge. First, it relates extinction to area, an underlying assumption of island biogeography theory (MacArthur, 1972; Schoener, 1983; Toft and Schoener, 1983; Diamond, 1984a; b; Pielou, 1979). Second, this crude relationship between habitat area and persistence of populations of mammals of different sizes provides a 'rule of thumb' for managers in the design of refuges to conserve not only specific species of animals and plants (Shaffer, Chapter 5), but also entire ecological communities.

The predicted area required to provide a given N_m, as expected, varies with the mammal's feeding ecology (herbivore *versus* carnivore) and its environment (temperate *versus* tropic). Generally, larger areas are required for carnivores than herbivores, tropic *versus* temperate populations and high *versus* low environmental variance. This indicates that carnivores in high variance tropical environments are most subject to extinction and herbivores in low variance temperate environments are least subject to extinction. Island biogeography theory examines extinction and area as average values without regard to the species or habitat. We can see, however, from the above analysis that a species' ecology (feeding, climate, and body mass) can dramatically change the relationship between area and extinction probability (Wright and Hubbell, 1983).

Carnivores are expected to require more area to forage over than herbivores since animal foods are less abundant than plant foods (McNab, 1963; Harestad and Bunnell, 1979). This implies that we must preserve larger areas to support a given carnivore population, as indicated in Figure 3.2b, c. On the other hand, population densities for a species are lower in tropical rather than temperate environments. Tropical densities may be lower due to greater species diversity in the tropics which may lead to a greater number and intensity of deleterious biotic interactions (e.g., competition, predation, disease, etc.). Lower tropical densities probably may not be attributable to lower food availability as resulting from lower productivity. For example, tropical grasslands from which the majority of the data come are some of the most productive environments. Lower densities require the preservation of larger areas to provide a given population size (Figure 3.2b, c).

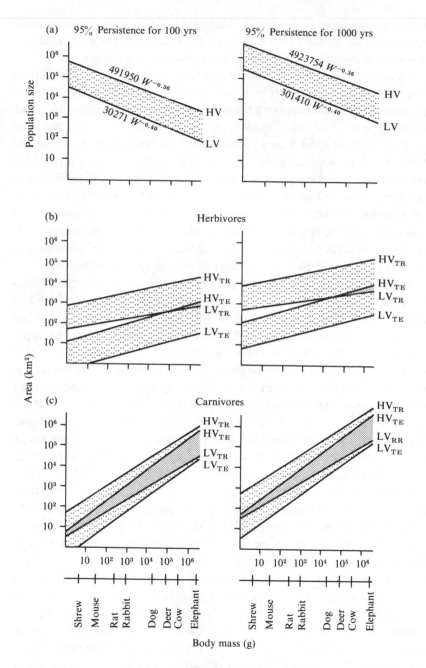

Figure 3.2.

Two final points need to be examined: are there any additional impacts on extinction that arise from differences in the natural history of species and how important is environmentally-induced variability for extinction? Carnivores were dropped in the analysis of Brown's (1971) and Patterson's (1984) data because the measure of environmental variability based on rainfall, water levels, or plant growth seemed more appropriate to reflect changes in the abundance of a herbivore's plant foods, rather than a carnivore's foods. If we assume, however, that variability in plant foods changes herbivore numbers which in turn change carnivore numbers, then the carnivore data can be compared with the predictions of the model using the V values in Box I (Figure 3.3). Again both study sites provide very similar regression equations (Figure 3.3). Even though this comparison employs the temperate carnivore's body mass dependent relationship to estimate N_m and the maximum V value, we find that the model predicts a much greater persistence time than observed for carnivores.

Given carnivore and herbivore populations of equal size, the model's predictions are supported more closely for herbivores; extinctions in carnivores are much greater than expected. In part this may arise because many of the carnivores have very specialized habitat requirements (J. A. Brown, pers. comm.). Nonetheless, this finding is counterintuitive since we usually think of mammalian carnivores as being 'K-selected' and the herbivores as more 'r-selected' (MacArthur and Wilson, 1967). Population numbers for 'K-selected' species are thought to vary less over time than population numbers of 'r-selected' species. Therefore, a comparison of 'K- and r-selected' species for population fluctuations may only

---

Figure 3.2. (a) presents the solution to the extinction model for the population size needed to persist 100 or 1000 years with a 95% probability for mammals of different body masses. The scale at the bottom of (a), (b), and (c) gives examples of mammals of different body masses but are not the mammals used in the calculations. HV and LV refer to the high and low variance values presented in Box I (V) that should bound the majority of 'real world' values (shaded region). The allometric regressions for population size at each variance (HV–LV) are presented.

(b) presents the conversion of the predicted N_m values for herbivorous mammals of different body masses into the necessary habitat area needed to sustain that population size. TR refers to tropical environments and TE refers to temperate environments. The shaded regions represent the expected 'real world' values bounded by HV and LV. The allometric equations used to convert N_m into area appear in Box I.

(c) presents a similar conversion of N_m into habitat area for carnivores.

be appropriate within a trophic level. In the case of carnivores, their populations are interacting (predator/prey) with herbivore populations, and this interaction, which is one step removed from environmental variations, might serve to amplify population variability.

Stochastic models of predator/prey interactions have suggested such a relationship (Leslie and Gower, 1960), and Pimm (1984) argues that stochastic fluctuations in r can lead to reductions in food chain length (i.e., disappearance of upper trophic levels). Empirically, this is substantiated by the greater extinction rates observed for carnivores (Terborgh and Winter, 1980; Diamond, 1984a; b).

Finally, the minimum population size (N) required to permit a 95% chance of persistence for a given time period can be examined for the impact of the relative environmental variance on r, (V/r). The minimum N increases dramatically over a small range of V/r values (Figure 3.4: $V/r = 1$ to 2) and then increases at a much slower rate. Therefore, the simple presence of environmentally-induced variance has a dramatic impact on extinction, but continued increases in variance become less and less important. The relationship in Figure 3.4 increases at a decreasing rate because large populations are less likely to be reduced to very low

Figure 3.3. The predicted persistence from the extinction model is plotted against the observed persistence for carnivorous, boreal, mammal species inhabiting mountaintops of different areas (same area categories as in Figure 3.1). The largest observed V value was employed (Box I). Great Basin mountaintops are plotted in (a), while (b) presents values for the Southern Rocky Mountains.

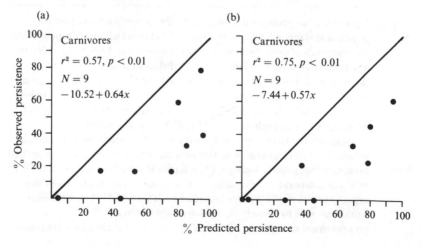

densities by variability. Consequently, once a population reaches a certain size the importance of environmental variation is of less consequence for extinction.

Conclusion

Overall, the extinction model (Goodman, Chapter 2) for random and environmental demographic variation appears to capture the important aspects of the extinction process. The estimates for the model's parameters that are presented here, although reflecting observed extinction patterns for mammals, do oversimply the dynamics and underestimate extinction probabilities. Nonetheless, for a specific group of animals, the analysis provides a first approximation of the necessary population sizes and habitat area for averting extinction over some time period. This has potential for the management of endangered species populations and the design of wildlife refuges (Shaffer, Chapter 5; Shaffer, 1981; 1983; Shaffer and Samson, 1985).

The simple analysis conducted here is by no means complete. Other taxa than mammals need to be examined in a similar manner and additional data sets for mammal extinctions also must be used to test the model (e.g., Sunda Shelf: Heaney, 1984). Nonetheless, the body size patterns in species extinction reported elsewhere are consistent with the predictions presented here (Diamond, 1984a; b; Terborgh and Winter, 1980; Schoener, 1983; Toft and Schoener, 1983). This is important since the models represent an underlying assumption of island biogeography

Figure 3.4. The effect of changing relative environmental variance (V/r) on the necessary mammalian population size for persistence is presented ($r = 0.125$, $T = 2000$ years or 95% of persisting 100 years).

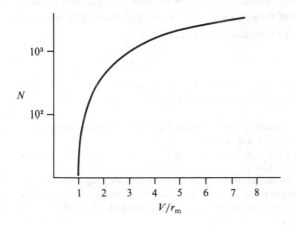

theory and link this theory with the area of evolutionary ecology dealing with life history or reproductive strategies.

The most complete data sets would be obtained from studying laboratory populations in variable environments, using species with short generation times (e.g., *Drosophila*). In addition, long-term field experiments, such as those in the Amazon rain forest on the extinction of populations in fragmented forests (Lovejoy *et al.*, 1984), must be conducted. Field studies can provide comparisons of laboratory results with field conditions and with species having longer generation times. These data currently are rare especially for species that have small populations or are threatened by man. A larger data base will provide a better basis for the design of parks and refuges to conserve the world's biota. Therefore, the model studied here, or a similar model, may provide a useful methodology for estimating the sizes of viable populations. This is the essence of the idea of MVP.

The concept of MVP, as addressed in this chapter, does not inspire optimism. By comparing the areas required for mammal persistence with the sizes of parks in the world (Frankel and Soulé, 1981), we can estimate the future success of man's conservation efforts if we assume management by 'benign neglect.' The largest mammalian carnivores (10–100 kg) can be expected to persist 100 years in 0–22% of the current parks but no park is large enough to guarantee persistence for 1000 years. For the largest mammalian herbivores (100–1000 kg), the future is brighter since 4–100% of reserves should permit persistence for 100 years and 0–22% will permit persistence for 1000 years. For larger mammals (>50 kg) to persist in evolutionary time (10^5–10^6 years), regions of 10^6 to 10^9 km^2 are required, assuming that major climatic variations do not occur. These calculations are in accord with estimates made by J. H. Brown (pers. comm.). Obviously, man must re-evaluate his conservation efforts and management schemes in light of these results if the larger mammals are to be preserved in nature without human intervention.

References

Blueweiss, L., Fox, H., Kudzma, V., Nakashima, D., Peters, R., and Sams, S. 1978. Relationships between body size and some life history parameters. *Oecologia (Berl.)* **37**: 257–72.

Brown, J. H. 1971. Mammals on mountaintops: nonequilibrium insular biogeography. *Am. Nat.* **105**: 467–78.

Calder, W. A. III. 1984. *Size, Function, and Life History*. Harvard University Press, Cambridge, Mass.

Calow, P. 1981. Resource utilization and reproduction. Pp. 245–70 *in* C. R. Townsend and P. Calow (eds.) *Physiological Ecology: An Evolutionary Approach to Resource Use*. Sinauer Associates, Sunderland, Mass.

Caughley, G. and Krebs, C. J. 1983. Are big mammals simply little mammals writ large? *Oecologia (Berl.)* **59**: 7–17.

Colinvaux, P. 1978. *Why Big Fierce Animals are Rare: an Ecologist's Perspective.* Princeton University Press, Princeton, New Jersey.

Damuth, J. 1981. Population density and body size in mammals. *Nature* **290**: 699–700.

Department of Environmental Health. 1960. *Drought flow of Michigan streams.* School of Public Health, University of Michigan.

Diamond, J. M. 1984a. 'Normal' extinctions of isolated populations. Pp. 191–246 *in* M. H. Nitecki (ed.) *Extinctions.* The University of Chicago Press, Chicago.

Diamond, J. M. 1984b. Historic extinction: a Rosetta Stone for understanding prehistoric extinctions. Pp. 824–62 *in* P. S. Martin and R. G. Klein (eds.) *Quaternary Extinctions: a Prehistoric Revolution.* The University of Arizona Press, Tucson, Arizona.

Feller, W. 1939. Die Grundlagen der Volterraschen Theorie des Kampfes ums dasein in wahrscheinlichkeitstheoretischer Behandlung. *Acta Biotheoretica* **5**: 11–40.

Fenchel, T. 1974. Intrinsic rate of natural increase: the relationship with body size. *Oecologia (Berl.)* **14**: 317–26.

Frankel, O. H. and Soulé, M. E. 1981. *Conservation and Evolution.* Cambridge University Press, Cambridge.

Fritts, H. C. 1966. Growth-rings of trees: their correlation with climate. *Science* **154**: 973–9.

Ginzburg, L. R., Slobodkin, L. B., Johnson, K., and Bindman, A. G. 1982. Quasiextinction probabilities as a measure of impact on population growth. *Risk Analysis* **2**: 171–81.

Goodman, D. (in press) The minimum viable population problem. I. The demography of chance extinction.

Hanson, F. B. and Tuckwell, H. C. 1978. Persistence times of populations with large random fluctuations. *Theor. Pop. Biol.* **14**: 46–61.

Harestad, A. S. and Bunnell, F. L. 1979. Home range and body weight – a reevaluation. *Ecology* **60**: 389–402.

Hayssen, V. 1984. Basal metabolic rate and the intrinsic rate of increase: an empirical and theoretical reexamination. *Oecologia (Berl.)* **64**: 419–21.

Heaney, L. R. 1984. Mammalian species richness on islands on the Sunda Shelf, Southeast Asia. *Oecologia (Berl.)* **61**: 11–17.

Hennemann, W. W. III. 1984. Commentary. *Oecologia (Berl.)* **64**: 421–3.

Horn, H. S. and Rubenstein, D. I. 1984. Behavioural adaptations and life history. Pp. 279–98 *in* J. R. Krebs and N. B. Davies (eds.) *Behavioural Ecology: An Evolutionary Approach.* Sinauer Associates, Sunderland, Mass.

Hubbell, S. P. 1979. Tree dispersion, abundance, and diversity in a tropical dry forest. *Science* **203**: 1299–1309.

Leigh, E. G., Jr. 1975. Population fluctuations, community stability, and environmental variability. Pp. 51–73. *In* M. L. Cody and J. M. Diamond (eds.) *Ecology and Evolution of Communities.* Belknap Press of Harvard University, Cambridge, Mass.

Leigh, E. G., Jr. 1981. The average lifetime of a population in a varying environment. *J. Theor. Biol.* **90**: 231–39.

Leslie, P. H. and Gower, J. C. 1960. The properties of a stochastic model for the predator–prey type of interaction between two species. *Biometrika* **47**: 219–34.

Lodge, R. W., Campbell, J. B., Smoliak, S., and Johnston, A. 1971. *Management of the western range.* Can. Dept. Agric. Publ. No. 1425.

Lovejoy, T. E., Rankin, J. M., Bierregaard, R. O., Jr., Brown, K. S., Jr.,

Emmons, L. M., and Van der Voort, M. E. 1984. Ecosystem decay of Amazon forest remnants. Pp. 295–325 *in* M. H. Nitecki (ed.) *Extinctions*. The University of Chicago Press, Chicago.

MacArthur, R. H. 1972. *Geographical Ecology: Patterns in the Distribution of Species*. Harper and Row, New York.

MacArthur, R. H. and Wilson, E. O. 1967. *The Theory of Island Biogeography*. Princeton University Press, Princeton, New Jersey.

McNab, B. K. 1963. Bioenergetics and the determination of home range size. *Am. Nat.* **97**: 133–40.

McNab, B. K. 1980. Food habits, energetics, and the population biology of mammals. *Am. Nat.* **116**: 106–24.

McNab, B. K. 1984. Commentary. *Oecologia (Berl.)* **64**: 423–4.

Millar, J. S. and Zammuto, R. M. 1983. Life histories of mammals: an analysis of life tables. *Ecology* **64**: 631–5.

Morth, H. T. 1967. *Investigation into the meteorological aspects of the variations in the level of Lake Victoria*. EAMD Memoirs, Vol. IV, No. 2.

Odum, E. P. 1971. *Fundamentals of Ecology*, Third Edition. W. B. Saunders Co., Philadelphia.

Patterson, B. D. 1984. Mammalian extinction and biogeography in the Southern Rocky Mountains. Pp. 247–93 *in* M. H. Nitecki (ed.) *Extinctions*. The University of Chicago Press, Chicago.

Peters, R. H. 1983. *The Ecological Implications of Body Size*. Cambridge University Press, Cambridge.

Peters, R. H. and Raelson, J. V. 1984. Relations between individual size and mammalian population density. *Am. Nat.* **124**: 498–517.

Peters, R. H. and Wassenberg, K. 1983. The effect of body size on animal abundance. *Oecologia (Berl.)* **60**: 89–96.

Pianka, E. R. 1970. On r- and K-selection. *Am. Nat.* **104**: 592–7.

Pielou, E. C. 1979. *Biogeography*. John Wiley and Sons, New York.

Pimm, S. L. 1984. Food chains and return times. Pp. 397–412 *in* D. R. Strong, Jr., D. Simberloff, L. G. Abele, and A. B. Thistle (eds.) *Ecological Communities: Conceptual Issues and the Evidence*. Princeton University Press, Princeton.

Richter-Dyn, N. and Goel, R. S. 1972. On the extinction of a colonizing species. *Theor. Pop. Biol.* **3**: 406–33.

Ricklefs, R. E. 1973. *Ecology*. Chiron Press, Newton, Massachusetts.

Rosenzweig, M. L. 1968. Net primary productivity of terrestrial communities: prediction from climatological data. *Am. Nat.* **102**: 67–74.

Roughgarden, J. 1979. *Theory of Population Genetics and Evolutionary Ecology: an Introduction*. Macmillan Publishing Co., New York.

Schaffer, W. M. and Gadgil, M. D. 1975. Selection for optimal life histories in plants. Pp. 142–57 *in* M. L. Cody and J. M. Diamond (eds.) *Ecology and Evolution of Communities*. Belknap Press of Harvard University, Cambridge, Mass.

Schmitz, O. J. and Lavigne, D. M. 1984. Intrinsic rate of increase, body size, and specific metabolic rate in marine mammals. *Oecologia (Berl.)* **62**: 305–9.

Schoener, T. W. 1983. Rate of species turnover decreases from lower to higher organisms: a review of the data. *Oikos* **41**: 372–7.

Shaffer, M. L. 1981. Minimum population sizes for species conservation. *Bioscience* **31**: 131–4.

Shaffer, M. L. 1983. Determining minimum viable populations sizes for the grizzly bear. *Int. Conf. Bear Res. Manage.* **5**: 133–9.

Shaffer, M. L. and Samson, F. B. 1985. Population size and extinction: a note on determining critical population sizes. *Am. Nat.* **125**: 144–52.

Slobodkin, L. B. 1960. Ecological energy relationships at the population level. *Am. Nat.* **94**: 213–36.

Slobodkin, L. B. 1962. Energy in animal ecology. *Advances in Ecological Research* **1**: 69–101.

Slobodkin, L. B. 1972. On the inconstancy of ecological efficiency and the form of ecological theories. *Trans. Conn. Acad. Arts and Sci.* **44**: 293–305.

Smith, F. E. 1954. Quantitative aspects of population growth. Pp. 277–94 *in* E. J. Boell (ed.) *Dynamics of Growth Processes*. Princeton University Press, Princeton, New Jersey.

Soulé, M. E., Wilcox, B. A., and Holtby, C. 1979. Benign neglect: a model of faunal collapse in the game reserves of East Africa. *Biol. Conservation* **15**: 259–72.

Strebel, D. E. 1985. Environmental fluctuations and extinction – single species. *Theor. Pop. Biol.* **27**: 1–26.

Stearns, S. C. 1976. Life-history tactics: a review of the ideas. *Quart. Rev. Biol.* **51**: 3–65.

Terborgh, J. and Winter, B. 1980. Some causes of extinction. Pp. 119–33 *in* M. E. Soulé and B. A. Wilcox (eds.) *Conservation Biology: An Evolutionary-Ecological Perspective*. Sinauer Associates, Sunderland, Mass.

Toft, C. A. and Schoener, T. W. 1983. Abundance and diversity of orb spiders on 106 Bahamian islands: biogeography at an intermediate trophic level. *Oikos* **41**: 411–26.

Tuomi, J. 1980. Mammalian reproductive strategies: a generalized relation of litter size to body size. *Oecologia (Berl.)* **45**: 39–44.

Western, D. 1979. Size, life history and ecology in mammals. *Afr. J. Ecol.* **17**: 185–204.

Western, D. and Ssemakula, J. 1982. Life history patterns in birds and mammals and their evolutionary interpretation. *Oecologia (Berl.)* **54**: 281–90.

Wright, S. J. and Hubbell, S. P. 1983. Stochastic extinction and reserve size: a focal species approach. *Oikos* **41**: 466–76.

Box I: a general extinction analysis

A general (body mass) solution to the extinction model is developed here for mammals. The necessary model parameters are taken from the literature and presented as functions of body mass. (W_g = body mass in grams.)

For mammals:

$r_m = 18.0W_g^{-0.36}$ (no./year)   (Caughley and Krebs, 1983)

N_m = (a) tropical herbivores: $648.0W_g^{-0.57}$ (no./km^2)

              (Peters and Raelson, 1984)

   (b) tropical carnivores: $10918.9W_g^{-1.02}$ (no./km^2)

              (Peters and Raelson, 1984)

   (c) temperate herbivores: $44693.7W_g^{-0.66}$ (no./km^2)

              (Peters and Raelson, 1984)

   (d) temperate carnivores: $95478.7W_g^{-1.14}$ (no./km^2)

              (Peters and Raelson, 1984)

Variation in rainfall, stream flow, lake levels, or tree growth ring width (Morth, 1967; Fritts, 1966; Lodge *et al.*, 1971; Department of Environmental Health, 1960; Belovsky, unpubl. data) are used to compute environmental variance (see text). The lowest environmental variance values were found for temperate forest rainfall and dry temperate forest tree growth rings, and the highest values were found for grassland rainfall (temperate and tropic) and moist temperate forest tree growth rings.

$$V = 1.43r \text{ to } 7.32r$$

This range of values encompasses the extremes in the studies cited above.

Using the above parameters, the expected persistence time can be computed for the extinction model. The model is solved for an expected persistence time of 20 000 years which provides a 95% probability of persistence for 1000 years (see text). The r^2 values refer to the correlation coefficients for the regression equations between mammal body mass and population size needed for a 20 000 year expected persistence time given high (HV) and low (LV) environmental variances.

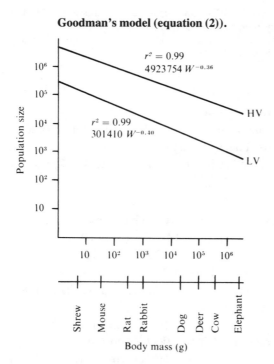

Goodman's model (equation (2)).

Appendix

The computer program is provided to solve the extinction model, equation (2). The program is written in BASIC and provides the option to solve for expected persistence time given population size, or to use an iterative process to solve for the population size needed to provide an expected persistence time. The population's mean growth rate and variance due to environmental fluctuations also must be entered.

```
1000 REM-GOODMAN'S EXTINCTION MODEL
1010 CLEAR
1020 PRINT "************************************************************"
1030 PRINT "************************************************************"
1040 PRINT "***                                                     ***"
1050 PRINT "***   N IS THE POPULATION SIZE                          ***"
1060 PRINT "***   T IS THE EXPECTED PERSISTENCE TIME                ***"
1070 PRINT "***                                                     ***"
1080 PRINT "***      DO YOU WISH TO SOLVE FOR N GIVEN T, THEN TYPE 0 ***"
1090 PRINT "***                                                     ***"
1100 PRINT "***      DO YOU WISH TO SOLVE FOR T GIVEN N, THEN TYPE 1 ***"
1110 PRINT "***                                                     ***"
1120 PRINT "************************************************************"
1130 PRINT "************************************************************"
1140
1150 INPUT PROMPT "WHAT IS YOUR CHOICE? ":A1
1160
1170 INPUT PROMPT "WHAT IS THE GROWTH RATE (R)? ":R
1180 INPUT PROMPT "WHAT IS THE VARIANCE OF R (V)? ":V
1190 LET F=1
1200 IF A1=1 THEN GOTO 1230        !BRANCH INTO SEARCH PROCESS
1210 INPUT PROMPT "WHAT IS THE DESIRED PERSISTENCE TIME (T)? ":T
1220 INPUT PROMPT "WHAT ARE THE GUESSES FOR UPPER AND LOWER N? ":K2,K1
1230 LET X1=0
1240 LET X2=0
1250 LET X3=0
1260 LET Y1=0
1270 LET Y2=0
1280 LET Y3=0
1290 LET Z1=0
1300 LET Z2=0
1310 LET Z3=0
1320 LET T1=0
1330 LET T2=0
1340 LET T3=0
1350 IF A1=0 THEN GO TO 1560
1360 INPUT PROMPT "WHAT IS THE POPULATION SIZE? ":N
1370 IF N>20 THEN LET T1-1.644    !LIMIT TO 1/I^2
1380 IF N>20 THEN GOTO 1420
1390 FOR P=1 TO N
1400     LET T1=(1/P^2)+T1
1410 NEXT P
1420 LET T1=(2/(V-R))*T1
1430 LET X1=((V+R)/(V-R))*T1/(2*R)
1440 LET M=N
1450 IF N>1000 THEN LET M=1000   !LIMIT TO LOOP LENGTH
1460 FOR P=1 TO M
1470     LET X2=X2+1/(P*(P*V-R))
```

```
1480 NEXT P
1490 LET X2=X2/R
1500 FOR P=2 TO M
1510    LET X3=X3+1/((((P-1)*V)-R)*((P*V)-R))
1520 NEXT P
1530 LET X3=X3*T1*V
1540 LET T=(X1-X2-X3)*((N-1)*V-R)
1550 GOTO 2280
1560 LET M1=K1
1570 IF K1>20 THEN LET T1=1.644    !LIMIT TO 1/P^2
1580 IF K1>20 THEN GOTO 1620
1590 FOR P=1 TO K1
1600    LET T1=(1/P^2)+T1
1610 NEXT P
1620 LET T1=(2/(V-R))*T1
1630 LET M2=K2
1640 IF K2>20 THEN LET T2=1.644    !LIMIT TO 1/P^2
1650 IF K2>20 THEN GOTO 1690
1660 FOR P=1 TO K2
1670    LET T2=(1/P^2)+T2
1680 NEXT P
1690 LET T2=(2/(V-R))*T2
1700 LET K3=(K1+K2)/2
1710 LET M3=K3
1720 IF K3>20 THEN LET T3=1.644    !LIMIT TO 1/P^2
1730 IF K3>20 THEN GOTO 1770
1740 FOR P=1 TO K3
1750    LET T3=(1/P^2)+T3
1760 NEXT P
1770 LET T3=(2/(V-R))*T3
1780 IF K3>1000 THEN LET M3=1000  !LIMIT TO LOOP LENGTH
1790 IF F<>1 THEN GOTO 2020
1800 LET X1=(V+R)/(V-R)*T1/(2*R)
1810 IF K1>1000 THEN LET M1=1000  !LIMIT TO LOOP LENGTH
1820 IF K2>1000 THEN LET M2=1000  !LIMIT TO LOOP LENGTH
1830 FOR P=1 TO M1
1840    LET X2=X2+1/(P*(P*V-R))
1850 NEXT P
1860 LET X2=X2/R
1870 FOR P=2 TO M1
1880    LET X3=X3+1/(((((P-1)*V)-R)*((P*V)-R))
1890 NEXT P
1900 LET X3=X3*T1*V
1910 LET T1=(X1-X2-X3)*((K1-1)*V-R)
1920 LET Y1=((V+R)/(V-R))*T2/(2*R)
1930 FOR P=1 TO M2
1940    LET Y2=Y2+1/(P*(P*V-R))
1950 NEXT P
1960 LET Y2=Y2/R
1970 FOR P=2 TO M2
1980    LET Y3=Y3+1/((((P-1)*V)-R)*((P*V)-R))
1990 NEXT P
2000 LET Y3=Y3*T2*V
2010 LET T2=(Y1-Y2-Y3)*((K2-1)*V-R)
2020 LET K3=(K1+K2)/2
2030 LET Z1=((V+R)/(V-R))*T3/(2*R)
2040 FOR P=1 TO M3
2050    LET Z2=Z2+1/(P*(P*V-R))
2060 NEXT P
```

```
2070 LET Z2=Z2/R
2080 FOR P=2 TO M3
2090    LET Z3=Z3+1/((((P-1)*V)-R)*((P*V)-R))
2100 NEXT P
2110 LET Z3=Z3*T3*V
2120 LET T3=(Z1-Z2-Z3)*((K3-1)*V-R)
2130 IF F=1 AND T2<T THEN GOTO 2240
2140 IF F=1 AND T1>T THEN GOTO 2260
2150 IF T3<T THEN LET K1=K3
2160 IF T3>T THEN LET K2=K3
2170 IF ABS(T3-T)<.001*T THEN GOTO 2272
2180 LET Z1=0
2190 LET Z2=0
2200 LET Z3=0
2210 LET T3=0
2220 LET F=2
2230 GOTO 1700
2240 INPUT PROMPT "PICK A LARGER UPPER VALUE FOR N - ":K2
2250 GOTO 1230
2260 INPUT PROMPT "PICK A SMALLER LOWER VALUE FOR N - ":K1
2270 GOTO 1230
2272 IF A1=0 THEN LET T=T3
2276 IF A1=0 THEN LET N=K3
2280 PRINT "***********************************************************"
2290 PRINT "***********************************************************"
2300 PRINT "***                                          ***"
2310 PRINT "***      MODEL PARAMETERS:                    ***"
2320 PRINT "***                                          ***"
2325 PRINT "***        ";
2330 PRINT USING "R=##.##":R;
2335 PRINT "                             ***"
2337 PRINT "***            ";
2340 PRINT USING "V=##.##":V;
2345 PRINT "                         ***"
2347 PRINT "***            ";
2350 PRINT USING "N=#######":N;
2355 PRINT "                    ***"
2357 PRINT "***            ";
2360 PRINT USING "T=#######":T;
2365 PRINT "                         ***"
2370 PRINT "***                                          ***"
2380 PRINT "**************************************"
2390 PRINT "**************************************"
2400
2410 INPUT PROMPT "DO YOU WISH TO CONTINUE? ":A$
2420 IF A$<>"YES" THEN GOTO 2450
2430 CLEAR
2440 GOTO 1020
2450 END
```

4

Minimum viable population size in the presence of catastrophes

WARREN J. EWENS
Department of Biology, University of Pennsylvania, Philadelphia, PA 19104

P. J. BROCKWELL
Department of Statistics, Colorado State University, Fort Collins, CO 80521

J. M. GANI
Department of Statistics, University of Kentucky, Lexington, KT 40506

S. I. RESNICK
Department of Statistics, Colorado State University, Fort Collins, CO 80521

There are two broad concepts of a minimum viable population (MVP) size. The first is a *genetic* concept, based on the rate at which genetic variation in a population is lost, and hence fitness decreased, through random genetic drift. The second is a *demographic* concept and is concerned with the probability of complete extinction of a population through random demographic forces. Although at an overall level these concepts are related, since inbreeding decreases fecundity and increases the death rate, present theory treats these as distinct concepts, since normal practice has been to assume the population size constant in defining and calculating the genetic MVP. For convenience, we also preserve this distinction in this chapter, and note that until a generalized theory covering both concepts is attempted, confusion may arise by the loose transfer of a numerical value of the MVP from the genetic to the demographic case, particularly the genetically derived values offered by Franklin (1980) and Soulé (1980).

For each of these two MVP concepts, the numerical value for the MVP eventually reached will depend on two assumptions. The first is the criterion chosen to define an MVP; for example, using the demographic concept, the size of the population which guarantees 95% probability of survival for y years clearly depends on the value chosen for y. The second assumption concerns the details of the model used to describe the population's behavior. The MVP will be affected by the broad features of the model, such as the geographical structure, the ceiling on population size, the birth and death rates (absolute or density-dependent), and so on. But it will also depend on more detailed features (e.g., numerical values of parameters) within the broad framework. As a result of this, a very wide range of values can reasonably be arrived at for the MVP for any given situation, and the view that a standard numerical value can be used as a 'rule' for MVP across a broad range of circumstances is misguided. These observations seem obvious enough, and would not be made here were it not for the fact that 'rule' values for MVP seem to be widely accepted. It seems more sensible, for any given situation, to disregard 'rule' values and, having decided on the criteria for MVP, to model the population of interest as accurately as possible so as to calculate the required value. In this connection, computer simulation might well provide the most useful approach (in particular for a demographically defined MVP), first because personal computers are ideally suited to this task, and secondly because theoretical calculations may be possible only for unduly simplified models. We report on such a simulation later, and note that a study following these suggestions is the recent grizzly bear simulation of Shaffer (1983).

Definition of the genetic MVP

We start by discussing the population genetics theory which underlies the calculation of any genetically based MVP size.

In the early days of population genetics theory, R. A. Fisher and Sewall Wright independently introduced a very simple mathematical model to describe the stochastic behavior of gene frequencies in a diploid population of fixed size N. (See Ewens (1979, p. 16) for a description of this model.) We consider some specific locus A in this population, admitting alleles A_1 and A_2, and assume that there are no complicating factors such that variations in population size, geographical structure, or two sexes, arise. Mainly for historical reasons, this model has assumed a central place in the theory against which other models are calibrated, as we note in a moment. The model has a number of well-known features, the main one of interest for us now being the following. Suppose two genes are taken at random from the population in generation t, and let P_t be the probability that these two genes are of different allelic types. In other words, if there are X genes of allelic type A_1 in generation t and thus $2N - X$ genes of allelic type A_2, then $P_t = X(2N - X)/2N(2N - 1)$. Then it is easy to show that

$$P_{t+1} = \left(1 - \frac{1}{2N}\right)P_t, \tag{1}$$

so that

$$P_t = \left(1 - \frac{1}{2N}\right)^t P_0, \tag{2}$$

where P_0 is the value of P_t in generation $t = 0$.

We therefore say that the mean population heterozygosity decreases at a geometric rate $1 - 1/2N$ per generation, or, more loosely, that the genetic variation in the population decreases at this rate.

As noted above, the Wright–Fisher model is very simplified. Suppose we introduce a more complicated model, involving say two sexes or geographical structure. Suppose also that in this more complicated model we find, at least for large t, that, defining P_t as above,

$$P_t = \lambda^t P_0, \tag{3}$$

where λ is the rate of decrease of heterozygosity in this model. Then we can say that in this more complicated model, the genetic variation decreases asymptotically at the same rate as a simple Wright–Fisher population of size N_e, if N_e satisfies

$$1 - \frac{1}{2N_e} = \lambda \tag{4}$$

or

$$N_e = \frac{1}{2}(1 - \lambda)^{-1}. \tag{5}$$

We thus call the value of N_e calculated from equations (5) or (6) the (eigenvalue) effective population size of the more complex model. For example, in the standard generalization of the Wright–Fisher model allowing for two sexes (see Ewens, 1979, pp. 106–8, for details), the value of λ satisfying equation (3) is, to a close approximation, $\lambda = 1 - (N_1 + N_2)/8N_1N_2$, where N_1 is the number of males in the population and N_2 the number of females, and this gives

$$N_e \approx 4N_1N_2/(N_1 + N_2) \tag{6}$$

Note that when $N_1 = N_2$, so that the two sexes are of equal numbers, the effective population size and the actual population size are effectively equal. The effective population size concept is also discussed in this volume by Lande and Barrowclough (Chapter 6), and some of the consequences of formulae such as equation (6) are discussed in Frankel and Soulé (1981, p. 38). For example, a population of 10 males and 1000 females loses genetic variation at the same asymptotic rate as a population of 20 males and 20 females. This is the sort of consideration which is taken into account when one calculates the rate at which a real population, involving perhaps two sexes, geographical structure, and cyclical changes in population size, loses genetical variation, and it is from this that the MVP size, i.e., the population size for which this rate of loss takes a given accepted value, is calculated. For example, if the sex ratio $N_1 : N_2$ is $1 : 10$, and the acceptable rate of decrease of genetic variation is 1%, then equations (4) and (6) show that we will require $N_e = 50$, and hence $N_1 = 14$, $N_2 = 140$, to achieve this rate of decrease. We therefore conclude that the MVP in this case is 154.

Definition of the demographic MVP

The definition of the genetic MVP outlined in the previous section is rather precise. Unfortunately, no such precision exists for the demographic MVP, no doubt because many definitions are possible and different definitions are desirable in different circumstances. The common feature of the definitions so far considered is that eventual extinction of the population is certain, and that the MVP is the size of the population which, with a given probability, will ensure the existence of the population for a stated period of time.

Having made these general comments, we turn to the main consideration of this chapter, namely the calculation of the MVP when 'catastrophic' events, entailing sudden decreases of population size or the entire elimination of subpopulations, can occur. We introduce and discuss two catastrophe models, one aimed at the calculation of a genetic MVP and the other at the calculation of a demographic MVP. We emphasize that these are but two of many catastrophe models that could be analyzed, and we use them more to illustrate the points made above than because they necessarily describe important real-world events.

Catastrophes: an example of a genetic MVP size

We turn now to the calculation of the genetically defined MVP using a catastrophe model introduced into the literature by Kimura and Maruyama (1980), having points of similarity with the well-known 'island' model of Wright (1969, p. 290).

Imagine a population of nN individuals, divided into n subpopulations each of size N. In each generation k subpopulations, chosen at random, become extinct (as a result of some catastrophe). The patch occupied by any such subpopulation is assumed filled by new arrivals from one of the remaining $n - k$ subpopulations, chosen at random and independently of whether this subpopulation has filled any other newly opened patch. Superimposed on this extinction and colonizing process is a random sampling of genes within each subpopulation, determining the genetic constitution within each new subpopulation.

Some preliminary and non-standard calculations of the effective population size in situations of this type were given by Kimura and Maruyama (1980), but it is possible to give more exact results than they have (Ewens, 1987). We do not go into the mathematical details here. It is sufficient to note that if, in generation t, two genes are drawn at random from the population t, then the probability P_t that these two genes are of different allelic types is of the form

$$P_t = A\lambda_1^t + B\lambda_2^t \tag{7}$$

where A and B are constants whose exact value is not important, and

$$\lambda_1 = 1 - \frac{1}{2N}, \tag{8}$$

$$\lambda_2 = [(n - k - 1)(n^2 - k)]/[n(n - 1)(n - k)]. \tag{9}$$

Equation (7) is quite revealing. Genetic variation is lost, in the model we consider, in two ways. The first is due to random genetic drift within subpopulations, and the rate at which genetic uniformity is reached within subpopulations is the standard Wright–Fisher value λ_1 (see equation (2)). The second is due to the replacement process of extinct subpopulations by descendants from other subpopulations: we may describe this as a loss of variation through the extinction process, and whose rate is measured by λ_2 (which, as expected, is independent of subpopulation size). Whichever is the larger of λ_1 and λ_2 (i.e., the within or the between subpopulation rates of loss of genetic variation) controls the ultimate rate at which genetic variation is lost, and using the argument which led to equation (5), the effective population size is

$$N_e = \frac{1}{2}(1 - \lambda_1)^{-1} = N \quad \text{if} \quad \lambda_1 > \lambda_2, \tag{10}$$

$$N_e = \frac{1}{2}(1 - \lambda_2)^{-1} \quad \text{if} \quad \lambda_2 > \lambda_1. \tag{11}$$

From these, a minimum viable population size can formally be found, as described above, by equating the acceptable rate of loss of genetic variation to $1 - (2N_e)^{-1}$.

However, it is possible to arrive at an over-hasty calculation of the MVP in this way. The form of the right-hand side in equation (7) is more complex than that in equation (2), and this of course arises because of the more complex model which leads to equation (7). This implies that it might be unwise to calculate N_e from equations (10) or (11) by equating 1 − $1/(2N_e)$ to a predetermined acceptable loss of genetic variation. It is more useful to return to equation (7) and to recall that λ_1 describes the rate of loss of genetic variation within subpopulations and λ_2 the rate of loss of variation because of subpopulation extinction. If it is impossible, by human intervention, to introduce genetic variation from one subpopulation into another, and if one focuses on the amount of genetic variation within one single subpopulation, then the rate λ_1 of loss of genetic variation within a subpopulation is what is important. In this case we should ignore equations (10) and (11) and find a MVP size by equating λ_1 to the acceptable rate loss of genetic variation. If, on the other hand, the introduction of genetic variation from one subpopulation to another is possible by human intervention, then it is natural to focus on the total population rather than any one subpopulation when assessing the rate of loss of genetic variation, and in this case equations (10) and (11) become more appropriate.

We conclude this section by emphasizing that the formulae given above, and to a large extent also the conclusions reached in the previous paragraph, depend strongly on the particular model we have assumed and described. It is clear that several variations to the model can be introduced which will significantly change these conclusions. The more important of these is the introduction of migration: if Nn is large, even a small migration rate between subpopulations would be sufficient to preserve genetic variation in the total population, and to a significant extent within each subpopulation, for very long periods.

Catastrophes: demographic models

We turn now to a demographic MVP calculation involving catastrophes. One of the most widely studied stochastic models is the birth-and-death process, for which, if the size of the population at time t is N, the probability that a birth occurs in the population in the small time interval $(t, t + \delta t)$ is $\alpha(N)\delta t$ and the probability of a death is $\beta(N)\delta t$. Models of particular interest are the constant coefficient case $\alpha(N) = \alpha$, $\beta(N) = \beta$, arising in many physical applications, and the linear coefficient case $\alpha(N) = \alpha N$, $\beta(N) = \beta N$ arising in some biological applications where birth rates and death rates are assumed to be proportional to the current population size. Goodman (Chapter 2) has given some of the properties of these models. In this section we consider the effects of a third event which may occur in the time interval $(t, t + \delta t)$, namely a catastrophe (with probability $\gamma(N)\delta t$). When a catastrophe occurs, each member of the population may die (with probability $1 - p$) or survive (with probability p), independently of the survival or otherwise of each other individual.

The mathematics of catastrophe processes is quite complicated (see, for example, Brockwell *et al.* (1982; 1983) and Brockwell (1985)), and it would be extremely difficult to derive simple mathematical formulae for any quantity of interest in any other than very simple models. Fortunately, however, some progress can be made in a model which reasonably describes the behavior of some biological populations, namely where $\alpha(N) = \alpha N$, $\beta(N) = \beta N$, and $\gamma(N) = \gamma$. The latter condition corresponds to catastrophes induced by factors extrinsic to the population, such as extreme weather conditions, rather than by factors intrinsic to the population, such as epidemics.

It can be shown, under the conditions of the preceding paragraph, that eventual extinction of the population is certain if $\alpha \leq \beta - \gamma \ln p$, and our aim is to consider characteristics of this extinction time as a function of the initial population size i.

The most useful starting point for the theory is to note that if the extinction times of the lines of descent of each of the initial i individuals were independent, the extinction time of the entire population would be the maximum of these i extinction times, and this would allow use of the statistical theory of extreme values (Gumbel, 1958). This theory asserts that, for large i,

Prob (population extinction time $\leq t$)

$$\approx \exp\left[-\exp\left(-\frac{t - a_1}{b_i}\right)\right],$$

$$(12)$$

where a_i and b_i are parameters depending on the initial population size i, given by

$$b_i = 0.7797\sigma_i, \quad a_i = \mu_i - 0.5772b_i,$$

$$(13)$$

μ_i and σ_i^2 being the mean and variance of the population extinction time. Strictly speaking, the extreme value theory just described cannot be used because the probabilistic behaviors of the lines of descent are not independent, being linked through the commonly experienced catastrophe events. Nevertheless, we have found, using a large number of simulations, that the probability (12) provides a very accurate approximation. Thus if we can find reasonably accurate expressions for μ_i and σ_i^2 as functions of α, β, γ, p, and i, we can use these to calculate a_i and b_i and hence use equation (12). While it is possible to calculate accurate values for μ_i and σ_i^2, the calculations are complicated and so we use here the so-called 'diffusion approximations' to these quantities which we have found give expressions which are usually within 20% of the correct values (with better accuracy for large i). These formulae are

$$\mu_i = (\ln i)/(\alpha - \beta - \gamma \ln p), \tag{14}$$

$$\sigma_i^2 = (\ln i)[\gamma(\ln p)^2]/(\alpha - \beta - \gamma \ln p)^3. \tag{15}$$

We can use these expressions as follows. First, choose values for α, β, γ, p, and i which characterize the population of interest. Second, calculate μ_i and σ_i^2 from these, using equations (14) and (15). Third, calculate a_i and b_i from μ_i and σ_i^2, using equation (13). Finally, suppose we wish to find the time t^* such that

Prob (population extinction time $\leqslant t^*$) = p^*,

for any given value p^*. Equation (12) shows that t^* is given by

$$t^* = a_i - b_i \ln (-\ln p^*). \tag{16}$$

In making the choice of parameter values, we note that in the absence of catastrophes, the mean lifetime for any individual is β^{-1} and the mean number of offspring is $\alpha\beta^{-1}$. Thus if, for example, we assume that the mean lifetime is 5 years and the mean number of offspring per individual is 1.2, we must put $\alpha = 0.24$, $\beta = 0.20$. Further, γ^{-1} is the mean time between catastrophes, so if we believe this mean time to be 10 years, we must put $\gamma = 0.1$. Suppose finally the probability p that an individual survives a catastrophe is 0.5. Then $\beta - \gamma \ln p$ is 0.26931 and since this exceeds α $(= 0.24)$, eventual extinction of the population is certain. Suppose now that i, the initial population size, is 1000. Then using equations (14) and (15), the mean and standard deviation of the extinction time of the population are 236 years and 115 years respectively. Substituting in equation (13) we get

$$b_{1000} = 89.508, \quad a_{1000} = 184.33.$$

Thus we can say, for example, using equation (16), that if t^* is the median time until extinction (i.e., if Prob (population extinction time $\leqslant t^*$) = 0.5), then

$$t^* = 184.33 - 89.508 \ln (-\ln 0.5) = 217 \text{ years.} \tag{17}$$

By using equation (16) with $p^* = 0.95$, we find that there is a 95% chance that the population has become extinct after 450 years.

If now we change the initial size of the population to 3000, we find from equations (14) and (15) that the mean and standard deviation of the population extinction time are 273 years and 124 years, respectively. Substituting into equation (13) we get

$$b_{3000} = 96.371, \quad a_{3000} = 217.37$$

and now the median extinction time is

$$217.37 - 96.371 \ln (-\ln 0.5) = 253 \text{ years}$$

or an increase of only 36 years over the value in equation (17). Comparison with equation (19) shows that the initial size of the population in this model is not a major factor in the length of time the population persists. Mathematically we can see this from equations (14) and (15). These equations show that it is the logarithm of the population size, which changes only slowly as the population size increases, which affects the parameters determining survival time characteristics. This conclusion, while severely dependent on the model we have chosen, sheds an unexpected light on the effect of the initial population size on the survival time.

Discussion and concluding remarks

There are several points which we have attempted to make in this chapter, and it is worthwhile summarizing some of them.

First, it is extremely difficult to analyze mathematically any model which can claim to reflect biological reality at all accurately – non-mathematicians are perhaps not aware of the severe limitations of mathematical theory and practice. As a result, any model which has been analyzed by mathematical methods is apt to be oversimplified and thus perhaps to omit essential features of the biological problem at hand. The calculation of the genetic MVP given above, for example, does not allow migration between subpopulations, and to the extent that migration does occur its conclusions should therefore be treated with caution. Further, if a model involving migration were to be analyzed mathematically, it should be checked whether the migration pattern (e.g., panmictic or nearest-neighbor) assumed in the analysis is appropriate.

Despite these caveats, a mathematical model can yield interesting conclusions which might apply more widely than the confines of the model itself. The conclusion reached in the analysis of the demographic MVP model, that the median extinction time depends on the logarithm of the initial population size, and hence only weakly on this initial size, is one such result.

Second, although at an overall level the genetic and demographic MVPs are related, current theory treats them as separate concepts, so that great caution should be exercised in transferring a conclusion reached, say, from a 'genetic' analysis to a 'demographic' problem. One of the outstanding problems of the theory is to arrive at an overall analysis synthesizing demographic and genetic aspects, and until this is done the problem just mentioned will remain.

References

Brockwell, P. J. 1985. The extinction time of a birth, death and catastrophe process and of a related diffusion model. *Adv. Appl. Prob.* **17**: 42–52.

Brockwell, P. J., Gani, J. M., and Resnick, S. I. 1982. Birth, immigration and catastrophe processes. *Adv. Appl. Probl.* **14**: 709–31.

Brockwell, P. J., Gani, J. M., and Resnick, S. I. 1983. Catastrophe processes with continuous state-space. *Austral. J. Statist.* **25**, (**2**): 208–26.

Ewens, W. J. 1979. *Mathematical Population Genetics*. Springer-Verlag, Berlin, Heidelberg, New York.

Ewens, W. J. 1987. The effective population size in the presence of catastrophes. To appear *in* M. W. Feldman (ed.) *Mathematical Evolutionary Theory*.

Frankel, O. H. and Soulé, M. E. 1981. *Conservation and Evolution*. Cambridge University Press.

Franklin, I. R. 1980. Evolutionary change in small populations. Pp. 135–49 *in* M. E. Soulé and B. A. Wilcox (eds.) *Conservation Biology. An Evolutionary-Ecological Perspective*. Sinauer Associates, Sunderland, Mass.

Gumbel, E. J. 1958. *Statistics of Extremes*. Columbia University Press, New York.

Kimura, M. and Maruyama, T. 1980. Genetic variability and effective population size when local extinction and recolonization of subpopulations are frequent. *Proc. Natl. Acad. Sci.* **77**, 6710–14.

Shaffer, M. 1983. Determining minimum viable population size for the grizzly bear. *Int. Conf. Bear Res. and Manage.* **5**, 133–9.

Soulé, M. 1980. Thresholds for survival: maintaining fitness and evolutionary potential. Pp. 151–70 *in* M. E. Soulé and B. A. Wilcox (eds) *Conservation Biology: An Evolutionary-Ecological Perspective*. Sinauer Associates: Sunderland, Mass.

Wright, S. 1969. *Evolution and the Genetics of Populations, Volume 2. The Theory of Gene Frequencies*. The University of Chicago Press, Chicago and London.

5

Minimum viable populations: coping with uncertainty

MARK SHAFFER
1937A Villa Ridge Drive, Reston, VA 22090

Chance extinctions: a growing concern

The Global 2000 Report to the President (1980) estimates that between 500 000 and 2 000 000 species – 15–20% of all species on Earth – could become extinct by the year 2000. Though direct exploitation and pollution will certainly be factors, the principal cause of this projected wave of extinctions is the continuing loss of wild habitats. Thus, habitat conservation and management will be the key elements in any program to minimize or reduce this expected diminution of the world's biotic diversity.

Given an expanding human population with rising economic expectations, competition for use of the world's remaining wildlands will be intense. Conservationists will often face the problem of determining just how little habitat a species can have and yet survive. At the same time, biologists are increasingly coming to recognize that extinction may often be the result of chance events and that the likelihood of extinction may increase dramatically as population size diminishes.

To see this, consider the life of an individual living thing. To fulfill life's potential, the individual must be conceived, go through an intricate developmental period, be born, further develop, mate, reproduce, and all the while survive. Anywhere along this continuum of events the individual may die. Death, when it occurs, will always be for some reason (exposure, lack of food, disease, aggression, accident, age) but the reasons are varied and not always intimately connected. Often they involve an element of chance, like being struck by an automobile, or being born during an exceptionally bad drought.

This variety of hazards and their own inherent uncertainty, taken together, make the life of any individual organism a probabilistic phenomenon – a continual roll of the dice. Death is the only certainty, but the time and circumstances are open to wager.

Extinction is to a population or species what death is to an individual. Because populations are collections of individuals, extinction is also an inherently probabilistic phenomenon. To be sure, other factors are often involved, but these operate against the ever-present background of chance.

There are two important corollaries of the chance element in life and death, persistence and extinction. First, the smaller the population, the more likely extinction is in any given period of time. Second, the longer the period of time, the more likely extinction is for a population of any given size.

If the likelihood of survival depends on both population size and time, then what degree of persistence constitutes preservation and how much habitat is necessary to achieve such preservation? This is the essence of the minimum viable population problem and the central question facing conservationists today.

The minimum viable population (MVP) concept (Soulé, 1980; Shaffer, 1981; Salwasser *et al.*, 1983; Gilpin and Soulé, 1986) has emerged as a recognition that extinction is a probabilistic phenomenon and that the likelihood of population survival cannot be evaluated without considering some time frame and some objective level of security. The concept has not lead to a universally applicable definition of what constitutes an MVP (for an illustrative example of a definition, see Shaffer, 1981), but along with related considerations of levels of genetic diversity necessary to maintain adaptation and evolution (Franklin, 1980; Soulé, 1980; Frankel and Soulé, 1981; Schonewald-Cox *et al.*, 1983; Salwasser *et al.*, 1983), it has made clear the importance of three key issues for conservation efforts, namely:

(1) the effect of various chance events on population persistence;
(2) the time frame to use in conservation planning; and
(3) the degree of security sought for the population(s) being conserved.

Only the first of these issues is subject to scientific solution. The latter two issues, while amenable to scientific advice and guidance, require a value judgement by society. How long should a population persist? How secure should that persistence be? The answers will entail economic, social, cultural, and political considerations.

This chapter focuses on the first issue. What types of chance events affect population persistence and what is the relationship of these events to population size, to time, and to each other? In this chapter, I review the findings of the previous chapters about the effects of chance events on population persistence: examine how these findings may be used to better estimate minimum viable population sizes and their area requirements; and attempt to relate the emerging picture of the limits to population viability to overall efforts to conserve biological diversity.

The limits to population viability

Not all the variation in the natural world is due to chance; much, if not most, is due to deterministic (cause-and-effect) relationships. Annual variations in forage production caused by annual variations in rainfall are an example. Chance merely adds to the deterministically based variability of natural systems. Some of what we attribute to chance may really be the workings of deterministic processes that are currently not understood. By definition, a chance or random event is one that is unpredictable, so there is little practical difference between a purely random event and the results of processes that, because they are not understood, remain unpredictable.

A process in which a variable outcome is random or uncertain is known as a stochastic process. Thus, stochasticity is variability due, at least in part, to chance or random events. Stochasticity is not a word that rolls easily from the tongue. Here the term uncertainty is used instead. Many of the factors that affect population dynamics, and thus, potentially, the likelihood of extinction, contain an element of uncertainty. These can be lumped into four broad classes (Shaffer, 1981).

(1) *Demographic uncertainty* resulting from random events in the survival and reproduction of individuals.
(2) *Environmental uncertainty* due to random, or at least unpredictable, changes in weather, food supply, and the populations of competitors, predators, parasites, etc.
(3) *Natural catastrophes* such as floods, fires, droughts, etc., which may occur at random intervals.
(4) *Genetic uncertainty* or random changes in genetic make-up due to the founder effect, genetic drift, or inbreeding, which alter the survival and reproductive probabilities of individuals.

All of these factors increase in importance – in the magnitude of their effects on population dynamics – with decreasing population size. Further, these factors may interact, as for example, an epidemic that reduces population size to a point where inbreeding depression becomes a factor by decreasing the demographic parameters of survival and reproduction.

The foregoing chapters explore the relationship of the probabilities of extinction to population size under the effects of the first three classes of uncertainty. Goodman (Chapter 2) presents a model that can incorporate the effects of demographic and/or environmental uncertainty. Belovsky (Chapter 3) explores the problem of parameter estimation for Goodman's model and presents some initial estimates for MVP sizes and their minimum area requirements (MAR) for mammals. His treatment introduces the allometric relationships of population growth rate and population density as factors in MVP and MAR determinations. Ewens *et al.* (Chapter 4) present two models of catastrophic effects on population persistence or its determinants. The first model examines the effects of catastrophes on the rate of inbreeding. The second model examines the effects of catastrophes on the probabilities of extinction due to demographic uncertainty. Each of these chapters deals with one or two, but not all three classes of uncertainty that affect population persistence. It remains to relate these treatments to each other and the minimum viable population overall. The focus of this integration is the single, isolated, unsubdivided population. As will be shown in Chapter 7 (see also Shaffer, 1985), more complex population patterns may complicate the following interpretation.

Figure 5.1 shows, in an idealized fashion, the functional form of the relationship of the expected time to extinction, or average persistence time, of a population as a function of that population's size for three

Figure 5.1. Functional forms of the relationship of the expected time to extinction, or average persistence time (T_K), to population size (K) for three classes of uncertainty.

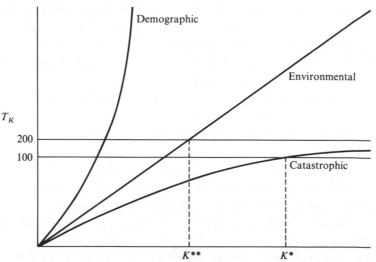

classes of uncertainty (demographic, environmental, and catastrophic). No relationship is shown for genetic uncertainty for reasons given in Chapter 10. These idealized relationships are based on the models and arguments presented in the preceding chapters (2–4).

Even on a scaleless, qualitative basis, several important conclusions emerge from a perusal of Figure 5.1. First, average persistence times increase geometrically with increasing population size under the effects of demographic uncertainty (Goodman, Chapter 2). This geometric relationship indicates that demographic uncertainty is only an important hazard for relatively small populations (on the order of 10s to 100s). This relationship depends on population growth rate; the lower the growth rate, the more slowly average persistence times increase with increases in population size. Nevertheless, beyond modest population sizes and/or growth rates, the average persistence times become so long as to make demographic uncertainty appear moot for conservation purposes.

More troublesome is the relationship of average persistence times under the effects of environmental uncertainty. Here persistence times do not increase geometrically with increasing population size. Rather, persistence times increase linearly with increases in population size (Goodman, Chapter 2). This relationship depends critically on the population growth rate and its variability, here presumed to be random and environmentally induced. This linear relationship means there is no critical population size that, once reached, ensures a high level of long-term security. A further complication is the finding that persistence times under the combined effects of demographic and environmental uncertainty take the form of a negative exponential distribution. Thus, roughly half of the populations of any given size will go extinct before even 70% of their expected persistence time has elapsed. The message is starkly clear: in a variable environment any loss in population size proportionally increases the chances of population extinction. True, the slope of the line and the variability around it will vary from species to species and habitat to habitat but the forms of the relationships will likely remain the same. To be very sure of retaining a species for very long may, depending on population growth rate and the degree of environmental variability, require either very large population sizes (on the order of 100s to 1 000 000s or larger (see Goodman, Chapter 2, and Belovsky, Chapter 3) or numerous populations.

The most distressing news lies in the curve for catastrophes (Ewens *et al.*, Chapter 4). Here, persistence times do not increase even linearly with population size but only with the ln of population size. This relationship depends not only on population growth rate but also on the severity and frequency of catastrophes. This relationship indicates that progressively larger and larger increases in population size yield diminishing dividends in terms of increased persistence times for any particular catastrophe scenario. In essence, this curve is a theoretical confirmation of the inevitability of extinction.

In Figure 5.1 the two curves and one line are portrayed as never intersecting. This may not always be the case. There may be ranges of population sizes and growth rates where demographic uncertainty is so severe that adding environmental and/or catastrophic uncertainty has no measurable impact on the expectation of persistence. Alternatively, there may be cases where environmental uncertainty proves more important than catastrophes in limiting the expectation of persistence. In fact, it may ultimately prove more realistic to view catastrophes as nothing more than the extremes of environmental uncertainty. But such cases are likely to be the exceptions with the patterns portrayed in Figure 5.1 the general rule.

Figure 5.1 contains no line or curve for the relationship of persistence times to population size under the effects of genetic uncertainty because no clear relationship emerges from a consideration of genetic factors (Lande and Barrowclough, Chapter 6). This is not to minimize the importance of genetic considerations but is a recognition of the complex relationship of genetic variation to population persistence. As Frankel and Soulé (1981) have shown, the key issue for conservation genetics is the relationship between genetic variation, individual fitness, and population viability. Despite the lack of a clear-cut understanding of this relationship there is a general consensus that, at least at the population level, and perhaps also at the individual level, viability, as measured by such traits as survival and/or reproduction, tends to increase with increasing heterozygosity, at least for many major animal taxa (Frankel and Soulé, 1981). The major exceptions to this rule appear to be selfing plants and invertebrates (Selander, 1983). Thus, it is widely accepted that maintaining genetic variation is crucial to maintaining individual fitness and population viability.

To date, much of the work on the MVP problem has focused on the genetic minima necessary to meet the requirements for short-term survival, continuing adaptation to environmental change, and, ultimately, continuing evolution into new forms (Senner, 1980; Franklin, 1980; Soulé, 1980; Frankel and Soulé, 1981; Schonewald-Cox *et al.*, 1983; Lehmkuhl, 1984). In general, inbreeding has been viewed as the principal threat to short-term survival and genetic drift as the principal threat to the loss of genetic variation thought essential to continuing adaptation.

Views on the potential for further evolution of large-bodied, tropical species are summarily dismal (Soulé, 1980). Several analyses (Senner, 1980; Franklin, 1980; Soulé, 1980; Frankel and Soulé, 1981) have led to the conclusion that effective population sizes, in the genetic sense (see Lande and Barrowclough, Chapter 6) on the order of 50 and 500 are necessary to provide short-term survival and continuing adaptation, respectively.

For most situations, the actual number of individuals necessary to provide effective populations of several hundred will range from the upper 100s to the 1000s, perhaps rarely the 10000s. But, as we have already seen earlier in this section, environmental and catastrophic uncertainty may require very much larger population sizes for a high level of security in the mid- to long-term (e.g., 95% probability of persistence for 100 or 1000 years, Goodman, Chapter 2; Belovsky, Chapter 3; Ewens *et al.*, Chapter 4). Although a clear picture of the functional form of the relationship of population persistence to population size under the effects of genetic uncertainty is still highly desirable, it now appears that, for the single, isolated, unsubdivided population, genetic considerations will not always, perhaps not often, set the lower limit to acceptable population size.

Applications to determining minimum viable population sizes

Figure 5.1 reveals there is now a clearer picture of the relative impacts of the various classes of uncertainty on population persistence. Demographic uncertainty poses the least threat while catastrophes pose the greatest; environmental uncertainty being somewhere in between. More importantly, a comprehensive model of the relationship of population persistence to population size under the *combined* effects of all forms of uncertainty, including genetic uncertainty, is still lacking. Consequently, the machinery to provide comprehensive estimates of population persistence is still not available, at least in an integrated form.

Despite this somewhat chaotic state of affairs, some useful guidance for management purposes may still be gained by a further examination of the form of the functional relationships in Figure 5.1. In Figure 5.1, two horizontal lines corresponding to conservation planning time frames of 100 and 200 years respectively, are shown. The first of these lines $(T_K(100))$ intersects all three functional relationships. Clearly a population size (K^*), corresponding to the intersection of the $T_K(100)$ line and the catastrophic uncertainty curve, would be of sufficient size so that its expected, or average, time to extinction would meet the planning time frame under the effects of all three classes of uncertainty. If the variance in T_K under the effects of all three classes of uncertainty were also known, K^* could be adjusted upward to provide a specified level of security, e.g., a 95% probability of persistence for at least 100 years. As Goodman's model (Chapter 2) demonstrates, such an adjustment might require a very much larger K^*.

The second horizontal line ($T_K(200)$) intersects only the demographic and environmental uncertainty relationships. A population (K^{**}) corresponding to the intersection of the $T_K(200)$ line and the environmental uncertainty line would be of sufficient size so that its expected time to extinction would meet the planning time frame of 200 years under the effects of demographic and environmental uncertainty. However, it is clear that no population size on the K axis will yield the desired expected time to extinction of 200 years under the effects of catastrophic uncertainty. If the species is to survive 200 years, management must ameliorate the prevailing catastrophe scenario or more than one population must be maintained.

Thus, if the functional forms of the relationship of population persistence to population size under the effects of each class of uncertainty could be derived, even independently, this information could be used to assess if an MVP exists for a given time frame and, if so, its size. Alternatively, if the relationships were such that no MVP satisfies the specified time frame, as was the case in the second example above, the analysis would indicate when more than one population is necessary to meet the specified planning time frame and which class of uncertainty mandates this action.

Because of the importance of environmental and catastrophic uncertainty as the principal threats to long-term population survival, it is important to further consider Belovsky's initial estimates of MVP sizes based on Goodman's model. Detailed life histories and data on demographic parameters are available for only a comparatively few organisms relative to the number which may require conservation efforts. But, as Belovsky points out, there is a general relationship between the size of an individual organism and certain population parameters such as density and population growth rate. This is true for a wide variety of taxa (Belovsky, Chapter 3). Further, though measures of variability in population parameters are often lacking, to a first approximation these can be assessed by employing levels of variability in components of a species' environment or habitat which likely drive, to some extent, a species' population dynamics (Belovsky, Chapter 3).

Employing this line of reasoning, Belovsky provides some initial estimates of MVP size and minimum area requirements (MAR) for various body size ranges of mammals. For illustrative purposes he deals with a standard of 95% probability of persistence for two time frames: 100 and 1000 years. His figures (Chapter 3) show the results. In brief, over a range of six orders of magnitude in mammalian body mass (10–10^6 grams), MVP sizes range from 100s to 1 000 000s of individuals corresponding to MARs of 10s to 1 000 000s of square kilometers. As body mass increases, MVP sizes decrease but density relations are such that, the larger the body mass, the larger the MAR necessary for the prescribed MVP. The degree of environmental variability can alter MVP sizes for a species of any given body mass by as much as two orders of magnitude. MARs are, as expected, larger for carnivores than herbivores and larger for tropical than for temperate species.

Clearly these 'ball park' figures span a considerable range and are open to considerable refinement, but what is most important is the reasoning that some initial guidance on MVPs and MARs can be gained simply from the relationships of growth rate and density to a species' body mass and from the levels of inherent variability in major environmental or habitat factors. Such parameters are among the most widely available and readily measured for a wide variety of species and habitats. This approach is worth pursuing in greater detail and for other major taxa. In particular, accurate measures of environmentally-induced variation in population growth rates are sorely needed.

Belovsky's test of Goodman's model against Brown's (1971) data on the extinction of small mammals on high altitude Great Basin habitat islands is instructive in its approach and encouraging in the congruency between prediction and observation. The island biogeographic literature contains numerous other data sets on faunal relaxation or turnover which could provide some other initial tests of this theoretical model. Moreover, Goodman's model shows such sensitivity of persistence times to environmental variability that empirical and experimental approaches to studying extinction now appear within the realm of practical reality, at least for very dynamic systems. In the absence of scientifically validated predictive relationships, conservation efforts must be guided in large part by theory and inference. But this should be accompanied at every practical opportunity by tests of the prevailing theory which can serve to refine management's directions. Tests of Goodman's model against suitable existing data and further selected experimental work, such as the World Wildlife Fund's Minimum Critical Size of Ecosystems Program (Lovejoy and Oren, 1981) are urgently needed.

It is not unlikely that further work with Goodman's model, especially the gathering of more detailed and precise measures of the variability in population growth rate, will lead to somewhat smaller MVPs for any given level of security. This is likely for two reasons. First, Belovsky's approach to deriving estimates of environmental variation does not take into account buffering mechanisms which may exist for many species in many habitats, such as prey switching by predators. Second, Goodman's model assumes that all individuals of the population, no matter how large the population, experience the same level of environmental variability. But as Soulé and Gilpin (pers. comm.) point out, the reasonableness of this assumption is likely negatively correlated with population size. That is, all else being equal, the larger the population, the larger its range. The larger a population's range, the less likely all parts of the range, and thus all members of the population, experience the same environmental inputs and their variations.

Similarly, further work with Ewens *et al.*'s model or with more sophisticated versions using available or derivable information on the frequency and severity of various catastrophe scenarios will provide a clearer range of MVP sizes for this factor. The literature on natural disturbance is vast and growing (Sousa, 1984). A further examination of this information could provide a basis for developing reasonable models of catastrophe dynamics, at least for sessile plant and animal populations.

Nevertheless, MVP sizes for high level (e.g., 95% probability of survival) mid- to long-term (e.g., 100 or 1000 years) security are likely to remain relatively large, especially in light of the current distribution of reserve sizes. Based on Belovsky's work, few, if any, existing reserves will prove large enough to provide a high level of mid-term security at least for the larger, rarer species. This accords with previous assessments of the long-term viability of major mammal species in African reserves based on species-area considerations (Soulé *et al.*, 1979). But there remains hope. Probably most species are naturally patchily distributed. Such species can be considered as a population of populations. This pattern has been termed a metapopulation (Levins, 1970). The above analyses have implicitly assumed a single, totally isolated population. Relaxing this assumption so that any population may receive migrants from outside could drastically alter projected persistence times. Lande and Barrowclough (Chapter 6), Ewens *et al.* (Chapter 4), and Gilpin (Chapter 7) discuss the importance of geographical population structure and migration for the maintenance of genetic variation, but these factors are also of importance to overcoming demographic, environmental, and catastrophic uncertainty as well. Indeed, a metapopulation strategy (e.g., more than one population) may be the only way of assuring a species persistence for any specified time frame. Moreover, multiple populations can allow for natural or man-mediated recolonization of those populations that do fail. To illustrate this point, consider a species with characteristics such that a population of 500 has, when all factors are considered, only 80% probability of persistence for 100 years. Adding a second, independent population, even in the absence of migration, would increase the probability of the species persistence in at least one of the populations to 96%. This is likely a greater increase in security than would occur from simply doubling the size of the original population.

Metapopulation dynamics is an emerging area both in ecological theory and management applications (Levins, 1970; Shaffer, 1985; Gilpin, Chapter 7). The dynamics of metapopulations promises to be complex but an understanding of such systems will prove essential to effective conservation efforts, particularly for the management of biological diversity in the context of multiple-use land management. Although the trade-offs between the number, size, and arrangements of reserves and the populations they contain are not yet clear, it is quite likely that metapopulation arrangements can aid significantly in reducing the size requirement for any single reserve, so long as the species involved can move or be moved among the various reserve units. This should aid greatly in management's efforts to fit nature into increasingly fragmented, man-dominated landscapes.

Implications for the conservation of biological diversity
The emerging picture of the limits to population viability has four immediate and important implications for efforts to forestall or ameliorate the impending extinction crisis. These are:

(1) extinction dynamics remain inadequately understood;
(2) preservation and endangerment are ill-defined;
(3) current nature reserves are too few in number and often too small;
(4) habitat conservation and management efforts, though substantial in some areas, are too diffuse and inadequately integrated.

Each of these implications will be discussed in turn.

Extinction dynamics
The preceding chapters (2–4) have provided a glimpse of the potential dynamics of the extinction process on a heretofore unrecognized scale. It now appears theoretically plausible that extinction may be a more likely event than has previously been appreciated, at least on a local scale. This corroborates, in a qualitative way, the increasing empirical body of evidence that localized extinction events are, in fact, commonplace

(Connell and Sousa, 1983). The fact that a high level of localized extinctions may occur unaccompanied by many global extinctions attests to the importance of environmental heterogeneity and both population size and number as buffers against the ultimate demise of a species.

Despite the theoretical progress reported in the preceding chapters and the continuing accumulation of empirical measures of localized extinctions, our capacity to precisely project a species' probabilities of extinction remains limited. This is so for three reasons. First, as pointed out earlier, theory has not advanced sufficiently to produce a comprehensive model of population dynamics that incorporates all four classes of uncertainty that can affect population persistence. Goodman's model captures the effects of demographic and environmental uncertainty but, ultimately, both genetic and catastrophic uncertainty must also be incorporated into one model.

Second, even for models now available, the necessary data for actual application are generally lacking and are both very costly and time-consuming to gather.

Finally, determining extinction probabilities requires projecting the state of the future for many relevant parameters with all the perils and pitfalls this implies. The inescapable reality is that we must project the dynamics of systems without having the opportunity to examine them empirically or experimentally.

Nevertheless, much can be done. Conceptually realistic models of population or metapopulation dynamics incorporating the effects of various sources of chance are slowly emerging (Ginzburg *et al.*, 1982; Shaffer, 1983; Gilpin, Chapter 7). Comprehensive models cannot be far away. At a minimum, general models of various life-history types (e.g., density-regulated vertebrate carnivores, predator and/or density-regulated vertebrate herbivores, catastrophe regulated invertebrates and plants, etc.) could be developed rather rapidly as learning and research tools and management aids. Providing available data for such models will also prove a major challenge, but here again much can be done. As Belovsky's work points out, even indirect or superficial estimates of certain parameters can serve to make a meaningful start. Moreover, future research can be directed toward better determining key parameters and relationships such as natural levels of environmental variation and their impact on population growth rates. Equally important, long-term monitoring of the 'experiments' we conduct through our current management practices can add greatly to our knowledge on population dynamics and extinction.

Defining preservation and endangerment

It should be clear that preservation, unqualified as to time and circumstance, is a meaningless term. A population large enough to be almost certain of persisting a century may not have a prayer of enduring a millennium. By the same token, there may be many more 'endangered' species than currently recognized. Without some acceptable definition of what constitutes successful preservation, society may squander limited resources, over-conserving some species to the fatal neglect of others. In fact, this may already be occurring. Current species management efforts tend to emphasize vertebrates, particularly birds and mammals, while the potentially more ecologically crucial invertebrates and plants are essentially ignored. Until we have a clearer picture of which species may be crucial to the continuation of basic life sustaining processes, all species should probably receive equal emphasis.

There are no easy answers to the problem of defining successful preservation or what really constitutes endangerment. The one certainty is that the issue is not strictly a biological or scientific matter. Of all the issues facing the conservation of biological diversity, the definition of preservation itself, in quantitative terms subject to objective evaluation, is both the most crucial and least addressed.

Current nature reserves are too small and too few

The vast majority of all nature reserves worldwide, including Biosphere Reserves, are under 10 000 km² in area (Frankel and Soulé, 1981). Yet, if Belovsky's estimates prove even reasonably close, many mammalian species, particularly the larger, more spectacular and immediately useful or interesting to man, will require reserves on the order of 100 000–1 000 000's of km² for a high probability (0.95) of persistence for even a century. This is assuming that each reserve is intended to support a full complement of its native mammalian fauna and does so independently of all other reserves or of surrounding, non-reserve areas without active management. This may seem an unduly restrictive assumption until it is realized that this situation already exists or is rapidly emerging for some species. Witness the tiger in various Indian reserves or the grizzly bear in Yellowstone National Park and adjacent National Forests. Many more examples are likely available but, oddly, there appears to be no survey of species already restricted to reserve areas.

Beyond considerations of individual reserve size, it is clear from Ewens *et al.*'s (Chapter 4) exploratory analysis of catastrophe dynamics that multiple reserves will be essential in many cases. Without a survey of how many species are already restricted to only one or a few reserves and an assessment of their persistence probabilities, the current extent of this problem cannot be gauged. However, it can only worsen.

Integrating conservation efforts

The values and benefits of biological diversity have been adequately stated (Ehrlich and Ehrlich, 1981; Oldfield, 1984; Myers, 1983). It is clear that the current and potential wealth of nature and our continuing ignorance of its true scope argue strongly for a concerted effort to systematically conserve a full range of existing species and the communities they form. Because most impending extinctions are thought to be related to the loss of wild habitats, increased habitat conservation and management are crucial to achieving systematic conservation.

Numerous systems of nature reserves or other categories of public lands which, to varying degrees, can serve as reserves for many species, already exist or are being planned in many nations. In addition, several international systems of reserves have been developed in recent years, notably the World Heritage Program, the Biosphere Reserve System, and the List of Wetlands of International Importance Especially as Waterfowl Habitat. These various systems of conservation lands have developed from various authorities and for various purposes. Often they have achieved, or are achieving, their original objectives, but with accelerating habitat loss and fragmentation in non-reserve areas, increasing pressure will be placed on all public lands to serve as reservoirs for biological diversity.

For example, in the United States, at the Federal level alone, there are four major systems of conservation lands: the National Park System, the National Wildlife Refuge System, the National Forest System, and the National Resource Lands. These four systems are managed by four different agencies in two separate departments and under numerous legislative authorities mandating various purposes and uses. All contribute substantially in one way or another to the conservation of biological diversity. Yet, no system alone is currently adequate to protect the full spectrum of biological diversity in the United States. Even taken together, gaps exist in terms of species or community representation.

More importantly, there is no national program outlining the goals, objectives, policies, and strategies necessary to achieve the systematic conservation of biological diversity in the United States that identifies what each system is to contribute and how such an overall program would be coordinated. To be sure, interagency cooperation exists, as with grizzly bear management in the Yellowstone ecosystem, but effective conservation efforts will require much more than an occasional, crisis-oriented approach (see Chapter 9).

The United States is widely considered one of the principal leaders in conservation worldwide. Yet if its own efforts to conserve biological diversity are fragmented among agencies and only loosely coordinated, lacking guidance from an overall program and policy, what must the situation be in other countries with a less well-developed conservation ethic?

Systematic conservation will require three major efforts:

(1) a classification of the elements of diversity (species, communities, ecosystems, and biomes) we wish to conserve;
(2) an assessment of the numbers, sizes, and locations of reserves necessary to conserve elements with some agreed upon level of security;
(3) active management of reserves to perpetuate their natural dynamics that may be disrupted by extensive non-reserve habitat alteration and fragmentation.

Accomplishing these tasks will require the utmost coordination between both disciplines (taxonomists, biogeographers, geneticists, demographers) and agencies (forestry, wildlife, parks, etc.).

Summary

The world faces an impending crisis of species' extinctions. With estimates ranging up to 20% of all species becoming extinct by the beginning of the twenty-first century, this event could rank as one of the major biological perturbations in Earth's history. Most of these projected extinctions would result from population reductions accompanying the accelerating loss of wild habitats. But there is still time to act.

Extinctions of populations and species may occur for many reasons, among which will be chance. The recognition of the probabilistic component of extinction and its dependence on population size and time has profound ramifications for efforts to avoid or minimize the impending extinction crisis. The minimum viable population concept is a formal recognition of the chance component of extinction and an effort to determine how far man's encroachment on remaining wild habitats can proceed before running an unacceptable risk of losing the biological diversity such habitats contain.

At present we lack an integrated predictive capability for determining the potential longevity of populations in relation to their size and structure. As currently understood for the single, isolated, unsubdivided population, natural catastrophes set the ultimate limit to persistence. But this limit may often be remote in time or very infrequent and within it the level of environmental variability will likely pose the most serious obstacle to persistence, at least for moderately large populations over moderate time frames.

Both demographic and genetic uncertainty are also important considerations but except for species already severely diminished (e.g., the California condor, *Gymnogyps californianus*), their effects will likely be swamped by environmental variability.

Initial attempts to estimate MVPs and MARs for unsubdivided populations of mammals provide a range of population sizes of 100s or 1 000 000s and areas up to millions of km^2 for high level mid- to long-term security (i.e., 95% probability of persistence for 100 or 1000 years, respectively). The range is set by population growth rates, their variability, and population density. These estimates of MVPs and MARs compare unfavorably with the size class distribution of current reserves but may be reduced by further theoretical, empirical, and experimental developments or by comprehensive planning and management providing multiple reserves for most species.

Conservation efforts must focus on four key issues. First, we must refine our theoretical, historical, and, where possible, empirical understanding of extinction dynamics. This may be most meaningfully accomplished by development of comprehensive stochastic simulation models of key species (those that are large, rare, and/or particularly subject to environmental variation) and a reassessment of available information to determine natural patterns of catastrophe and levels of inherent environmental variability.

Second, as a society, we must come to grips with what we really mean by preservation. Does a 95% probability of persistence for 100 years make extinction sufficiently remote or all too imminent?

Third, it is clear, based on the crude estimates of extinction probabilities above, that the size and number of current nature reserves are likely insufficient to provide a high level of long-term security for at least some mammalian species, especially those that are large or rare.

Fourth and finally, the various types of public lands and various conservation programs must be increasingly coordinated under some integrated plan and policy for the systematic conservation of biological diversity if the impending tide of extinction is to be stemmed at all.

References

Brown, J. H. 1971. Mammals on mountaintops: nonequilibrium insular biogeography. *Am. Nat.* **105**: 467–78.

Connell, J. H. and Sousa, W. P. 1983. On the evidence needed to judge ecological stability or persistence. *Am. Nat.* **121**: 789–824.

Ehrlich, P. and Ehrlich, A. 1981. *Extinction: The Causes and Consequences of the Disappearance of Species*. Random House, New York.

Frankel, O. H. and Soulé, M. E. 1981. *Conservation and evolution*. Cambridge University Press, Cambridge.

Franklin, I. R. 1980. Evolutionary change in small populations. Pp. 135–50 *in* M. E. Soulé and B. A. Wilcox (eds.) *Conservation Biology: An Evolutionary-Ecological Perspective*. Sinauer Associates, Sunderland, Mass.

Gilpin, M. E. and Soulé, M. E. 1986. Minimum Viable Populations: the processes of species extinctions. Pp. 13–34 *in* M. E. Soulé (ed.) *Conservation Biology: The Science of Scarcity and Diversity*. Sinauer Associates, Sunderland, Mass.

Ginzburg, L., Slobodkin, L. B., Johnson, K., and Bindman, A. G. 1982. Quasiextinction probabilities as a measure of impact on population growth. *Risk Analysis* **2**: 171–81.

The Global 2000 Report to the President: Entering the Twenty-first Century, Vol. 2, Technical Report. Gerald O. Barney, Study Director, Washington. Government Printing Office, 1980, pp. 328–31.

Lehmkuhl, J. F. 1984. Determining size and dispersion of minimum viable populations for land management planning and species conservation. *Environ. Manage.* **8**(2): 167–76.

Levins, R. 1970. Extinction. Pp. 77–107 *in* M. Gustenhaver (ed.) *Some Mathematical Questions in Biology*, Vol. II. American Mathematical Society, Providence, Rhode Island.

Lovejoy, T. E. and Oren, D. C. 1981. The minimum critical size of ecosystems. Pp. 7–12 *in* R. L. Burgess and D. M. Sharpe (eds.) *Forest Island Dynamics in Man-dominated Landscapes*. Springer-Verlag, New York.

Myers, N. 1983. *A Wealth of Wild Species. Storehouse for Human Welfare.* Westmier Press, Boulder, Colorado.

Oldfield, M. L. 1984. *The Value of Conserving Genetic Resources*. US Department of the Interior, National Park Service, Washington, DC.

Salwasser, H., Mealey, S. P., and Johnson, K. 1983. Wildlife population viability – a question of risk. *Trans. N. Am. Wildl. Natur. Rs. Conf.* **48**, 421–37.

Schonewald-Cox, C., Chambers, S. M., McBryde, B., and Thomas, W. L. 1983. *Genetics and Conservation: A Reference for Managing Wild Animal and Plant Populations*. Benjamin Cummings Co., Menlo Park, Calif.

Sclander, R. K. 1983. Evolutionary consequences of inbreeding. Pp. 201–15 *in* C. Schoenwald-Cox, S. M. Chambers, B. McBryde and W. L. Thomas (eds.) *Genetics and Conservation: A Reference for Managing Wild Animal and Plant Productions*. Benjamin Cummings Co., Menlo Park, Calif.

Senner, J. W. 1980. Inbreeding depression and the survival of zoo populations. Pp. 209–44 *in* M. E. Soule and B. A. Wilcox (eds.) *Conservation Biology: An Evolutionary-Ecological Perspective.* Sinauer Associates, Sunderland, Mass.

Shaffer, M. L. 1981. Minimum population sizes for species conservation. *Bioscience* **31**: 131–4.

Shaffer, M. L. 1983. Determining minimum viable population sizes for the grizzly bear. *Int. Conf. Bear Res. Manage.* **5**: 133–9.

Shaffer, M. L. 1985. The metapopulation and species conservation: The special case of the Northern Spotted Owl. Pp. 86–99 *in* R. J. Gutierrez and A. B. Carey (eds.) *Ecology and Management of the Spotted Owl in the Pacific Northwest.* Gen. Tech. Rep. PNW-185. Portland, Or: US Dept Agric., Forest Serv., Pacific Northwest Forest and Range Exp. Stn.

Soulé, M. E. 1980. Thresholds for survival: maintaining fitness and evolutionary potential. Pp. 151–70 *in* M. E. Soulé and B. A. Wilcox (eds.) *Conservation Biology: An Evolutionary-Ecological Perspective.* Sinauer Associates, Sunderland, Mass.

Soulé, M. E., Wilcox, B. A., and Holtby, C. 1979. Benign neglect: a model of faunal collapse in the game reserves of East Africa. *Biol. Conserv.* **15**: 259–72.

Sousa, W. P. 1984. The role of disturbance in natural communities. *Ann. Rev. Ecol. Syst.* **15**: 353–91.

6

Effective population size, genetic variation, and their use in population management

RUSSELL LANDE
Department of Biology, University of Chicago, Chicago, IL 60637

GEORGE F. BARROWCLOUGH
Department of Ornithology, American Museum of Natural History, New York, NY 10024

A fundamental fact of population genetics is that in closed populations (i.e., without immigration) the presence of only a small number of individuals, sustained over several generations, will lead to the depletion of genetic variation. Thus, the number of individuals is a crucial parameter in determining the amount of genetic variability that can be maintained in a population. This, in turn, influences the probability of long-term survival of a population because genetic variation is requisite for evolutionary adaptation to a changing environment. Thus, maintaining population numbers and genetic variation must be a central theme of plans for long-term population management.

In the last decade there have been several discussions of the role of population genetics in the management and conservation of threatened species (e.g., Soulé and Wilcox, 1980; Frankel and Soulé, 1981; Schonewald-Cox *et al.*, 1983); such references provide a useful background for persons interested in this topic. Here we extend this treatment in four ways. First, we suggest criteria for the management of populations from a genetic perspective. We show how the effective size of a population, the pattern of natural selection, and rates of mutation interact to determine the amount and kinds of genetic variation maintained. Time scales associated with the different processes are also discussed. Second, we review methods for estimating the effective size of populations. This concept is central to assessments of the rate of loss of genetic variation caused by random genetic drift in a finite population. Practical methods are suggested for estimating the effective sizes of local populations subject to the simultaneous influences of variance in progeny production, fluctuation in adult sex ratio, changing population size, and overlapping generations. Methods for jointly dealing with these variables have not previously been available. Third, the influence of geographic structure of populations on the maintenance of genetic variability is summarized. Fourth, we give an overview of direct methods of measuring genetic variation for different types of characters and discuss how these can be integrated with estimates of effective population size in management programs.

Genetic considerations for long-term population survival

The problem of specifying the number of individuals necessary to make a population viable, from a genetic point of view, is not a simple one. Clearly, genetic variation must be established and maintained in order to prevent the deleterious effects of inbreeding and to allow evolutionary change. However, as described below, the quantity of genetic variation in a population is a function not only of *effective population size*, but also of the *type of genetic variation* being considered, and the *nature of selection* acting on that variation. Additionally, the analysis of these three factors may differ according to whether one takes a short-term, *non-equilibrium perspective* or a long-term, *equilibrium view*.

Effective population size

In the absence of natural selection, mutation, immigration, and other deterministic evolutionary forces, the combined effects of the random segregation of genes into gametes in a finite diploid population and the unequal reproduction among individuals due to environmental effects will produce random changes in the frequencies of alleles at polymorphic loci. This phenomenon, known as random genetic drift, tends to diminish genetic variation and eventually produces fixation of one allele (homozygosity) at each genetic locus. For example, consider an ideal population of constant size and discrete, non-overlapping generations, with N diploid, monoecious (hermaphroditic) individuals reproducing by random sampling of gametes from an infinite gametic pool to which each individual contributes equally. This model entails a binomial (or approximately Poisson) distribution of number of progeny among individuals, with a mean of two offspring per parent. For an allele with initial frequency p in the population, the variance in allelic frequency among repeated samples of N offspring is $p(1 - p)/2N$. From this variance it can be shown that the expected heterozygosity, $\overline{H}$, (that is, the average proportion of heterozygous genotypes at a locus) declines by a factor of $1 - 1/2N$ per generation (Wright, 1931). That is,

$$\overline{H}_{t+1} = (1 - 1/2N)\,\overline{H}_t,$$

where time, t, is measured in generations. If the population size is not very small, that is $N \gg 1$, then heterozygosity, either at a particular locus or across the entire genome, decays at an approximately exponential rate on a time scale of $2N$ generations:

$$\overline{H}_t = H_0\, e^{-t/2N}.$$

Thus, after $2N$ generations the expected heterozygosity is only e^{-1}, or 0.37, of the initial heterozygosity, H_0. The rate of loss of genetic variation in such a case is a function of the size of the population, N.

Wright (1931) introduced the concept of effective population size to calibrate the amount of random genetic drift in actual populations with a non-binomial (or non-Poisson) distribution of progeny numbers, separate sexes, or fluctuations in population size. The concept was later extended to populations with overlapping generations. The effective size of a population, N_e, is the size of the ideal population that would undergo the same amount of random genetic drift (measured by the sampling variance in allelic frequencies per generation or the rate of loss of selectively neutral heterozygosity) as the actual population. Effective population size has proven useful in the design and analysis of artificial breeding programs, and in understanding evolution in natural populations, although few attempts have been made to incorporate the simultaneous operation of the several complicating factors encountered in real populations.

The effective size of a population is sometimes used to measure the amount of inbreeding in a population that is finite, but otherwise randomly mating. In actual populations, though, matings between relatives can produce considerable inbreeding beyond that resulting from finite population size; pedigree analysis provides a more general tool for analyzing the degree of inbreeding (Wright, 1969: Chapter 7; Crow and Kimura, 1970: Chapter 3). We will therefore restrict our discussion of effective population size to its meaning in terms of random genetic drift, and consider inbreeding as a separate subject.

Kinds of genetic variation

It is important to distinguish among different types of genetic variation. The familiar *single-locus, Mendelian polymorphisms* have guided much of evolutionary thinking. However, in eukaryotic organisms, a great deal (perhaps most) of adaptive evolution is based on *quantitative* (polygenic) *characters* that vary in meristic (countable) or continuous fashion. In addition, chromosomal or *karyotypic variants* can sometimes be found segregating within or among populations. The effect of population size on each of these categories may be distinct.

Equilibrium and non-equilibrium approaches

The maintenance of genetic variation can be viewed from a non-equilibrium or an equilibrium perspective. In the *non-equilibrium* approach we can ask how long it will take to lose genetic variation by random drift, what the maximum tolerable rate of loss is, or, once it is lost, how rapidly will genetic variation be regained by mutation in a large population? In the *equilibrium* approach the questions center on how much genetic variation of a given type is maintained in a population with a certain spatial and temporal structure. The non-equilibrium approach is most applicable for short-term dynamics, especially following major changes in population structure or environment. The equilibrium approach is applicable for consideration of the long-term adaptability of a population. Both approaches are essential for population management, and we will see that the meaning of short and long time scales can differ tremendously for the different kinds of genetic variation.

Forms of selection

The presence or absence of natural selection, and the form of selection, if present, is central to the maintenance of genetic variation. The assumption of selective neutrality conveniently permits us to predict evolutionary consequences if effective population size is sufficiently small for random genetic drift to overpower selection. In this context the meaning of small population depends on the type of genetic variation and the form and intensity of selection acting on it, as shown below.

Directional selection favors an extreme expression of a trait and, with sufficient genetic variation, produces a secular trend in allelic frequency or in the mean value of a quantitative character. Balancing and stabilizing selection favor an intermediate expression of a trait; this can maintain a stable polymorphism for a single-gene character by conferring a hetero-zygote advantage. However, stabilizing selection tends to deplete the genetic variance in quantitative characters (e.g., Waddington, 1960; Scharloo, 1964; Wright, 1969: Chapter 4).

Quantitative genetic variation

There is evidence to suggest that most major phenotypic changes in evolution result from the accumulation of quantitative polygenic modification of existing phenotypes, rather than from single genes of major effect (Wright, 1968; Lande, 1981; Coyne, 1983). For the majority of characters in which mutations of large effect do occur, polygenic mutations of small effect occur far more frequently (Muller, 1949: p. 432; Gregory, 1965). In comparison with the low rates of spontaneous mutation for single genes of large effect, the total spontaneous rate for minor mutations at all loci influencing a particular quantitative character may often be on the order of 10^{-2} per gamete per generation or more (Sprague *et al.*, 1960; Russell *et al.*, 1963; Hoi-Sen, 1972; Mukai *et al.*, 1972). Additionally, mutations of large effect are almost always deleterious because of their main effect and pleiotropic effects on other characters. Fisher (1958: pp. 41–4) reasoned that, in a population evolving toward a multivariate optimum phenotype involving the mutual adjustment of many characters, the probability that a random (undirected) mutation of minor effect increases adaptation is nearly 1/2. For random mutations of major effect the probability of adaptation is rather small. This has been confirmed by the experience of geneticists with major mutants in the laboratory. Studies of natural populations have demonstrated that the genetic basis of phenotypic differences in quantitative characters among populations, races, and species is usually polygenic (Wright, 1968: Chapter 15; Lande,1981; Coyne, 1983).

The total genetic variance of a quantitative character in a population can be partitioned into components representing (1) the statistically additive effects of alleles within and among loci, (2) variance components due to dominance of alleles at the same locus, and (3) epistatic interactions between alleles at different loci. Phenotypic correlations between relatives can be used to estimate all of these components of genetic variance. The most important is usually the additive genetic variance. It is the major source of resemblance between parents and offspring that results in an evolutionary response to selection. A certain fraction of the epistatic genetic variance also contributes to the resemblance of parents and offspring, but for most quantitative characters (excluding major components of fitness such as viability and fecundity) the epistatic component of genetic variance is usually small and can be neglected (Falconer, 1981). The fraction of the total phenotypic variance attributable to the additive effects of genes is called the narrow-sense heritability of a character, h^2. This can be estimated from parent–offspring correlation or from the rate of change of the mean phenotype in a population subject to artificial selection (Falconer, 1981).

Neutral genes. Franklin (1980) employed an equilibrium model for the maintenance of additive genetic variance in quantitative characters by mutation in the absence of selection. He suggested that an effective population size of $N_e = 500$ would be sufficient to maintain typical levels of heritable variation. Because this number has been incorporated into population management plans (e.g., the Siberian tiger species survival plan: Seal, 1983; Seal and Foose, 1983/84), it seems worthwhile to review its derivation and to consider alternative models for the maintenance of polygenic variation, as well as those for single-locus traits.

Franklin observed that purely additive genetic variance is lost by random genetic drift at the same rate as heterozygosity, a fraction of $1/2N_e$ per generation, and that this is likely to be reasonably accurate for most traits (in which the genetic variance is largely additive). The input of additive genetic variance per generation from mutation was taken to be roughly 10^{-3} of the environmental variance (σ_e^2) that would be expressed in a highly inbred or genetically homogeneous line. This was based on data summarized by Lande (1976) for bristle counts in *Drosophila* (and quantitative characters in corn and mice; the mutational variance parameters for the *Drosophila* characters have since been confirmed by Hill (1982) using more extensive data). Thus, according to Franklin, 'we expect an approximate equilibrium between gain and loss when $1/2N_e = 10^{-3}$, that is, $N_e = 500$.'

A literal interpretation of this statement could be misleading because an equilibrium between mutation and random genetic drift will eventually be achieved for any value of N_e. The amount of genetic variance maintained, however, will depend on the effective population size. More explicitly, the change per generation in the expected amount of purely additive genetic variance, $\overline{\sigma_g^2}$, with a mutational input of genetic variance of σ_m^2 per generation, in the absence of selection, is

$$\Delta\overline{\sigma_g^2} = -\overline{\sigma_g^2}/2N_e + \sigma_m^2.$$

This yields an equilibrium expected value of

$$\overline{\sigma_g^2} = 2N_e\sigma_m^2.$$

Of course with random genetic drift the actual genetic variance will fluctuate with time around this expected value. Note that in this model there is no upper limit to the amount of genetic variance that can be maintained; given this constant mutational input of variance, the genetic variance expected at equilibrium is proportional to the effective population size. In order to maintain a heritability of about 0.5, which is typical for many characters including the *Drosophila* bristle traits (Falconer, 1981: Chapter 10), it is necessary that the genetic and environmental variances be about equal, $\sigma_g^2 = \sigma_e^2$, and, with $\sigma_m^2 = 10^{-3}\sigma_e^2$, the above formula gives $2 \times 10^{-3}N_e = 1$, that is, $N_e = 500$. This appears to be the logic underlying Franklin's derivation (M. Soulé, pers. comm.).

Stabilizing selection. The situation is rather different when natural selection is acting. The most common form of natural selection on quantitative characters is probably stabilizing selection toward an intermediate optimum phenotype (Haldane, 1954). Fluctuating directional selection caused by a moving optimum may also be common, but this does not substantially alter the amount of genetic variance maintained by polygenic mutation in a large population (Lande, 1977). If weak stabilizing selection on a quantitative character is described by a bell-shaped fitness function with a width ω (analogous to the standard deviation of a normal or Gaussian curve), the additive variance maintained by mutation and recombination in a very large population is approximately

$$\sigma_g^2 = \sqrt{2n_E\sigma_m^2\omega^2},$$

where n_E is the effective (or minimum) number of loci influencing the character (Lande, 1976; 1977). Thus, stabilizing selection places an upper limit on the amount of additive genetic variance that can be maintained, theoretically, in a large population.

Random genetic drift contributes to the reduction in additive genetic variance caused by stabilizing selection when finite population size is introduced to this model. Evidently, when the expected rate of loss of genetic variance by random genetic drift is less than that from stabilizing selection, a small population will maintain nearly as much genetic variance as a very large population. The minimum effective population size for which this holds was considered by Lande (1980). An approximate formula for the proportional rate of loss of additive genetic variance by stabilizing selection in a very large population in terms of some frequently measured parameters is h^2L/n_E. Here L is the selective load on the population when the mean phenotype is at the optimum, i.e., the decrement in mean fitness of individuals in the population relative to the fitness of the optimum phenotype. This has often been observed to be in the range of a few to several % for characters in a variety of organisms (Haldane, 1954; Johnson, 1976: Chapter 7). The effective number of loci has been estimated to range from about five or ten up to 20 for various characters (Wright, 1968: Chapter 15; Lande, 1981). Thus, for typical characters with a moderate heritability in the range of $h^2 = 0.3$ to 0.6, the proportional rate of loss of additive genetic variance from stabilizing selection in a large population is on the order of 10^{-3}, with the possibility of substantial differences among characters. This agrees reasonably well with the order of magnitude of the proportional input from mutation

$$\sigma_m^2/\sigma_g^2 = 10^{-3}\sigma_e^2/\sigma_g^2 = 10^{-3}(1 - h^2)/h^2$$

which, at equilibrium, must balance the loss from stabilizing selection in a very large population. Comparing these figures to the proportional rate of loss of additive genetic variance expected from random genetic drift, $1/2N_e$, it can be concluded that if

$$1/2N_e < h^2L/n_E \approx 10^{-3},$$

then a population with $N_e \gtrsim 500$ individuals can maintain nearly as much genetic variance in typical quantitative characters as an indefinitely large population. In view of the uncertainties about the several parameters involved in this argument, and the substantial differences in them that must actually exist between species and even among various characters in the same population, this figure cannot be regarded as being very precise.

Recovery rate of quantitative variation. Now consider the fate of a population that has passed through very small numbers for an extended period, and lost most of its genetic variability. If the population regains a large size, above the critical value of N_e just described, it can regenerate typical levels of heritable variation in quantitative characters by spontaneous mutation on a time scale of a few hundred to a few thousand generations. (The precise time depends on the linkage relations of the loci, the system of mating in the population, and the mutation and selection parameters specified above (Lande, 1977; 1980).) This contrasts with the restoration of genetic variation by mutation in single-locus characters, which may be orders of magnitude slower, as shown in the following section.

Other models of quantitative characters have been proposed in which the amount of additive genetic variance maintained in mutation–selection equilibrium in a large population is somewhat less than in those described here (Bulmer, 1980; Turelli, 1984). However, we doubt that the differences in the models are sufficient to alter greatly the foregoing conclusions.

Single-locus polymorphisms

Although evolution in quantitative characters is certainly essential for adaptation in eukaryotes, the relative importance of evolution in single-gene traits for adaptation is not well known. Additionally, the maintenance of selectively neutral and even deleterious polymorphisms is not irrelevant for the adaptive potential of a population: genetic variation that is presently non-adaptive may serve as the basis for future adaptation to environmental changes. Here we consider the interaction of such single-locus variation with population size.

Neutral variation. A model of single-locus selectively neutral polymorphism that has been useful in the analysis of molecular data is one in which every allele mutates at a rate μ per generation, with each new mutant of a type not currently existing in the population (Malécot, 1969; Kimura and Crow, 1964). An implication of this model is that there are a very large number of possible alleles at a locus. At equilibrium between mutation and random genetic drift, the expected heterozygosity is

$$\overline{H} = 4N_e\mu/(1 + 4N_e\mu).$$

Thus, if N_e is much greater than $1/4\mu$, the expected equilibrium heterozygosity is high, whereas if N_e is much less than $1/4\mu$ the heterozygosity is expected to be quite low. Because representative mutation rates for single loci are in the range of 10^{-5} to 10^{-7} per locus per generation (Schlager and Dickie, 1967; Dobzhansky, 1970; Chapter 3), it is clear that very large effective population sizes, on the order of a quarter million individuals or more, are needed to maintain intermediate or high levels of heterozygosity for selectively neutral alleles at a locus.

Recovery rate of neutral variation. If most of the heterozygosity has been lost due to random genetic drift during an extended period of small population size, and the population subsequently expands to a large effective size, $N_e > 1/4\mu$, it will take a very long time, on the order of $1/\mu$ = 10^5 to 10^7 generations, for mutation to restore the high levels of heterozygosity that are typical of many loci in natural populations (Nei *et al.*, 1975). This time scale contrasts sharply with the corresponding one for quantitative characters.

Deleterious variation. There are populations in which an important adaptive change has evolved from a mutation in a single gene. Empirical findings on natural and domesticated populations, and theoretical analysis, suggest that strong directional selection sustained over several generations is usually necessary for adaptive evolution of a major mutation with its associated deleterious pleiotropic effects (Lande, 1983). Some of the best-known examples occur in artificially disturbed populations and include the evolution of resistance to pesticides and diseases. We therefore need to consider the maintenance of genetic variation by recurrent mutation to deleterious alleles on which future adaptations may be built.

Suppose that mutations occur at a given locus from the normal allele, A, to the deleterious allele, a, at the rate μ per generation. The mutant homozygote has fitness $1 - s$, and the mutant heterozygote has fitness $1 - cs$ relative to the fitness of 1 for the normal homozygote. Here c is a measure of the dominance of the mutant. (c varies from zero to one, a value of one implies complete dominance and a value of zero represents a completely recessive allele.) Because the selective disadvantage of the mutant allele will keep it rare in a large population, reverse mutation from a to A can be ignored. In a very large randomly mating population, if the mutant is completely recessive, then a will reach an equilibrium frequency of approximately $\sqrt{\mu/s}$. If the mutant is partially dominant, so that most of the selective elimination occurs in heterozygotes ($c \gg \mu/s$), then the equilibrium frequency is lower, approximately μ/cs (Wright, 1969: Chapter 3; Crow and Kimura, 1970: Chapter 5).

The founding of a very small population from an historically large one, with subsequent continued random genetic drift, leads to a rapid increase in the expression of recessive deleterious alleles, some of which may become fixed if they are not actually lethal when homozygous. The loss of fitness upon rapid inbreeding, whether due to small population size or frequent matings between close relatives in a large population, is known as inbreeding depression. The complementary phenomenon of hybrid vigor (or heterosis), upon crossing different inbred lines, can be largely traced to the fixation of deleterious recessive mutations during inbreeding. It is not necessary to postulate widespread heterozygote advantage; there is little evidence for that (Lewontin, 1974; Nei, 1983). Other factors, which are not well understood, also contribute to inbreeding depression. Stabilizing selection on quantitative characters can produce a substantial component of inbreeding depression (Lande and Schemske, 1985). Stabilizing selection, together with developmental instability of homozygotes (if this is not an artifact of canalized development (Lande, 1980)), could create a general heterozygote advantage (Lerner, 1954; Lewontin, 1964).

Detailed information from *Drosophila* species indicates that roughly half of the inbreeding depression in viability is caused by rare recessive lethal and sublethal mutations at many loci (Simmons and Crow, 1977). In most species of higher animals and plants with historically large outcrossing populations, the average individual is heterozygous for one or more recessive lethal equivalents, i.e., lethal alleles or deleterious mutants at two or more loci that together are lethal (Wright, 1977: Chapters 2 and 3). The experience of animal breeders indicates that rapid inbreeding in a very small population recently founded from a large one produces substantial decreases in body size, viability, and fecundity, and frequently leads to the extinction of the population (Falconer, 1981). The slower the rate of inbreeding, or, in the present context, the larger the effective population size immediately after a population crash, the greater the opportunity for selection to eliminate recessive deleterious mutations and, consequently, the less inbreeding depression manifested. Most inbreeding depression can probably be avoided if N_e is at least a few dozen, corresponding to an increase in the average inbreeding coefficient of at most a few % per generation. Below we show how these quantities can be estimated.

In contrast to the potentially severe results of rapid inbreeding, the equilibrium genetic load from deleterious mutations in a very large population (the proportional loss in mean fitness) is equal to the mutation rate for a locus with complete recessive mutations, and about twice the mutation rate for a locus with incompletely recessive mutations. The total equilibrium genetic load from deleterious mutations at all loci probably causes not more than a few % selective mortality in most species (Crow, 1952).

The expected equilibrium frequency of recessive lethal mutations in a finite population depends on whether they are completely or incompletely recessive. For a locus with completely recessive lethal mutations ($c = 0$ and $s = 1$) in a very large randomly mating population ($N_e > 1/2\mu$) the equilibrium frequency is expected to be close to the deterministic value of $\sqrt{\mu}$, whereas in a small population ($N_e < 1/2\mu$) the expected equilibrium frequency is much lower, approximately $\mu\sqrt{2\pi N_e}$. For a locus with incompletely recessive lethal mutations ($1 > c \gg \mu$ and $s = 1$) the expected equilibrium frequency under random mating, approximately μ/cs, is independent of the effective population size (Wright, 1969: Chapter 13; Crow and Kimura, 1970: Chapter 9).

In *Drosophila melanogaster*, for example, the majority of lethal mutations are incompletely recessive, with $c \cong 0.025$, and there are about 5000 lethal-producing loci with an average mutation rate per locus per generation of $\mu = 2 \times 10^{-6}$ (Simmons and Crow, 1977). Therefore, in randomly mating populations, the problem of inbreeding depression due to recessive lethal mutations cannot be avoided even in populations that are kept at intermediate or small effective population sizes. However, in closely managed populations, e.g., in zoological gardens, it is possible to purge a population of most of the recessive lethals and eliminate most of the potential inbreeding depression attributable to that cause (Lande and Schemske, 1985). This can be accomplished by allowing a few or several % of inbreeding through matings between close relatives and allowing natural selection to act on the progeny (i.e., by not deliberately equalizing inbred and non-inbred family sizes).

Recovery rate of deleterious variation. Following an extreme population crash, and the attendant inbreeding depression, if a population does survive it will have lost the rare mildly deleterious alleles at most loci (while fixing some at other loci) and will be purified of nearly all recessive lethal alleles. For fully recessive mutations, if the population subsequently achieves a very large, stable size and is randomly mating, it will regain these polymorphisms on a time scale of $1/\sqrt{\mu s}$ generations. For incompletely recessive mutations, the polymorphism will be regained on a time scale of $1/cs$ generations independently of population size (Lande and Schemske, 1985). Judging from the *Drosophila* data, the potential for severe inbreeding depression due to recessive lethal mutations will be regained within about fifty to a few hundred generations. Time scales for the regeneration of mildly deleterious polymorphisms, which may serve as the foundation for later adaptations, are somewhat longer.

Recommendations. The overall pattern of interaction of kinds of genetic variation, nature of selection, and effective population size is summarized in Table 6.1. It is clearly not going to be possible to maintain large quantities of single-locus polymorphism in many managed populations, at least in those of larger vertebrates. On the other hand, large amounts of such variation ($H > 0.1$) are not routinely found in many natural populations (Nevo, 1978). Many undisturbed vertebrate populations have observed heterozygosities of less than three to four %. Consequently, managers should not necessarily be alarmed by such values in populations of birds and large mammals. It does seem both realistic and desirable, however, to maintain evolutionarily important amounts of

Table 6.1. *Effective population sizes necessary for mutation to maintain significant quantities of genetic variation at equilibrium.*

Type of variation	Nature of selection	Necessary effective population size	Recovery time (generations)
Quantitative	Neutral	~500	10^2–10^3
Quantitative	Stabilizing, or fluctuating optimum	~500	10^2–10^3
Single-locus	Neutral	10^5–10^6	10^5–10^7
Single-locus	Deleterious (incompletely recessive)	Independent of N_e (always present unless inbred)	~10^2

quantitative genetic variation in most managed populations by maintaining effective population sizes of the order of at least several hundreds of individuals.

Estimation of effective population size

Having discussed the relationship between the quantity of genetic variation of various kinds that is maintained in a population and the effective population size, N_e, we turn to the problem of estimating N_e. The effective size of a population is the number of individuals in an ideal population that would have the same genetic properties (in terms of random genetic drift) as an actual population with its own complicated pattern of demographics, sex ratio, etc. A method for determining the effective size of an actual population is described below.

If generations are discrete and non-overlapping, it is relatively simple to estimate the effective size of a single panmictic population given data on numbers of males and females, variance in progeny numbers (which may vary between sexes), and fluctuations in population size (Wright, 1969: Chapter 8; Crow and Kimura, 1970: Chapter 7). Although few species of vertebrates have discrete generations, we will use this case to illustrate some general principles pertaining to effective population sizes. The situation is more complex when generations overlap because, in a growing or shrinking population, lifetime progeny production is no longer an adequate descriptor of individual fitness, and generation times may differ between sexes. Here we suggest a method for incorporating the influence of overlapping generations with the other factors listed above to calculate the effective size of a single population. We assume that the population is randomly mating and closed to immigration. In the next section we discuss the influence of population subdivision and migration among populations.

Discrete non-overlapping generations

Sex ratio. From the sampling variance in gene frequency per generation, the effective population size in a particular generation can be computed:

$$N_e = 4[(1/N_{em}) + (1/N_{ef})]^{-1},$$

where N_{em} and N_{ef} are the effective numbers of males and females as defined below.

Variance in progeny number. Letting k represent the number of progeny produced by an individual during its lifetime, the effective numbers of males and females can be expressed in terms of the actual numbers, N_m and N_f, and the mean and variance of k for each sex, as:

$$N_{em} = (N_m \overline{k_m} - 1)/[\overline{k_m} + (\sigma^2_{km}/\overline{k_m}) - 1]$$

and

$$N_{ef} = (N_f \overline{k_f} - 1)/[\overline{k_f} + (\sigma^2_{kf}/\overline{k_f}) - 1].$$

These expressions can be derived from a formula of Pollak (1977) by using the identities $k_m N_{m,t} = k_f N_{f,t} = N_{t+1}$, where $N_{m,t}$ and $N_{f,t}$ are the numbers of males and females in generation t, and $N_t = N_{m,t} + N_{f,t}$. (The present expressions differ from those of Crow and Kimura (1970) because those authors assumed independent sampling of male and female gametes, which is violated in a non-ideal population.)

Some insight into these formulae can be gained by examining particular situations. If the sex ratio at birth (or after parental expenditure has ended) is close to $1:1$, the mean number of progeny per individual must then be nearly equal for the two sexes because they contribute the same total number of gametes to the next generation, $\overline{k_m} = \overline{k_f}$. The variances in progeny number, however, may differ between the sexes, usually being larger in males, especially in polygamous species (Wade and Arnold, 1980). Even if the actual numbers of males and females are equal, a larger variance of progeny number in males implies that the effective number of males is less than that of females. In real populations, the variance of progeny number generally exceeds the mean progeny number in both sexes (Crow and Kimura, 1970: p. 363) so that the effective number of individuals of either sex is less than the actual number present in any generation. Unequal effective numbers of males and females also contribute to decreasing the effective size within a generation.

For a given number of parents, N, the maximum effective population size occurs if the actual numbers of males and females are equal and there is no variance among individuals in progeny production: then $N_e = 2N$. This is the best that can be achieved, even in closely managed populations. In such circumstances random genetic drift is attributable entirely to Mendelian segregation in heterozygotes. The only way to further reduce the rate of loss of variability by random genetic drift in a population of a given size is by subdivision of the population. This results in a decrease of heterozygosity, but preserves genetic variability through fixation of different alleles in different subpopulations. However, extreme subdivision into very small isolated subpopulations (less than a few dozen individuals) should be avoided because of the likelihood of deleterious consequences from inbreeding depression.

Fluctuations in population size. When the size of the population fluctuates, the effective numbers in different generations, $N_e(1)$, $N_e(2)$, . . . , $N_e(t)$, can be combined to yield a long-term effective population size using the formula

$$(1 - 1/2N_e)^t = \prod_{i=1}^{t} (1 - 1/2N_e(i)]$$

or, solving this,

$$N_e = 1/2\left[1 - \left\{\prod_{i=1}^{t} [1 - 1/2N_e(i)]\right\}^{1/t}\right].$$

The well-known approximation to this expression, employing the harmonic mean of the effective numbers in each generation,

$$N_e \cong t/ \sum_{i=1}^{t} 1/N_e(i),$$

is valid only for fluctuations occurring on a short time scale, during which gene frequencies remain nearly constant (Wright, 1968: p. 214; Crow and Kimura, 1970: p. 360). The harmonic mean therefore should not be used in long-term management programs.

A salient feature of both the harmonic mean approximation and the more precise formula is that the generations with the smallest effective population size have a disproportionate influence on the long-term value of N_e. It is of interest that even in the most extreme situation, when the population is reduced to a single mating pair of individuals, $N_e = 2$ (with $\bar{k}_m = \bar{k}_f = 2$, and $\sigma^2_{km} = \sigma^2_{kf} = 0$), at most about 25% of the heterozygosity or additive genetic variance in quantitative characters is expected to be lost in a single generation. Hence a sudden population crash followed by a rapid recovery to a large effective size is not necessarily disastrous in terms of depleting genetic variance (Lewontin, 1965; Lande, 1980; Templeton, 1980); only rare alleles are likely to be lost in a single generation. Moreover, recessive lethal and detrimental mutations will retard the loss of genetic variance at other loci, especially those to which they are linked, due to linkage disequilibrium generated by random genetic drift. In high-fecundity organisms, which can recover quickly from a population crash, there is ample opportunity for selection to prevent the fixation of deleterious mutations and to reverse the harmful results of brief periods of inbreeding. For these reasons, either several generations of severe inbreeding in a small population or repeated crashes to a few individuals in a short span of time are necessary to deplete rapidly most of the genetic variance from an initially large population.

Table 6.2. *Sample distribution of numbers of offspring for three generations of a growing population.*

Generation	Males	No. offspring	Females	No. offspring
1	A	9	A, B	4
	B	3	C	3
			D	1
2	A	9	A	5
	B	5	B, C	4
	C, D	3	D	3
			E, F	2
			G, H	0
3	A	12	A, B	5
	B	9	C, D	4
	C	7	E, F, G	3
	D	5	H, I, J, K	2
	E	3	L	1
	F, G, H	0		

Example. The above formulae allow one to compute effective population size while simultaneously taking into account the effects of skewed sex ratio, non-Poisson variance in progeny number, and fluctuating population size. Consider the sample data in Tables 6.2 and 6.3 for an initially small, but steadily growing population.

For the first generation, the effective numbers of males and females can be calculated using the formulae for variance in offspring number. For example,

$$N_{em} = (2 * 6.0 - 1)/[6.0 + (18.00/6.0) - 1] = 1.38$$

We also obtain $N_{ef} = 4.12$. Note that the effective number of females is slightly greater than the actual number because the variance in reproductive success is less than the mean. Then, using the formula for sex ratio, we compute the effective number of total individuals in generation 1:

$$N_e = 4[(1/1.38) + (1/4.12)]^{-1} = 4.13.$$

In a similar fashion, we find N_{em} and N_{ef} for the second generation to be 3.39 and 6.62. The overall effective size, N_e, in generation 2 is 8.97. For the third generation, $N_{em} = 4.30$ and $N_{ef} = 13.73$. Note that the effective number of males is substantially smaller than the actual number because of the large variance among males in reproductive success. The overall N_e is 13.10.

Finally, using the formula for fluctuating population size, we compute

Table 6.3. *Sample demographic parameters for a growing population (data in Table 6.2) with a skewed sex ratio and variance in progeny number.*

Generation	No. males	No. females	$\overline{k}_m$	$\overline{k}_f$	σ^2_{km}	σ^2_{kf}
1	2	4	6.0	3.0	18.00	2.00
2	4	8	5.0	2.5	8.00	3.43
3	8	12	4.5	3.0	20.86	1.64

the equivalent effective size for the population over this three generation period:

$$N_e = 1/2\langle 1 - \{[1 - 1/(2 * 4.13)] * [1 - 1/(2 * 8.97)] \\ * [1 - 1/(2 * 13.10)]\}^{1/3}\rangle = 6.91.$$

Thus, the rate of loss of genic variability from the growing population, over this three generation interval, is the same as that expected from a population of constant effective size of 6.91. Even though the population has become substantially larger by the third generation, the overall effective size remains strongly influenced by the number of individuals at the initial bottleneck.

Overlapping generations

This is the case that applies to the great majority of animal species. We assume that the population is censused at regular intervals that are short in comparison to the generation time of either sex. For convenience, time and age are measured in units of the census interval (years if the censuses are conducted annually). We also assume that population size is large enough and environmental change slow enough that the age distribution of the population is nearly stable.

In calculating the contribution of each individual to future generations, progeny produced at each age must be discounted by the growth rate of the population (Charlesworth, 1980; Lande, 1982). The lifetime contribution of an individual to a population with a stable age distribution, which is currently growing at the exponential rate r (which may be positive or negative) per unit time, is defined as

$$k = e^{rT} \sum_{x=1}^{d} e^{-rx} l_x m_x$$

where $\overline{T}$ is the average generation time defined below, d is the maximum age at death, and m_x is the number of progeny produced between the ages of $x - 1$ and x. The survivorship of an individual, l_x, is defined as unity if it was alive at age $x - 1$, and is zero for all ages greater than or equal to the age at death. The exponential growth rate of the population per unit time is the unique real root of the equation

$$\sum_{x=1}^{d} e^{-rx} \overline{l_x m_x} = 2$$

in which $\overline{l_x m_x}$ is the average value of survivorship times fecundity at age x in the current population; the factor of 2 accounts for sexual reproduction. Theoretically, in a population with a stable age distribution and sex ratio, r can be obtained from either the male or the female lifetable with m_x applied only to offspring of the corresponding sex, and with 1 replacing 2 on the right side of the previous equation. It should be noticed that the relative contribution (or fitness) of an individual with a given schedule of reproduction depends on the growth rate of the population, r, which may change with time. Both m_x and r, as well as the generation times and effective numbers of individuals below, should be re-evaluated at each census. Because the lifetime reproduction of each individual must be known, the calculations from the data in any particular census can only be carried out after a lag of more than one generation.

The generation times for the two sexes are defined as their average ages at reproduction, discounting progeny by the growth rate of the population:

$$T_{\mathrm{m}} = (1/2) \sum_{x=1}^{d} x e^{-rx} \overline{l_{x\mathrm{m}} m_{x\mathrm{m}}}$$

and

$$T_{\mathrm{f}} = (1/2) \sum_{x=1}^{d} x e^{-rx} \overline{l_{x\mathrm{f}} m_{x\mathrm{f}}}.$$

These may differ substantially when the sexes mature at different ages. The average generation time is

$$\overline{T} = (T_{\mathrm{m}} + T_{\mathrm{f}})/2.$$

Because the sampling variances in the frequencies of genes derived from males and females are inversely proportional to their generation times, the effective population size *per average generation* can be shown to be

$$N_{\mathrm{e}} = 4(\overline{T}/N_{\mathrm{em}} T_{\mathrm{m}} + \overline{T}/N_{\mathrm{ef}} T_{\mathrm{f}})^{-1},$$

where N_{em} and N_{ef} are the effective numbers of males and females per average generation. By analogy with the discrete generation case, and based in part on Hill's (1972, 1979) model of an age-structured population of constant size, we define the effective numbers of the two sexes per average generation by the same formulae as above for discrete generations, but with the altered definition of k, and with N_{m} and N_{f} being the total number of males and females in all age classes. To account for the effects of aging, we suggest that in calculating $\overline{k}$ and σ_k^2 for surviving males and females, individuals of age x should be weighted by their expected reproductive value,

$$v_x = (1/2)\overline{l^{-1}}\, e_x^{rx} \sum_{y=x}^{d} e^{-ry}\, \overline{l_y m_y},$$

where the averages are taken over all individuals (surviving and dead) of the same age and sex. This gives their expected contribution to the future growth of the population (Fisher, 1958), with $v_0 = 1$ at conception (averaged over all individuals of both sexes) and $v_x = 0$ after death or last reproduction. Reproductive value weighting may also help to allow for departures from a stable age distribution; it has been used in this context for the analysis of selection (Crow, 1978; Charlesworth, 1980: pp. 67–8), and random genetic drift is similar to random fluctuating selection.

Following Hill we can define the effective population size *per unit time* as $N_e^* = N_e \overline{T}$. This is useful in calculating the expected proportional rate of loss of selectively neutral heterozygosity or additive genetic variance in quantitative characters caused by random genetic drift. This rate is approximately $1/2N_e^*$ per unit time. Fluctuations in the effective population size per unit time in different census periods, $N_e^*(1)$, $N_e^*(2)$, ..., $N_e^*(t)$, can be accounted for using the same formula as in the case of discrete generations to obtain a long-term effective population size per unit time.

It must be emphasized that there are factors that limit the accuracy of these formulae. In many populations it is not feasible to estimate all of the appropriate demographic parameters, and educated guesses must be relied upon. Further, the expected rate of loss of selectively neutral genetic variation in populations with overlapping generations only asymptotically approaches $1/2N_e^*$ per unit time (Charlesworth, 1980: Chapter 2; Hill, 1972; 1979; and references therein), so that in very small populations, or ones with a rapidly changing age distribution, these formulae must be regarded merely as rough approximations. This caveat also applies to the formulae for populations with discrete generations and separate sexes; for example, under continued sib-mating, the asymptotic rate of loss of neutral heterozygosity is 19.1% per generation instead of the 25% indicated by the preceding equations (Wright, 1931; 1969: Chapter 7). The formulae given here should nevertheless be sufficiently accurate for most practical purposes in population management programs.

Unfortunately, at the present time the detailed effects of overlapping generations are insufficiently understood to warrant generalizations about the interaction of different life history schedules and random genetic drift or the decrease in heterozygosity.

Subdivided populations

Realistically, not all managed populations will consist of a single panmictic unit. Many, perhaps most, natural populations possess some geographic structure. A species whose range is composed of more or less geographically isolated patches, interconnected through patterns of gene flow, extinction, and recolonization, is said to form a *metapopulation*, or population of subpopulations. Persons responsible for the long-term survivorship of such populations may have to consider the effects of the metapopulation structure on the quantity and geographical distribution of the genetic variation maintained. We consider here two classes of situations. In the first, the individual subpopulations are relatively persistent, but may have various geographical structures and degrees of connectedness. In the second case, we consider the situation where subpopulations are ephemeral and global persistence is the result of frequent recolonization.

Stable populations

Theoretical models have been developed to investigate the effects of geographical structure of populations for several different configurations. One set of models involve geographically continuously distributed populations. These have been called 'isolation-by-distance' models, and have been investigated for both linear and two-dimensional situations. Other sets of models are appropriate for cases in which the individuals of a population are organized into discrete colonies or patches of habitat. In situations of the latter type in which the pattern of gene flow among colonies is independent of relative geographical proximity, the 'island' model of population structure is appropriate. Alternatively, if gene flow is usually to adjacent colonies, then 'stepping-stone' models of population structure are used. A useful review of these models and their results can be found in Slatkin (1985).

Isolation-by-distance models. This model originated with Wright (1943). Individuals are assumed to be continuously distributed throughout an extensive one- or two-dimensional range. Individual dispersal distances, from birthsite to breeding site, are assumed to have a mean zero and standard deviation σ. Because this distance (σ is frequently termed the root-mean-square dispersal distance) is finite, it will take a number of generations for genes to 'flow' across the range of the species. Wright

(1943, 1951) and Dobzhansky and Wright (1947) investigated the properties of this type of geographical structure by treating the continuous population as a series of 'neighborhoods' grading into each other. Wright (1969: p. 295) defined a neighborhood as the 'area from which the parents of central individuals may be treated as if drawn from random.' Each neighborhood was taken to be of size $2\sqrt{\pi}\rho\sigma$ for linear cases and $4\pi\rho\sigma^2$ for two-dimensional situations. Here ρ is the density of the population. Note that $4\pi\rho\sigma^2$ is the number of individuals in a circle of radius 2σ; as in our previous discussion of N_e, this number requires correction for cases of non-unity sex ratio, non-Poisson distribution of offspring numbers, fluctuating densities, and overlapping generations. In addition, Wright (1969) provides a correction for non-Gaussian dispersal distributions.

With an isolation-by-distance type of population structure, some of the genetic variation in the population is distributed among subpopulations or neighborhoods. The magnitude of such spatial heterogeneity will depend on the local neighborhood size and the total geographical extent of the population; its magnitude can be evaluated with a coefficient, F_{st}. In the framework of an analysis of variance (Cockerham, 1973), F_{st} is the component of genetic variance distributed among subpopulations. F_{st} can vary from zero to one; it becomes one when different subpopulations are fixed for alternative alleles. Given local neighborhoods of size N_e, and a total of K such neighborhoods in the total population, F_{st} can be estimated as

$$(1 - t_K)/(1 + t_K),$$

where t_K is approximately

$$\exp - \{(1/N_e) * [\ln (K - 0.5) + 0.5772]$$
$$+ [1/(2N_e^2)] * [1.6449 - 2/(2K - 1)]$$
$$+ [1/(3N_e^3)] * [1.202 - 2/(2K - 1)^2] + \ldots \}$$

(Wright, 1951: p. 350). In practice the first two or three terms are adequate for the summation because the series converges rapidly. It should be noted that this model is not mathematically very precise (Felsenstein, 1975; Malécot, 1975; Slatkin, 1985), and so results must only be treated as order of magnitude estimates, at best.

F_{st} can also be thought of as the inbreeding coefficient of a subpopulation with respect to the total population. If its value is large, then some of the problems associated with inbreeding, such as an increased expression of recessive deleterious alleles, can occur in the subpopulations, even in the absence of matings among close relatives. However, dispersal must be severely limited and population density must be low for this to be a real problem.

Maruyama (1977) has considered a similar, continuous population density model, and addressed the problem of the conditions under which the total population can be treated as a single panmictic unit for the purpose of analyzing random genetic drift and the maintenance of genic heterozygosity. He found that for linear situations, the population can be considered panmictic if $\rho\sigma^2 > L/10$, where ρ and σ are defined as above, and L is the total linear range of the population. For an area continuum, the population can be considered panmictic if $\rho\sigma^2 > 1$. Nagylaki (1974) has obtained a qualitatively similar result with a more exact treatment. Panmixia is thus easily achieved for the two-dimensional cases ; however, significant differentiation is common for linear situations: as L gets large, it becomes very unlikely that $\rho\sigma^2$ will exceed $L/10$.

Example. As an example, consider the case of the spotted owl (*Strix occidentalis*), a bird that prefers old-growth redwood and Douglas-fir forests in the Pacific northwest region of the United States. Barrowclough and Coats (1985) investigated the population genetics of this more or less continuously distributed species using an isolation-by-distance model. Radio-tracking of dispersing juveniles produced a distribution of dispersal distances whose standard deviation was 33.56 km. The density of these owls is approximately 0.037 km^{-2}. Therefore, the number of owls in a neighborhood is approximately

$$4\pi(0.037)(33.56)^2 = 523.7$$

A correction for variance in offspring numbers, overlapping generations, and non-normality of the dispersal distribution resulted in an estimate of the effective size of a neighborhood of about 220. In the range of the subspecies of concern, there are approximately ten such neighborhoods. Therefore, using Wright's formula, and taking N_e as 220 and K as 10, expected F_{st} was computed to be 0.007. Thus, less than 1% of the genetic variance is expected to be distributed among neighborhoods for this species. Likewise, using Maruyama's formula,

$$\rho\sigma^2 = 0.037(33.56)^2 = 48.67,$$

which is greater than 1.0, so for the purpose of estimating the effects of random genetic drift and loss of genic variability, the population of the spotted owl can currently be considered as a single panmictic unit of approximate effective size 220 * 10 or 2200 individuals.

Stepping-stone models. Not all species are continuously distributed in space. For species that have a clumped or colonial distribution and for which the probability of intercolony gene flow is a decreasing function of distance, the relevant model is one of the stepping-stone models of population structure. One- and two-dimensional stepping-stone models have been developed by Kimura and Weiss (1964) and Weiss and Kimura (1965).

Consider an array of colonies, each of effective size N_e. (If the colonies vary in size, then assume each has a size equivalent to the harmonic mean of the actual distribution of sizes.) Assume each colony exchanges a fraction, m, of its members with adjacent colonies each generation, and a fraction, m_∞, with the population as a whole (long distance migration). In a linear array of colonies, $m/2$ are exchanged with each of the two adjacent colonies; $m/4$ are exchanged with each of the four adjacent colonies in a two-dimensional configuration. Note that in practice there may be very large standard errors associated with estimates of m and m_∞; in fact, m_∞ is frequently taken to be of the same order as mutation, say 10^{-5}. Then, F_{st} among a large number of colonies can be estimated as

$$F_{st} = 1/(1 + 2N_eC_o),$$

where

$$C_o = 2(2m * m_\infty)^{1/2}$$

for linear arrays, and

$$C_o^{-1} = [1/(\pi m)][(1/M_1)K(1/M_1) + (1/M_2)K(1/M_2)]$$

for two-dimensional arrays. Here

$$M_1 = (1 + m_\infty/m) \quad \text{and} \quad M_2 = [1 - (2 - m_\infty)/m],$$

and $K(\cdot)$ is the complete elliptic integral of the first kind. Needless to say, these calculations are best performed on a computer.

In practice, the number of colonies may not be infinite; for such cases the actual expected differentiation may be approximated by the product of the above estimate of F_{st} and a correction factor for finite colony number. For a linear case, that factor is

$$\left[1 - 1/n - (2/n^2) \sum_{i=1}^{n} (n - i)r(i)\right],$$

where n is the number of colonies and

$$r(i) = \exp - (2m_\infty/m)^{1/2}i.$$

For a two-dimensional case, the correction factor for a finite number of colonies is

$$\left\{1 - 1/(n_1n_2) - [2/(n_1n_2)^2]\left[\sum_{i=1}^{n_1} (n_1 - i)n_2r(i, 0)\right.\right.$$
$$+ \sum_{j=1}^{n_2} n_1(n_2 - j)r(0, j)$$
$$\left.\left. + 2 \sum_{i=1}^{n_1} \sum_{j=1}^{n_2} (n_1 - i)(n_2 - j)r(i, j)\right]\right\},$$

where n_1 and n_2 are the numbers of colonies along the x and y axes (n_1n_2 is the total number of colonies) and

$$r(i, j) = [C_o/(\pi m)]K_0[(4m_\infty/m)^{1/2}\rho],$$

where $K_0[\cdot]$ is the modified Bessel function of zeroth order and $\rho = (i^2 + j^2)^{1/2}$ is the Cartesian distance between the origin and a colony at position (i, j).

The above equations will enable one to compute the magnitude of genetic differentiation among colonies. It may also be of interest to know whether the population as a whole can be treated as a single, panmictic unit for purposes of comparing the genetical size to the guidelines presented in Table 6.1. In general, the number of migrants that must be exchanged among adjacent colonies per generation to maintain effective panmixia is somewhat larger than that required for the island model (see next section). Malécot (1975) obtained a minimum value of gene flow of 1.25 individuals per generation for a two-dimensional case. Using a computer simulation, Crow and Aoki (1984) obtained a similar result: the number of migrants per generation required to maintain panmixia was between one and two. For a linear case, Malécot found that unless the number of migrants was of the order of $(n_1N_e)^{1/2}$ or more, differentiation would take place among colonies. Again, as with the isolation-by-distance model, a linear population results in significant differentiation relative to a two-dimensional situation. (As Slatkin (1985) points out, however, this is only true for evolutionary short periods of time. Two-dimensional configurations can actually result in greater differentiation for intervals over which mutation becomes important – 1000s of generations.)

The potential for significant reduction of genetic variation *within* subpopulations is considerably greater for stepping-stone populations than for continuously distributed ones. This is because the probability of dispersal across unsuitable habitat may be very small for low vagility organisms. In fact, if the probability of successful gene flow among colonies is very low, it may be necessary to consider each colony separately for purposes of estimating the extent of individual heterozygosity. In a series of small, well-isolated colonies, much of the genetic variance will be distributed *among* rather than *within* colonies. Of course, if estimates of m are available, the extent of this problem can be computed using the above formulae for calculating F_{st}.

Island model. This model presupposes a large number of colonies, each of effective size N_e (or harmonic size if colonies differ in size), and each of which exchanges a fraction, m, of its individuals each generation randomly with an immigrant gene pool made up from contributions from all colonies. Thus, in this model, physical proximity does not influence the probability of gene flow. Consequently, this model is unrealistic for many natural populations, but may be appropriate for zoological gardens or reserves where gene flow is mediated by managers.

The model was developed by Wright (1943) and subsequently elaborated by Maruyama (1970), Nei *et al.* (1977), and Ewens (1979). The equilibrium amount of differentiation among colonies can be computed as approximately

$$F_{st} = (1 - m)^2/[2N_e - (2N_e - 1) * (1 - m)^2].$$

Crow and Kimura (1970) find that for this island model of geographic structure, the total population can be treated as effectively panmictic if m is greater than about $1/(4N_e)$. Wright (1969) obtained the same result, but emphasized that even when m is an order of magnitude greater there can be some non-negligible differences in allelic frequency among colonies.

Summary. Based on the foregoing models, a subdivided population can be considered approximately panmictic if the separate colonies exchange on the order of one or more migrants with each other per generation. This is less true of linear population structures than of two-dimensional ones. Formulae have been presented for the computation of the approximate amount of differentiation among colonies, given estimates of the effective size of the local neighborhoods or colonies and the amount of gene flow among them. All of the formulae and conclusions are based on approximations, inexact models, and assumptions that will frequently be violated (e.g., Slatkin, 1985). Thus, at least occasional direct monitoring of the genetics of subdivided populations is desirable to check on the accuracy of the predictions based on these models (see chapter summary).

The general effect of population subdivision is to somewhat *increase* the total genic variation in the metapopulation system, but at the expense of decreasing the variation within subpopulations. That is, some of the variation within subpopulations (heterozygosity) is converted to variation among subpopulations (F_{st}). To some extent this may be favorable: it forms the basis for Wright's shifting balance theory of evolution (Wright, 1970); however, if too pronounced it can lead to inbreeding difficulties within the subpopulations. This can be a real problem with small colonies of low vagility organisms. Managers can artificially achieve panmixia by moving as few as one or two individuals at random into each subpopulation per generation, provided the transferred individuals actually produce offspring.

Ephemeral populations

There may be cases in which managers are faced with the problem of maintaining a viable population of a species composed of several or numerous subpopulations, each of which has a relatively high probability of extinction. For example, the species may be ecologically restricted to a particular successional stage, for example, tree-fall areas in lowland tropical forests or recently burned patches of forest or grassland. The local populations may be subject to frequent severe epidemic diseases or parasites, or perhaps it is a fugitive species restricted to small, offshore islands with reduced competition and predation but with very small numbers of individuals. Many species in a wide variety of taxa may be characterized by this metapopulation structure (Ehrlich, 1983).

The long-term persistence of such species depends upon a balance between the frequent extinctions of subpopulations and recolonizations of newly suitable patches of habitat or areas where the earlier subpopulation has become extinct. The colonization process may frequently involve a small propagule. Hence, this type of metapopulation dynamics, with frequent local bottlenecks of population sizes during colonization events, can result in the maintenance of reduced quantities of genetic variance. Ewens *et al.* (Chapter 4) have developed a mathematically precise model for such an ephemeral population structure with the assumption of no immigration among populations. Here we investigate models in which there is some genetic interchange among extant populations. Slatkin (1977) and Maruyama and Kimura (1980) have begun the investigation of such situations, and we review these preliminary results here. We note, however, that genetic variation is irrelevant if a population goes extinct. An ephemeral population structure will require intensive demographic monitoring and, depending on the vagility of the organism and the geographic distances involved, occasional artificial introductions (see other chapters on genetics and demography in this volume).

Maruyama and Kimura (1980) consider the case of a number of colonies, n, each of harmonic effective size N. (Colonies are founded by a small number of individuals and then rapidly grow to some large size before becoming extinct. N is the harmonic mean of this temporal sequence of population numbers over the tenure of a subpopulation; see Island model section above). Let μ, m, and λ be the per generation mutation, gene flow, and extinction rates, respectively. For the island model of geographic structure (see above), with respect to the maintenance of selectively neutral heterozygosity, the overall effective size of the entire set of populations is found to be approximately

$$N_e = N + n/[4(\mu + \lambda + m)] + nN(\mu + m)/(\mu + \lambda + m) .$$

We note that some of the variables in this formula are difficult to measure in practice; this is especially true of μ, λ, and m. In addition, Ewens *et al.* (Chapter 4) have pointed out that this definition of effective population size is a bit unorthodox; nevertheless, simulations in part support the results, and some qualitative implications of the result are of interest. Using rough approximations to the parameters, managers may at least be able to obtain an order of magnitude estimate of N_e.

Among the variables that managers may be able to adjust through manipulations, overall effective population size is positively influenced by colony size and number, and by gene flow among colonies. N_e, and hence the amount of genetic variation maintained in the system, is inversely related to subpopulation extinction rate. In particular, if λ is at all large compared to m, then overall N_e can be greatly reduced with respect to the total apparent effective size of the species, nN.

It may or may not be possible for manipulation to result in a decrease in subpopulation extinction rate. That will depend on the specific ecological situation. If it is feasible, however, then N_e may be substantially increased if a major reduction in λ can be achieved. Additionally, it may be possible to increase N_e by increasing the size of the initial propagules. For example, a recolonization could be artificially started with a few dozens of individuals rather than with a single fertilized female; this would result in the maintenance of more heterozygosity.

Artificially promoting gene flow among colonies, m, can also be used to increase N_e. This, however, along with a practice of taking propagules from a mixture of colonies, will result in a change in the distribution of genetic variation in the system. Mixed propagules and substantial gene flow among colonies will lead to more genetic variation being maintained within, rather than among, subpopulations (Slatkin, 1977; see section on inbreeding depression, below).

Monitoring the genetics of managed populations

Estimates of effective population size
The calculations described in the preceding sections are useful for the relatively short-term prediction of the impact of management practices on the loss of genetic variability due to the effects of random drift. Over a period of many generations, however, predictions based on these equations may prove inaccurate for a number of reasons. Random genetic drift is, of course, a stochastic process; our treatment of it in computing the sampling effects due to finite population size, sex ratio, variance in progeny number, and fluctuations of numbers of individuals

has dealt with expectations (or averages) and so is subject to error. Additionally, these calculations of sampling effects are explicitly for neutral genes. Heterozygote advantage or inbreeding depression, for example, may result in the maintenance of more variation than the formulae indicate. Finally, the formulae themselves are in some cases approximations (e.g., the case of overlapping generations). Thus, long-term population management programs should also involve some form of direct monitoring of genetic variation.

Direct measurement of genetic variation

Single-locus variation. It is possible to monitor the levels of genic variation for several different classes of genes, e.g., blood group antigens, restriction sites in mitochondrial and nuclear DNA, etc., but the most convenient polymorphisms for such purposes are the structural gene polymorphisms revealed by electrophoresis. This technique is widely known and many countries have laboratories capable of surveying and monitoring such variation. Discussion of techniques and the meaning of the variation can be found in Brewer (1970), Shaw and Prasad (1970), Lewontin (1974), Harris and Hopkinson (1976), and Kimura (1983). Nei (1978) presents a method for obtaining an unbiased estimator of genic heterozygosity. The method presumes Hardy–Weinberg frequencies obtain in the sampled population. Let x_{ij} be the frequency of allele i at locus j. Single-locus heterozygosity at locus j can be estimated as:

$$h_j = 2n_j\left(1 - \sum_i x_{ij}^2\right)/(2n_j - 1),$$

where n_j is the number of individuals examined for locus j, and the summation is over all alleles segregating at that locus. Overall heterozygosity, H, is estimated as

$$H = (1/L) \sum_j h_j,$$

where L is the total number of loci sampled, and the summation is over all loci $j = 1$ to L. An alternative possibility is to compute heterozygosity directly from the observed frequencies of actual heterozygotes at each locus.

These statistics can be monitored over time to ensure that variability does not rapidly decay. Unfortunately, there is no objective standard to which absolute level of heterozygosity can be compared. Genetic heterozygosity in natural populations varies greatly from taxon to taxon

(Nevo, 1978) and its evolutionary meaning is controversial (Lewontin, 1974). Moreover, as mentioned above, it takes hundreds of thousands or millions of years for single-locus heterozygosity to recover from the effects of severe bottlenecks. Thus, the level of heterozygosity in a managed population may actually be a reflection of demographic events that the source population experienced in the very distant past. Nevertheless, it is now relatively easy and inexpensive to monitor this variation using blood or tissue samples from 20 to 30 individuals for 30 to 40 loci (Nei, 1978; Gorman and Renzi, 1979). A trend of loss of this variability would be easily observed and could serve as a warning to managers that selection or random genetic drift is a problem in their stock. A caveat is necessary here, however. Note that we are not advocating the use of electrophoresis for the selection of particular individuals with specific electrophoretic genotypes for mating purposes; that would represent a form of artificial selection and would result in the decrease of genetic variation at other loci. Rather, the use of electrophoresis is recommended strictly for the purpose of monitoring genetic variation, not manipulating it.

Quantitative variation. The level of genetic variation for quantitative traits can be monitored with heritability studies. Persons interested in maintaining quantitative genetic variation in managed populations will want to know that at least some of the phenotypic variation in a population has an additive genetic component. An evolutionary response to selection is based on such variation. Narrow-sense heritability is the ratio of the additive genetic variance to the total phenotypic variance, and thus can be used to monitor the level of quantitative genetic variation in a population.

The narrow-sense heritability, h^2, of a particular quantitative trait can be estimated as the slope of the regression of the value of the trait in offspring on the value in the midparent. (The midparent value is the mean of the values in the two parents.) In some cases the male parent may be unknown; in such cases, h^2 can be calculated as twice the regression of the offspring on the female parent. Alternative methods based on full-sib and half-sib families are also available (Falconer, 1981). A significantly greater slope of regression of offspring on female parent than on male parent indicates a maternal effect (or X-linkage); in such cases h^2 is best estimated as twice the slope of the regression of offspring on male parent, or from the resemblance between paternal half-sib families (Falconer, 1981). For an example of the calculation of heritability, see Hartl (1981: pp. 159–60). Typical levels of heritability for many traits are of the order of 0.3 to 0.7; however, for traits closely related to fitness, e.g., viability, litter size, etc., heritability values are often considerably lower.

Management programs probably should involve monitoring the heritability of some quantitative trait(s) that are expected to be moderately to highly heritable, such as body length or height at a specific age. Lengths and widths of permanent molar teeth in mammalian species are convenient in being easily measured on live individuals and independent of age, with heritabilities around 0.5 in human and mouse populations. The animals on which the regression is computed must all be from roughly the same location. Genetic–environmental interactions may yield an artificially high estimate of h^2 if measurements taken in more than one environment are pooled.

In zoological gardens it will be relatively easy to monitor heritability of representative quantitative traits, such as size, because pedigrees will be known for many animals. In semi-wild or managed natural populations, however, this may prove expensive, and monitoring may mean sampling heritability at intervals of several generations. Heritability estimates may be subject to large (but computable) standard errors, and so sample sizes of several dozens of offspring distributed among many families may be requisite. In spite of these difficulties, we believe this monitoring is worth pursuing because quantitative genetic variation is crucial to the long-term adaptation of populations.

Chromosomal polymorphisms. Karyotypic analysis and such techniques as G- and C-banding can be used to monitor chromosomal polymorphisms. For example, inversion polymorphisms are commonly found in many mammals and birds (e.g., Shields, 1982). Techniques for karyological analysis are discussed in Patton (1967) and Shields (1983). The level of variability in a population can be estimated using the same equations as those given for electrophoretic monitoring.

Chromosomal polymorphisms are not common in all groups of organisms. Thus, if segregating chromosomal variants are found, they can be used as indicators of variability and for its monitoring; however, the lack of such variability does not imply a fatal homozygosity that requires immediate action. Moreover, different types of karyological variation require differing interpretation. Inversion polymorphisms may lock in favorably interacting gene combinations. In some cases, though, segregating inversions and translocations can lead to fertility problems in heterozygotes.

Inbreeding depression. It is difficult or impossible to measure the exact level of inbreeding in a population. In practice, one measures the inbreeding coefficient relative to the original level of inbreeding in some source population.

We assume a pedigree is available for the individuals of interest. Then the inbreeding coefficient of an individual, I, can be computed as

$$F_I = \sum (1/2)^i (1 + F_A),$$

where i is the number of individuals (except I) in a closed path through an ancestor common to both parents of individual I (i.e., a closed path is one with inbreeding); F_A is the inbreeding coefficient (if known) of ancestor A, and the summation is over all possible closed paths in the pedigree leading to individual I. For example, in Figure 6.1, individual I is inbred through two paths, one tracing back to A, and a second one to B. There are three individuals in the B loop, and five in the A loop. We assume F_A and F_B are zero. Therefore,

$$F_I = (1/2)^3 + (1/2)^5 = 0.156.$$

For further examples of such calculations, see Ballou (1983).

The severity of inbreeding depression can be found by computing the correlation of fertility, viability, etc., with the inbreeding coefficient (e.g., Templeton and Read, 1983). It is not uncommon for a 10% increase in F to result in a 10% reduction in traits closely associated with fitness, such as body size, fecundity, and longevity (Falconer, 1981: Chapter 14; Ralls *et al.*, 1979; Frankel and Soulé, 1981).

There may be some cases in which it is important to determine if inbreeding depression is a serious current or potential problem, especially if the population has been small for an extended period, or if there is a history of known or suspected inbreeding. For such cases, if pedigrees are

Figure 6.1. A simple pedigree with inbreeding.

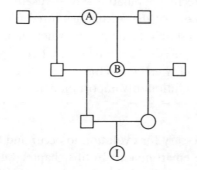

Table 6.4. *Recommended techniques for monitoring genetic variation in managed populations.*

Nature of genetic variation	Monitored index	Technique
Single-locus	Overall heterozygosity	Electrophoresis of 30–40 loci
Quantitative	Narrow-sense heritability	Offspring–parent regression or sib analysis
Chromosomal	Heterozygosity	Karyology; G-, C-banding
Deleterious genes	Inbreeding depression	Correlation of fitness-related traits with inbreeding coefficients computed from pedigrees

available, the above formula should be employed to ascertain the potential severity of the problem.

Unfortunately, however, pedigrees are difficult and expensive to obtain for natural and semi-wild populations. It may be feasible in some cases to arrange for a generation or two of full-sib mating in order to see how severe the problem is. However, the number of cases in which the necessary time and effort is worthwhile will be limited. Deliberately encouraging close inbreeding will be a waste of valuable stock if the number of individuals in a population is limited.

Recommendations

In Table 6.4 we list some recommended techniques for direct monitoring of genetic variation in managed populations. Although predictions based on estimates of effective population size are useful for the short-term, we believe one or more of the techniques listed for direct measurement of genetic variation should be employed where long-term management of a population is required. If resources are strictly limited, occasional computation of heritability estimates for quantitative genetic variation may provide the most evolutionarily important data.

Summary

Genetic variation is necessary for evolution to occur and hence for adaptation to changes in the environment. In this chapter we have shown that it is the genetical effective size that is the primary variable of importance to biologists concerned with monitoring or managing the genetic variation present in a population. Consequently, in practice it often will be necessary either to measure the effective size of a population, or to monitor the level of genetic variation directly. We have provided suggestions for methods of doing both, and it is recommended that managers pursue both options to ensure long-term viability of species under their aegis.

Many species will not consist of a single, panmictic unit. We have therefore reviewed approximate methods for computing the effects of geographical structure on the maintenance of genic variability. Unfortunately, the simplicity of presently available models may require some rough approximations to the real world.

Of particular importance is the finding that the genetic variation of a population cannot be considered a single entity. Quantitative variation must be considered separately from single-locus variation, as must neutral variation from selected variation. The effective sizes of populations necessary to maintain significant amounts of each type of variation at equilibrium differ, as do the time scales involved in their recovery following loss. For many taxa, it may be less easy to maintain quantities of single-locus variation than quantitative variation. We strongly feel that every effort should be made to preserve evolutionarily important amounts of quantitative genetic variation by maintaining effective population sizes of at least several hundreds of individuals. A population of that size can maintain nearly as much genetic variation in most quantitative characters as an indefinitely large population.

Genetic variation should be a central theme of plans for the long-term maintenance of populations. However, as has been pointed out elsewhere in this volume, on a short time scale demographic factors, such as the size and growth rate of a population, may take precedence in management practices because genetic variation is not important if the population becomes extinct. Of course, demography and genetics are not independent; actions taken to increase the population size or its rate of increase will also result in a reduction in the rate of loss of genetic variability. Once the short-term persistence of the population is ensured, management practices can be adjusted to enhance the maintenance of genetic variability and the potential for long-term evolution. Populations on the verge of extinction, which may be virtually devoid of genetic variability (and perhaps with reduced fitness as the result of inbreeding), should not be considered hopeless (e.g., Brown *et al.*, 1985) because, if the population regains moderate or large numbers, genetic variation can be regenerated by mutation, thus restoring the potential for adaptive evolution. Even the deleterious effects of major mutations fixed in a small population through inbreeding and random genetic drift can be counteracted by polygenic modifiers of individually small effect. This has often been observed in laboratory stocks of major mutants in *Drosophila*, which tend to gradually revert to wild type through natural selection.

References

Ballou, J. 1983. Calculating inbreeding coefficients from pedigrees. Pp. 509–20 *in* C. M. Schonewald-Cox, S. M. Chambers, B. MacBryde, and W. L. Thomas (eds.) *Genetics and Conservation: A Reference for Managing Wild Animal and Plant Populations*. Benjamin/Cummings Publ. Co., Menlo Park, Calif.

Barrowclough, G. F. and Coats, S. L. 1985. The demography and population genetics of owls, with special reference to the conservation of the spotted owl (*Strix occidentalis*). Pp. 74–85 *in* R. J. Gutiérrez and A. B. Carey (eds.) *Ecology and Management of the Spotted Owl in the Pacific Northwest*. Gen. Techn. Report PNW-185. USDA Forest Service, Pacific Northwest Forest and Experimental Sta., Portland, Oreg.

Brewer, G. J. 1970. *An Introduction to Isozyme Techniques*. Academic Press, New York.

Brown, P., Wilson, R., Loyn, R., and Murray, N. 1985. *The Orange-bellied Parrot – An RAOU conservation statement*. RAOU Report No. 14. Royal Austral. Ornithol. Union, Moonee Ponds, Victoria, Australia.

Bulmer, M. J. 1980. *The Mathematical Theory of Quantitative Genetics*. Oxford University Press, Oxford.

Charlesworth, B. 1980. *Evolution in Age-structured Populations*. Cambridge University Press, Cambridge.

Cockerham, C. C. 1973. Analyses of gene frequencies. *Genetics* **74**: 679–700.

Coyne, J. A. 1983. Genetic basis of differences in genital morphology among three sibling species of *Drosophila*. *Evolution* **37**: 1101–18.

Crow, J. F. 1952. Dominance and overdominance. Pp. 282–97 *in* J. W. Gowen (ed.) *Heterosis*. Iowa State College Press, Ames, Iowa.

Crow, J. F. 1978. Gene frequency and fitness change in an age-structured population. *Ann. Hum. Genet.* **42**: 335–70.

Crow, J. F. and Aoki, K. 1984. Group selection for a polygenic behavioral trait: Estimating the degree of population subdivision. *Proc. Natl. Acad. Sci., USA* **81**: 6073–7.

Crow, J. F. and Kimura, M. 1970. *An Introduction to Population Genetics Theory*. Harper and Row, New York.

Dobzhansky, T. 1970. *Genetics of the Evolutionary Process*. Columbia University Press, New York.

Dobzhansky, T. and Wright, S. 1947. Genetics of natural populations. XV. Rate of diffusion of a mutant gene through a population of *Drosophila pseudoobscura*. *Genetics* **32**: 303–24.

Ehrlich, P. R. 1983. Genetics and the extinction of butterfly populations. Pp. 152–63 *in* C. M. Schonewald-Cox, S. M. Chambers, B. MacBryde, and W. L. Thomas (eds.) *Genetics and Conservation. A Reference for Managing Wild Animal and Plant Populations*. Benjamin/Cummings Publ. Co., Menlo Park, Calif.

Ewens, W. J. 1979. *Mathematical Population Genetics*. Springer-Verlag, Berlin.

Falconer, D. S. 1981. *Introduction to Quantitative Genetics*, 2nd ed. Longman, London.

Felsenstein, J. 1975. A pain in the torus: some difficulties with models of isolation by distance. *Amer. Nat.* **109**: 359–68.

Fisher, R. A. 1958. *The Genetical Theory of Natural Selection*, 2nd ed. Dover, New York.

Frankel, O. H. and Soulé, M. E. 1981. *Conservation and Evolution*. Cambridge University Press, Cambridge.

Franklin, I. R. 1980. Evolutionary changes in small populations. Pp. 135–49 *in* M. E. Soulé and B. A. Wilcox (eds.) *Conservation Biology. An Evolutionary-Ecological Perspective*. Sinauer Associates, Sunderland, Mass.

Gorman, G. C. and Renzi, J. 1979. Genetic distance and heterozygosity estimates in electrophoretic studies: Effects of sample size. *Copeia* 1979: 242–9.

Gregory, W. C. 1965. Mutation frequency, magnitude of change and the probability of improvement in adaptation. *Radiat. Biol.* **5** (Suppl.): 429–41.

Haldane, J. B. S. 1954. The measurement of selection. *Proc. Intl. Congr. Genet.* (*Caryologia*, Suppl. 6) **9**: 480–7.

Harris, H. and Hopkinson, D. A. 1976. *Handbook of Enzyme Electrophoresis in Human Genetics*. North-Holland Publ., Amsterdam, Netherlands.

Hartl, D. L. 1981. *A Primer of Population Genetics*. Sinauer Associates, Sunderland, Mass.

Hill, W. G. 1972. Effective size of populations with overlapping generations. *Theor. Pop. Biol.* **3**: 278–89.

Hill, W. G. 1979. A note on effective population size with overlapping generations. *Genetics* **92**: 317–22.

Hill, W. G. 1982. Predictions of response to artificial selection from new mutations. *Genet. Research* **40**: 255–78.

Hoi-Sen, Y. 1972. Is sub-line differentiation a continuing process in inbred strains of mice? *Genet. Research* **19**: 53–9.

Johnson, C. 1976. *Introduction to Natural Selection*. University Park Press, Baltimore, Md.

Kimura, M. 1983. *The Neutral Theory of Molecular Evolution*. Cambridge University Press, Cambridge.

Kimura, M. and Crow, J. F. 1964. The number of alleles that can be maintained in a finite population. *Genetics* **49**: 725–38.

Kimura, M. and Weiss, G. H. 1964. The stepping stone model of population structure and the decrease of genetic correlation with distance. *Genetics* **49**: 561–76.

Lande, R. 1976. The maintenance of genetic variability by mutation in a polygenic character with linked loci. *Genet. Research* **26**: 221–35.

Lande, R. 1977. The influence of the mating system on the maintenance of genetic variability in polygenic characters. *Genetics* **86**: 485–98.

Lande, R. 1980. Genetic variation and phenotypic evolution during allopatric speciation. *Amer. Nat.* **116**: 463–79.

Lande, R. 1981. The minimum number of genes contributing to quantitative variation between and within populations. *Genetics* **99**: 541–53.

Lande, R. 1982. A quantitative genetic theory of life history evolution. *Ecology* **63**: 607–15.

Lande, R. 1983. The response to selection on major and minor mutations affecting a metrical trait. *Heredity* **50**: 47–65.

Lande, R. and Schemske, D. W. 1985. The evolution of self-fertilization and inbreeding depression in plants. I. Genetic models. *Evolution* **39**: 24–40.

Lerner, I. M. 1954. *Genetic Homeostasis*. Oliver and Boyd, London.

Lewontin, R. C. 1964. The interaction of selection and linkage. II. Optimum models. *Genetics* **50**, 757–82.

Lewontin, R. C. 1965. Comment. Pp. 481–4 *in* H. G. Baker and G. L. Stebbins (eds.) *The Genetics of Colonizing Species*. Academic Press, New York.

Lewontin, R. C. 1974. *The Genetic Basis of Evolutionary Change*. Columbia University Press, New York.

Malécot, G. 1969. *The Mathematics of Heredity*. W. H. Freeman, San Francisco, Calif.

Malécot, G. 1975. Heterozygosity and relationship in regularly subdivided populations. *Theor. Pop. Biol.* **8**: 212–41.

Maruyama, T. 1970. Effective number of alleles in a subdivided population. *Theor. Pop. Biol.* **1**: 273–306.

Maruyama, T. 1977. Stochastic problems in population genetics. *Lecture Notes in Biomathematics*, Vol. 17. Springer-Verlag, Berlin.

Maruyama, T. and Kimura, M. 1980. Genetic variability and effective population size when local extinction and recolonization of subpopulations are frequent. *Proc. Natl. Acad. Sci. USA* **77**: 6710–14.

Mukai, T., Chigusa, S. I., Mettler, L. E., and Crow, J. F. 1972. Mutation rate and dominance of genes affecting viability in *Drosophila melanogaster*. *Genetics* **72**: 335–55.

Muller, H. J. 1949. Redintegration of the symposium on genetics, paleontology, and evolution. Pp. 421–45 *in* G. L. Jepsen, E. Mayr, and G. G. Simpson (eds.) *Genetics, Paleontology and Evolution*. Princeton University Press, Princeton, New Jersey.

Nagylaki, T. 1974. The decay of genetic variability in geographically structured populations. *Proc. Natl. Acad. Sci., USA* **71**: 2932–6.

Nei, M. 1978. Estimation of average heterozygosity and genetic distance from a small number of individuals. *Genetics* **89**: 583–90.

Nei, M. 1983. Genic polymorphism and the role of mutation in evolution. Pp. 165–90 *in* M. Nei and R. K. Koehn (eds.) *Evolution of Genes and Proteins*. Sinauer Associates, Sunderland, Mass.

Nei, M., Chakravarti, A. and Tateno, Y. 1977. Mean and variance of F_{st} in a finite number of incompletely isolated populations. *Theor. Pop. Biol.* **11**: 291–306.

Nei, M., Maruyama, T., and Chakraborty, R. 1975. The bottleneck effect and genetic variability in populations. *Evolution* **29**: 1–10.

Nevo, E. 1978. Genetic variation in natural populations: patterns and theory. *Theor. Pop. Biol.* **13**: 121–77.

Patton, J. L. 1967. Chromosome studies of certain pocket mice, genus *Perognathus* (Rodentia: Heteromyidae). *J. Mammal.* **48**: 27–37.

Pollak, E. 1977. Effective population numbers and their interrelationships. Pp. 115–44 *in Proceedings of the Washington State University Conference on Biomathematics and Biostatistics*. Washington State University, Spokane, Wash.

Ralls, K., Brugger, K., and Ballou, J. 1979. Inbreeding and juvenile mortality in small populations of ungulates. *Science* **206**: 1101–03.

Russell, W. A., Sprague, G. F., and Penny, L. H. 1963. Mutations affecting quantitative characters in long-time inbred lines of maize. *Crop. Sci.* **3**: 175–8.

Scharloo, W. 1964. The effect of disruptive and stabilizing selection on the expression of *cubitus interruptus* in *Drosophila*. *Genetics* **50**: 553–62.

Schlager, G. and Dickie, M. M. 1967. Spontaneous mutations and mutation rates in the house mouse. *Genetics* **57**: 319–30.

Schonewald-Cox, C. M., Chambers, S. M., MacBryde, B., and Thomas, W. L. 1983. *Genetics and Conservation: A reference for managing wild animal and plant populations*. Benjamin Cummings Publ. Co., Menlo Park, Calif.

Seal, U. S. 1984. An analysis of the demography and genetics of captive Amur tigers and a preliminary captive propagation plan. *Internl. Tigerzuchtbuch* **9**: 5–19.

Seal, U. S. and Foose, T. 1983/84. Siberian tiger species survival plan: a strategy for survival. *J. Minn. Acad. Sci.* **49**(3): 3–9.

Shaw, C. R. and Prasad, R. 1970. Starch gel electrophoresis of enzymes – a compilation of recipes. *Biochem. Genet.* **4**: 297–320.

Shields, G. F. 1982. Comparative avian cytogenetics: A review. *Condor* **84**: 45–58.

Shields, G. F. 1983. Bird chromosomes. *Current Ornithol.* **1**: 189–209.

Simmons, M. J. and Crow, J. F. 1977. Mutations affecting fitness in *Drosophila* populations. *Ann. Rev. Genet.* **11**: 49–78.

Slatkin, M. 1977. Gene flow and genetic drift in a species subject to frequent local extinctions. *Theor. Pop. Biol.* **12**: 253–62.

Slatkin, M. 1985. Gene flow in natural populations. *Ann. Rev. Ecol. Syst.* **16**: 393–430.

Soulé, M. E. and Wilcox, B. A. (eds.) 1980. *Conservation Biology. An evolutionary-ecological perspective*. Sinauer Associates, Sunderland, Mass.

Sprague, G. F., Russell, W. A., and Penny, L. H. 1960. Mutations affecting quantitative traits in the selfed progeny of doubled monoploid maize stocks. *Genetics* **45**: 855–66.

Templeton, A. R. 1980. Modes of speciation and inferences based on genetic distances. *Evolution* **34**: 719–29.

Templeton, A. R. and Read, B. 1983. The elimination of inbreeding depression in a captive herd of Speke's gazelle. Pp. 241–61 *in* C. M. Schonewald-Cox, S. M. Chambers, B. MacBryde, and W. L. Thomas (eds.) *Genetics and Conservation: A reference for managing wild animal and plant populations*. Benjamin/Cummings Publ. Co., Menlo Park, Calif.

Turelli, M. 1984. Heritable genetic variation via mutation–selection balance: Lerch's zeta meets the abdominal bristle. *Theor. Pop. Biol.* **25**: 138–93.

Waddington, C. H. 1960. Experiments on canalizing selection. *Genet. Research* **1**: 140–50.

Wade, M. J. and Arnold, S. J. 1980. The intensity of sexual selection in relation to male sexual behavior, female choice, and sperm precedence. *Animal Behaviour* **28**: 446–61.

Weiss, G. H. and Kimura, M. 1965. A mathematical analysis of the stepping stone model of genetic correlation. *J. Appl. Probab.* **2**: 129–49.

Wright, S. 1931. Evolution in Mendelian populations. *Genetics* **16**: 97–159.

Wright, S. 1943. Isolation by distance. *Genetics* **28**: 114–38.

Wright, S. 1951. The genetical structure of populations. *Ann. Eugenics* **15**: 323–54.

Wright, S. 1968. *Evolution and the Genetics of Populations*. Vol. 1. *Genetic and Biometric Foundations*. University of Chicago Press, Chicago, Ill.

Wright, S. 1969. *Evolution and the Genetics of Populations*. Vol. 2. *The Theory of Gene Frequencies*. University of Chicago Press, Chicago, Ill.

Wright, S. 1970. Random drift and the shifting balance theory of evolution. Pp. 1–31 *in* K. Kojima (ed.) *Mathematical Topics in Population Genetics*. Springer-Verlag, Berlin.

Wright, S. 1977. *Evolution and the Genetics of Populations*. Vol. 3. *Experimental Results and Evolutionary Deductions*. University of Chicago Press, Chicago, Ill.

7

Spatial structure and population vulnerability

MICHAEL E. GILPIN
Department of Biology [C-016], University of California at San Diego, La Jolla, CA 92093

Population extinction can result from many factors. Even though most cases are hidden from observers, its processes can be viewed in different ways. The other chapters of this book focus on single features of species biology that contribute to species extinction. Superficially, this chapter treats yet another factor: the extension of the spatial stage on which the extinction drama is played. Nonetheless, space is something different. It affects and is, in turn, affected by the other aspects of species biology that contribute to extinction.

The spatial extension of ecological systems, which considers the actual locations of organisms in the landscape, is not routinely incorporated into theoretical formulations of population genetics, demography, population dynamics, and community ecology. Our theories typically present variables such as N's and p's that summarize, with a single number, the ecological and genetical states of a system over some conceptually delimited region of physical space. That is, N is a count of all the animals in this space; it does not tell where they are, or how they are clumped or otherwise associated. Similarly, p represents a gene frequency in a 'population' of organisms, but the region over which this estimate is valid is not normally specified.

This reluctance to address questions of spatial extension results from at least two important considerations. First, it is quite difficult in a field study to keep track of the locations of organisms, especially of the motile vertebrates that are normally considered in MVP studies. Second, the computational problems of dealing with space in a theoretical manner are formidable and usually cannot be treated with anything but digital computers. Fortunately, in many ecological generalizations space is of secondary importance and can safely be left from the description. But the omission of spatial structure can be serious in the analysis of population vulnerability, where an unusually high premium must be placed on precision. This chapter assesses the important role played by space, especially the patchiness of habitats, in characterizing the MVP of a species.

To give an intuitive basis for the discussion to follow, some stereotypic representations of space are given in Figure 7.1. Figure 7.1a is a point; as

Figure 7.1. Some ways in which spatial extension is considered in theoretical models of population biology. Figure 7.1a is a 'zero-dimensional' representation in which all dynamic change occurs at a point. Figure 7.1b shows space as extending uniformly along a single dimension. Figure 7.1c shows the spatial background varying at a constant rate along a single spatial dimension. Figure 7.1d shows a unimodal variation of the spatial background. Figure 7.1e shows large discontinuous changes in habitat quality along a single spatial dimension, yielding discrete patchiness. Figure 7.1f is the same as Figure 7.1e except that the spatial extension is along two spatial dimensions.

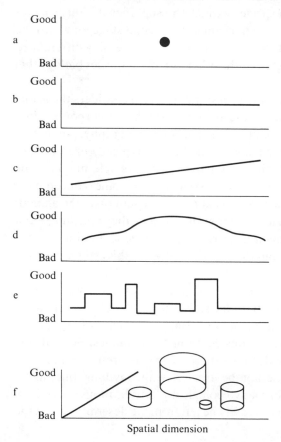

Spatial dimension

silly as this seems, this is the normal, albeit tacit, assumption about spatial structure. This zero-dimensional structure allows the lumping that goes into the typical state variables for gene frequencies and census counts, i.e., p's and N's. Figure 7.1b shows space extended in a single dimension but otherwise homogeneous. It is likely, but not certain, that the population will distribute itself over this space uniformly; if so, one is justified in lumping the total count of animals in a single state variable such as N. Yet biological interactions even against a uniform spatial background can produce non-homogeneous spatial distributions and thereby cause problems for population vulnerability analysis (PVA, Gilpin and Soulé, 1986). Such non-uniformity can be produced by social behaviors. Clumping for defense against predators is one obvious example. Figure 7.1c and d recognize that gradients and other non-uniformities exist in the spatial background of the species population; these may be thought to exist along a single axis. Such continuous spatial variation definitely plays a role in the management of endangered species population. For instance, one would probably want to locate the population in the 'optimal' portion of its potential range, where the species growth rate or carrying capacity is likely to be higher. These central versus marginal considerations are not nearly so serious as the one- and two-dimensional patchiness depicted in Figure 7.1e and f, where discrete patches of the area are habitable and the intervening regions are not. A population distributed over such an environment will be patchy, with the collection or set of local populations constituting the so-called 'metapopulation.' It is these latter cases of discrete patchiness on which this chapter will focus.

As a more realistic approach to grasping the issue of metapopulations, some examples in which the spatial structure of a species has bearing on its MVP are briefly mentioned and illustrated. The grizzly bear (*Ursus arctos*) has population isolates in the Cabinet–Yaak region of Idaho and in the Yellowstone ecosystem; the 'mainland' for this system is the much larger patch in Canada that extends into the United States in the area around and including Glacier National Park. This is illustrated schematically in Figure 7.2a. The black-footed ferret (*Mustela nigripes*) was confined to islands of its host population, the prairie dog (*Cynomys leucurus*), and probably had a patchy structure in its recent population history. Figure 7.2b and c show possible examples of this. Third, but possibly incorrectly, the spotted owl (*Strix occidentalis*) is often addressed from the standpoint of SOMAs (Spotted Owl Management Areas) on patches of old-growth Douglas fir. The possible problem with this is that these spatial units are pair-bonded spotted owl families whose behavior is properly the subject of demography. A more important aspect of spatial structure of this species concerns how the SOMA's will be clustered to form regional isolates. This is shown in Figure 7.2d. Figure 7.2e and f show other spatial structures relevant for conservation biology. Figure 7.2f presents the question of how far a species might penetrate a peninsular, while Figure 7.2e raises the issue of paths of stepping stones in colonization. More specific analysis of these examples will be provided under the various sections of population vulnerability analysis, below.

Some basic definitions

The archetypal candidate for PVA is a species that occupies a region of two-dimensional landscape that is composed of a mosaic of habitable patches. For proper analysis there must, of course be some *a priori* method to identify such patches without reference to the distribution of the study species itself. For example, soil characteristics often define patches for plants, and perennial plants can define habitable patches for animals. Given the patches, one must assume that it is possible

Figure 7.2. Some patterns of two-dimensional spatial patchiness. Each case shows habitable patches, indicated by dark ovals, in a 'sea' of inhospitable habitat. See text for comparisons to actual species situations and configurations.

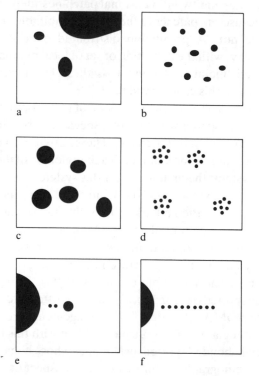

to census individual patch populations and to somehow obtain or otherwise infer the dynamic character of the flow or movement of animals between these patches. To talk about this system, one can index the patches from 1 to Z (or a two-dimensional system such as is used in chess might be utilized). Each patch can be considered to have a certain local 'carrying capacity,' k_i, which would be related to the size and habitat quality of the patch. In practice, this would be taken as the 'equilibrium' population size of the study species in the absence of disturbance; it is similar to the maximum N that Goodman (Chapter 2) uses. One then defines x_i as the actual state of occupancy of the ith patch, 1 for occupied and 0 for absent. The global index P (not to be confused with gene frequency) is the total fraction of the patches occupied, that is, the sum of x_i divided by Z. The total population size is

$$N = \sum_{i=1}^{Z} x_i k_i$$

where this assumes that each occupied patch is at its local carrying capacity.

A very important aspect of metapopulation behavior is the flow of individuals between patches. There are a number of different features of, and modes for, this flow. The flow of immigrants has significance for the genetic differentiation of the patches, the population dynamics of each patch (the 'rescue effect' of Brown and Kodric-Brown, 1977), and the island biogeography of the entire system. There are a large number of configurations for the distribution of patches (e.g., Figure 7.2). Clearly, rates of flow depend on the degree of isolation, normally mediated by physical distance and the character of the intervening habitat. Thus, a basic parameter of this system is the distance, d_{ij}, between adjacent patches i and j.

Of equal importance to PVA is the extinction of local populations on the individual patches themselves. This depends on many factors that are, in fact, the subject of the other chapters of this volume. Suffice it to note that the extinction probability will doubtless be related to the area of the patch. For some kinds of organisms and habitats, and for some time scales and areas of patches, the local populations will not go extinct, for others they will. This is an extremely important distinction for the discussion of metapopulation dynamics to follow. We shall call the two cases 'fixed' and 'winking.' For the fixed case, the local populations do not go extinct, thus making the migration between patches of more importance to genetics than to population dynamics. With the winking or turnover of local populations, patchiness may become the most important aspect of PVA, as the very persistence of the system will depend on rates of patch extinction and recolonization.

Population vulnerability analysis

To put the following discussion of spatial structure into a context, we graphically review the approach to population vulnerability analysis (PVA) developed by Gilpin and Soulé (1986). Gilpin and Soulé stressed the interaction of processes, with extinction resulting more from feedback loops than from single shocks. Figure 7.3 shows the major loops which they identify. This figure shows the species population as a unit with its full biology and state-summarizing statistics represented in the large circle. The environment can shock or perturb this system in various ways.

Figure 7.3. Components of population vulnerability analysis. The large circle represents the species population under consideration. The lower half of this circle contains the population variables (or statistics) that are used for the analysis. A 'major shock' strikes the population and can produce, through reduced growth and fragmentation, immediate extinction. Or, it can set up feedback loops involving fragmentation, demographic fluctuations, inbreeding, and loss of adaptability, that affect the population and which may mutually exacerbate each other, thereby indirectly causing extinction.

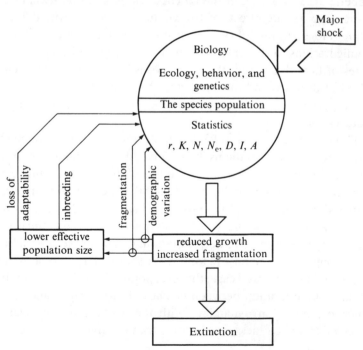

These shocks lead directly to lower growth, small size, and possibly greater spatial heterogeneity or fragmentation. The consequences of these immediate effects can be directly fed back to the population, or they can affect the genetical state of the population in such a way as to cause inbreeding depression and the erosion of selectable variation. Figure 7.3 does not graphically represent space. Figure 7.4 suggests how multiple patch systems might interact. Unfortunately, the complexity that space adds to this scheme is so great that no single figure can represent it.

For the case of local turnover of populations ('winking'), two cases need to be distinguished. First, the winking can contribute to the accumulating impact of demographic instability, loss of genetic variation, and catastrophes, each of which then leads to the possible extinction of the metapopulation. Second, and more likely, these demographic and genetic factors lead to a continuous increase in the rates of patch turnover until recolonization is no longer sufficient to keep pace with local extinction, causing the extinction of the metapopulation.

The following discussion treats under separate subheadings the subjects of the other chapters of this book, i.e., genetics (inbreeding and total variance), demography, and environment (disturbance and catastrophe). Lastly, we treat the full dynamics of the archipelago of patches (the metapopulation). There are several good reasons for this sequence. First, we are traveling from the better to the least understood. Second, the earlier topics tend to influence the later topics; for example, inbreeding can exacerbate the population response to a catastrophe. Nonetheless, the process of PVA, as emphasized by Gilpin and Soulé (1986) is one of quantifying or estimating the probability of feedback processes that lead

Figure 7.4. The same scheme as represented in Figure 7.3 but taking place over three spatially distinct subpopulations.

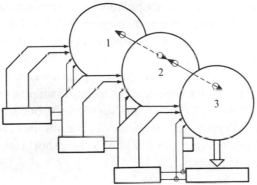

to 'vortices' into which a population spirals to its extinction. Each of the phenomena below can influence, and can be influenced by, each of the others.

Genetics: inbreeding

Normally outbred species suffer effects of inbreeding if husbanded in small numbers (Ralls, Brugger, and Ballou, 1979). The associated inbreeding depression may be manifested in a number of ways, with the most typical being an increase in infant mortality. As a rule-of-thumb based on domestic animals, an N_e of less than about 50 disposes a population to inbreeding depression (Soulé, 1980; Franklin, 1980).

A possible field example of this is in the grizzly bear population in the Yellowstone National Park ecosystem which has had a total population size of about 100 for the last five generations and an N_e of less than a third of this during this period. This species has shown reduced litter sizes in the last generation (Chris Servheen, pers. comm.), possibly the result of inbreeding.

A metapopulation structure can increase inbreeding. A population is genetically isolated if there is fewer than one effective migrant entering the population per generation (Chapter 6); to be 'effective,' a migrant must actually breed. Thus, the Yellowstone population of grizzly bears should only show inbreeding depression if fewer than one bear per decade successfully enters from the more northern population in the area of Glacier National Park.

If patch populations do turn over, each patch population will have gone through a recent genetic bottleneck during the colonization period. Such bottlenecks will greatly exacerbate inbreeding. Maruyama and Kimura (1980) have produced an analytical model for this process. Their model, which is unrealistic from an ecological perspective, can produce dramatic lowerings of N_e for the entire metapopulation, and thus for each population in it. Gilpin (1987) has performed a computer simulation study that more exactly accounts for the ecology of the process and has applied this to the curious case of the cheetah (*Acinonyx jubatus*), which has very little genetic variation and which has various physiological handicaps (O'Brien *et al.*, 1983). Gilpin (1987) gives one numeric example where a metapopulation does not drop below 1026 individuals yet has an N_e of 10, two orders of magnitude lower. This should make managers cautious in dismissing the possibility of inbreeding in cases where a 'snapshot' census of the population yields a large number.

Genetics: total variance

Loss of genetic variance is caused by the same force that produces inbreeding, that is, the genetic sampling of alleles in a population that has a low effective population size. Genetic variation is a population level phenomenon. The time scale on which it may pose a threat to the continued existence of a species is inter-generational. Early in the history of PVA, the emphasis was on the loss of genetic variation (Franklin, 1980; Soulé, 1980), since a population without genetic variation cannot adapt genetically to any change in its environment. Now, however, environmental stochasticity and habitat fragmentation are recognized as possibly more significant factors, at least in the short term.

From one standpoint, population subdivision without turnover enhances the preservation of genetic variance (Chesser *et al.*, 1980), but one must be careful of the scale on which one measures this. Clearly, a small, inbred patch population cannot have much genetic variance. Yet somewhat paradoxically, a system of patch populations considered at the regional level may have more genetic variance than would a single large population of the same total size. There are two reasons for this. First, local populations may go to fixation for different alleles. Second, the selection pressures may be different in different environmental patches. In any case, the genetic variation between patches can be very useful in protecting the species from extinction. Different patches might contain the genetic variants that could survive strong selection pressures, such as a disease, or a change in vegetation.

In cases where there is frequent turnover of patch populations, each local population will have derived all of its genetic variation from a recent pair of founders, and the effects of local drift and past selection will be overwhelmed. The metapopulation will have a very homogeneous structure of low genetic variance, as has apparently happened with the cheetah (O'Brien *et al.*, 1983) and may have occurred for such animals as the black-footed ferret, whose population structure may be similar to the cheetah's, thus causing it to lose much of its genetic variation. One manifestation of loss of genetic variation is increased sensitivity to epidemic diseases, because the population is not likely to have a heterogeneous immunological structure. Viral diseases have recently spread through populations of each species (O'Brien *et al.*, 1985; May, 1986).

Demographic stochasticity

Goodman (Chapter 2) describes demographic stochasticity as a completely individual level phenomenon, making the simplifying assumption that each animal behaves independently regarding birth and death events. Clearly, there are many exceptions such as bad winters, failures of resources, plagues of predators, and the like, that are correlated events for all individuals. These correlations over time between demographic events for individuals can be factored out, leaving the residuals to be called demographic stochasticity.

The above demographic correlations occur along a time axis. Space may also produce a correlation of demographic events. Butterfly populations occurring at different elevations on a mountain may receive very different signals from their environments. Long-term studies such as those on Euphydryas butterflies are doubtless the source of much valuable knowledge in this regard (Ehrlich, 1983). This problem is only beginning to receive the theoretical attention that it deserves (Goodman, Chapter 2).

Environmental stochasticity and catastrophes

Environmental stochasticities include the bad winters, resource failures, etc., mentioned in the last section. With such an environmental event, the entire population receives the shock. Such perturbations affect some parameter of the population's growth, such as the r or the K of the logistic growth model. The probability of extinction is calculated on the basis of diffusion equations for some fixed period of time (see Roughgarden, 1979 for a good review).

Mark Shaffer (1981) had a particularly telling and pertinent treatment of the joint effects of demographic and environmental stochasticity. In modelling grizzly bear dynamics, he employed a hierarchal treatment of chance birth and death phenomena. Based on 12 years of population data for the grizzly, the probabilities of good and bad years could first be assessed, and then the individual probabilities of birth and death given the character of the year could be obtained. Shaffer then used Monte Carlo techniques to simulate the process. He showed that populations in the size range of 50 to 100 would have difficulty surviving the joint action of these forces for more than a century. All future models of stochastic dynamics should incorporate inputs from both demography and the environment.

In considering the impact of environmental stochasticity on spatial patchiness, the critical variable is the degree to which the environment acts in a correlated fashion between the patches of the metapopulation. This correlation may vary with the type of environmental force in question. For example, a 'local catastrophe' to a single patch population may not be a catastrophe to the entire metapopulation. Other environmental perturbations will have a larger spatial scale for their action.

Volcanism, regional pollution, pandemics, large fires – these can affect the metapopulation as a unit. To the extent that the metapopulation suffers completely correlated environmental disturbances, the analysis of Goodman (Chapter 2) and Ewens *et al.* (Chapter 4) will hold.

Extinction and recolonization dynamics

Up to this point in the development of the argument, the metapopulation has not been viewed as directly contributing to its own extinction. At worst, populations on a particular patch might turn over and lose genetic variation. Thus, patchiness has been a condition or contributing factor that exacerbates some other process related to population survival. In cases where local populations do, however, undergo extinction and recolonization, it is not guaranteed that recolonization will keep up with local extinction.

Patch extinction depends on the PVA factors enumerated above; that is, genetic, demographic, and environmental forces acting within the patch. Patch recolonization depends on the geometrical arrangement of the metapopulation relative to the rate of interchange. It depends on whether neighboring patches are occupied, how big they are, and how near they are. Consider the one-dimensional case illustrated in Figure 7.5. The sinusoidal line represents quality of habitat, while the two horizontal lines represent the minimal habitat quality acceptable to a species. The upper line is that for a relatively inbred species, because it has lost flexibility and general fitness, and it requires better habitat quality to compensate. What this does, in the metaphor of the figure, is to reduce the number of habitable patches (lower Z), decrease the carrying capacity of each patch (which reduces the flux of colonists to adjacent patches),

Figure 7.5. A hypothetical situation in which the condition of genetic inbreeding interacts with habitat background to produce a condition of spatial patchiness. See text for further discussion.

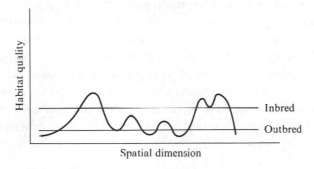

Spatial dimension

and increases the average distance between patches. In theory, these can quite easily shift the balance of extinction and recolonization such that the metapopulation goes extinct.

There was considerable work on the dynamics of metapopulations around the start of the 1970s. Much of it (e.g., Levins, 1970) was of a very abstract character. These studies typically ignored all aspects of geometry, that is, patch size and patch separation, and merely followed the dynamics of the variable P, the fraction of the patches occupied. A suggestive lesson from these studies was that there is a threshold value of P below which the system quickly collapses. There is, however, a danger that this result is not robust. In systems where the patches are of quite different sizes it is not reasonable to expect that the variable P will adequately describe the system. For example, if a system comprises one patch of 1000 ha and two patches of 10 ha, a P of 0.667 with the large patch extinct is considerably worse than a P of 0.333 with the large patch colonized. With the grizzly bear, for example, the current habitat fragments are of quite different size, and an extinction of the Canadian population is more serious than a catastrophe that eliminates, say, the Cabinet–Yaak population. For the spotted owl, it is likely that the aggregation of SOMAs will be of critical importance to management plans.

The approach used to model the dynamics of such ensembles of patches is based on the work of Gilpin and Diamond (1976) on the dynamics of archipelagos, of Gilpin (1980) on stepping-stone island systems, of Gilpin (1981) on peninsular diversity patterns, and of Diamond and Gilpin (1983) on narrow land bridge connections. The rules for this analysis are based on three observations:

(1) larger islands produce more migrants;
(2) the probability of immigration falls exponentially with distance;
(3) the probability of extinction is inversely related to the area of the patch (that is, the carrying capacity of the patch).

The dynamic simulation of such systems produces patches that wink in and wink out with varying frequencies and varying pairwise correlations. The work on such models is in its early stages. A general observation (Gilpin, unpublished) is that the dynamics of the system produce a spatial correlation that produces regions of high patch colonization and that these regions wander slowly in a random manner over the grid of possible sites. This observation could have importance for the work on the spotted owl system, but it may be tested with data from field observations and experiments.

Conclusions

PVA requires an integrated study of a number of dynamically connected feedback loops (Gilpin and Soulé, 1986). Spatial structure plays an almost ubiquitous role in these dynamics. First, spatial heterogeneity is often a given quantity that must be properly incorporated in the analysis of both genetics and environmental stochasticities. Second, it may be that island biogeographic dynamics, the extinction and recolonization of patch populations, dominates the system, with other aspects of PVA, e.g., inbreeding and environmental stochasticity, acting as parameter inputs.

Many rules of thumb (Diamond, 1975; Wilcove *et al.*, 1986) have been devised to help managers decide among alternative spatial configurations for systems of reserves. Although these were devised for the preservation of total diversity, they generally hold for questions of single species persistence. What this chapter has emphasized, however, is the necessity to consider the rate of colonization and of local population turnover that result under patchiness and to compute their impact on questions of genetics and demography. This requires an understanding of the correlations of events on different patches, some of which are produced by the turnover dynamics and some of which are dependent on the scale of regional environmental variation.

The analysis sketched in this chapter requires a significant input of data. Studies of genetics may be required to indicate the past history of patch size and turnover and the flow of migrants between patches. Close studies of demography can indicate the degree to which environmental events are uncorrelated between patches. Studies of community ecology can indicate the probabilities of extinctions due to predation, competition and disease. All of this can be fashioned into a systems model which can then permit reasonable investigation for alternative scenarios of management action. We should not expect exact and comprehensive models for any single species in the near future. Rather, the community of conservation biologists, including managers, field biologists, and theoreticians, must learn how to incorporate data into such systems models, and then, using a case study approach, learn how to make relative judgements among the possible courses of management action.

Summary

Many species populations are patchily distributed over a gridwork of their acceptable habitats. This necessarily moves some questions regarding their persistence to a regional level: the metapopulation composed of an interacting system of local populations that suffer extinction and are recolonized from within the region. Thus, it is not simply the total size of the population that is important to population vulnerability analysis, but also the geometrical character of its distribution and the dynamical aspects of the flow of its member individuals between nodes of the network of habitable patches (i.e., immigration). Patchiness affects all the features of population genetics and population demography that have a bearing on the question of MVP. Subdivision exacerbates the problem of inbreeding. And patchiness with frequent local extinction and recolonization can greatly lower the effective population size, N_e, thereby contributing to loss of genetic variance of the entire metapopulation. The seriousness of environmental stochasticity as discussed by Goodman (Chapter 2) is less in situations where different patch populations experience uncorrelated environments; the same holds for the consideration of catastrophes. Finally, there is the problem posed by the patchiness itself: the dynamic interplay between extinction and recolonization may not remain properly balanced and the entire metapopulation may go extinct.

References

Brown, J. H. and Kodric-Brown, A. 1977. Turnover rates in insular biogeography: effects of immigration on extinction. *Ecology* **58**: 445–9.

Chesser, C. H., Smith, M. H., and Brisbin, I. L. Jr. 1980. Management and maintenance of genetic variability in endangered species. *International Zoo Yearbook* **20**: 146–54.

Diamond, J. M. 1975. The island dilemma: lessons of modern biogeographic studies for the design of natural preserves. *Biological Conservation* **7**: 129–46.

Diamond, J. M. and Gilpin, M. E. 1983. Biogeographical umbilici and the origin of the Philippine avifauna. *Oikos* **41**: 307–21.

Ehrlich, P. R. 1983. Genetics and the extinction of butterfly populations. Pp. 152–63 *in* C. Schonewald-Cox *et al.* (eds.) *Genetics and Conservation*. Benjamin/Cummings, Menlo Park, Calif.

Franklin, I. R. 1980. Evolutionary change in small populations. Pp. 135–49 *in* M. E. Soulé and B. A. Wilcox (eds.) *Conservation Biology: An Evolutionary-Ecological Perspective*. Sinauer Associates, Sunderland, Mass.

Gilpin, M. E. 1980. The role of stepping-stone islands. *Theor. Pop. Biol.* **17**: 247–53.

Gilpin, M. E. 1981. Peninsular diversity patterns. *Am. Nat.* **118**: 291–6.

Gilpin, M. E. 1987. Metapopulation structure and effective population size: the case of the cheetah. *Evolution* (in press).

Gilpin, M. E. and Diamond, J. M. 1976. Calculation of immigration and extinction curves from the species–area–distance relation. *PNAS* **73**: 4130–4.

Gilpin, M. E. and Soulé, M. E. 1986. Minimum Viable Populations: the processes of species extinctions. Pp. 13–34 *in* M. E. Soulé (ed.) *Conservation Biology: The Science of Scarcity and Diversity*. Sinauer Associates, Sunderland, Mass.

Levins, R. 1970. Extinction. Pp. 75–108 in *Some Mathematical Questions in Biology*. American Mathematical Society, Providence, R.I.

Maruyama, T. and Kimura, M. 1980. Genetic variability and effective population size when local extinction and recolonization of subpopulations are frequent. *PNAS* **77**: 6710–14.

O'Brien, S. J., Wildt, D. E., Goldman, D., Merril, C. R., and Bush, M. 1983. The cheetah is depauperate in genetic variation. *Science* **221**: 459–62.

O'Brien, S. J., Roelke, M. E., Newman, A., Winkler, C. A., Meltzer, K. D., Colly, L., Evermann, J. F., Bush, M., and Wildt, D. E. 1985. Genetic basis for species vulnerability in the cheetah. *Science* **227**: 1428–34.

Ralls, K., Brugger, K., and Ballou, J. 1979. Inbreeding and juvenile mortality in small populations of ungulates. *Science* **206**: 1101–3.

Roughgarden, J. 1979. *Theory of Population Genetics and Evolutionary Ecology: An Introduction*. Macmillan, New York.

Shaffer, M. L. 1981. Minimum population sizes for species conservation. *Bioscience* **31**: 131–4.

Soulé, M. E. 1980. Thresholds for survival: maintaining fitness and evolutionary potential. Pp. 151–69 in M. E. Soulé and B. A. Wilcox (eds.) *Conservation Biology: An Evolutionary-Ecological Perspective*. Sinauer Associates, Sunderland, Mass.

Wilcove, D., McClellan, C., and Dobson, A. 1986. Habitat fragmentation in the temperate zone. Pp. 237–56 in M. E. Soulé (ed.) *Conservation Biology: Science of Diversity and Scarcity*. Sinauer Associates, Sunderland, Mass.

8

Managing critically endangered species: the Sumatran rhino as a case study

LYNN A. MAGUIRE
School of Forestry and Environmental Studies, Duke University, Durham, NC 27706

ULYSSES S. SEAL
VA Medical Center, 54th St and 48th Ave South, Minneapolis, MN 55417

PETER F. BRUSSARD
Department of Biology, Montana State University, Bozeman, MT 59717

The saving of critically endangered species is costly, and it is likely to conflict with other societal objectives. Methods are needed for clarifying and resolving such conflicts. In this chapter we will discuss an analytical tool called decision analysis (Raiffa, 1968). Decision analysis provides an explicit framework for identifying species in immediate danger of extinction, defining cases that may require intervention, evaluating the risks and benefits of alternate management strategies, and assessing whether or not the management efforts required to prevent a species' extinction can be justified in terms of their costs to society.

Why is an explicit framework needed? Conservation biology is essentially a crisis discipline (Soulé, 1985); neither time nor abundant economic resources are on its side. Difficult choices often must be made, usually in the absence of adequate data. When the outcomes of alternate actions are uncertain, it is hard to anticipate intuitively which one will be best. Furthermore, there are often several criteria for evaluating outcomes, such as minimizing costs versus maximizing protection; one action may seem to be best under the former criterion but a second far more desirable under the latter. Decision analysis provides a means of evaluating alternatives in a logical and repeatable manner; it is also a useful tool for communicating alternate management plans to others so that they can be persuaded to endorse one or more of them.

We will show how probabilities of extinction (pE) can be estimated and how these pE can be used to identify critically endangered species. Then we will suggest management procedures (interventions) that might be used to decrease pE in different situations and show how decision analysis can be used to choose the best alternative when the outcomes of these interventions are uncertain. We will illustrate the use of decision analysis with a specific example: assessing the status of the Sumatran rhinoceros *Dicerorhinus sumatrensis* and evaluating several management alternatives which recently have been proposed to save it from extinction.

Identifying species of concern

For the purpose of this chapter, we will call a species extinct when no breeding pairs remain. We will define the extinction probability for a species as the probability that habitat and/or population trends will result in no breeding pairs within two or three generations. We emphasize that two or three generations is a very short time horizon, and we do not advocate its use except for critically endangered species where options for longer-term management will be lost forever if short-term recovery programs are not successful.

A species' pE may be estimated from empirical studies, from analytical models of population processes, from computer simulations, or from subjective assessments by researchers or managers. In a few cases, empirical data on the loss of species diversity under various habitat and population trends are available; e.g., data on attrition from continental islands and from national parks (Wilcox, 1980).

Analytical models of population processes have been used to estimate pE (e.g., MacArthur and Wilson, 1967; MacArthur, 1972; Richter-Dyn and Goel, 1972; Leigh, 1981), but many of these have severe limitations (Brussard, 1985; Goodman, Chapter 2; Shaffer and Samson, 1985). Analytical models may provide a preliminary assessment of population trends under certain circumstances; examples in this book are those of Goodman (Chapter 2), and Ewens *et al.* (Chapter 4).

Simulation models can also be useful for estimating pE for particular species (e.g., Shaffer and Samson, 1985). These models may include both species-specific biological information (such as estimates of available habitat and potential rate of population increase) and sociological variables pertaining to the local human population. The latter might include estimates of poaching activity, type of agriculture, grazing impacts of domestic animals, and potential for catastrophes, disease, or habitat degradation. Unfortunately, data are scarce for building simulation models for many endangered species.

In many situations estimates of pE must be based on experience with related species and on general knowledge of local environmental and sociopolitical conditions. Methods of eliciting these subjective estimates are available (Behn and Vaupel, 1982; Spetzler and Stael von Holstein, 1975). Once determined, they can be used in the same way as probabilities obtained from empirical data or models.

Some factors influencing pE can be anticipated with appreciable certainty; others are fundamentally uncertain. For example, factors influencing pE for the Javan rhino *Rhinoceros sondaicus* over the next few generations include habitat destruction from timber harvests, increased mortality from poaching, and limitations on the area available for reserves. These can be estimated with some confidence. On the other hand, the impacts on pE of epidemic diseases, severe typhoons, fire, or volcanic eruptions are truly uncertain, but nevertheless important, especially as the range of the species shrinks. The recent outbreak of an undiagnosed fatal disease in Javan rhino populations (Oryx, 1982) and the loss of eight million acres of rhino habitat to fire in Borneo in 1983 (Geo, 1985) illustrate this point.

The expected impact of an event on pE is a function of (1) the probability that the event will occur and (2) the consequences for population survival if it does. For example, if the probability of epidemic disease is 0.1, the probability of extinction (pE), if an epidemic occurs, is 0.95, and pE in the absence of an epidemic is 0.85, then E(pE), the expected value for pE, is:

$$E(pE) = [p(epidemic)][pE(epidemic)] + [p(no\ epidemic)]$$
$$[pE(no\ epidemic)] = (0.1)(0.95) + (0.9)(0.85) = 0.86.$$
$$(1)$$

Once calculated, this value can be used to determine if the probability of extinction for this species is unacceptably high.

'Acceptable' levels of pE vary among taxonomic categories, among social and economic groups in society, and among political entities. In developing countries where human demands on resources are already overwhelming, pEs that are acceptable to local governments may shock visiting scientists from industrial nations.

Criteria are also often biased taxonomically. For example, the US Forest Service is specifically charged with maintaining viable populations of native and desired non-native vertebrates on National Forest lands. There is no mention of invertebrates in current Forest Service regulations, although some, such as the spectacular Nokomis fritillary butterfly *Speyeria nokomis* are in more immediate danger of extinction than are many vertebrates. Similarly, current standards for placing species on official endangered lists emphasize mammals and birds over other taxonomic groups, although there is little biological justification for doing so. In the United States the bald eagle *Haliaeetus leucocephalus*, the national symbol, has received far more attention than other species equally threatened with extinction.

The social assessment of whether or not the pE for a particular species is unacceptably high often is made implicitly through budget decisions or the lobbying efforts of special interest groups. Fortunately, there are explicit procedures for assigning values in situations involving multiple interest groups and conflicting goals (Keeney and Raiffa, 1976) which provide a more deliberate method of evaluating pEs and deciding which species need intervention.

The process of debating alternatives for endangered species management can itself change social and governmental attitudes toward extinction. For example, international meetings to discuss management of the Sumatran rhino increased concern for the fate of this species among all participants, including both Malaysian and Indonesian authorities. Probabilities of extinction that seemed acceptable before the meetings are now considered unacceptable. There is now broad support for a species survival plan involving several governments as well as private conservation groups.

An analysis of Sumatran rhino management

We will illustrate the use of decision analysis in the management of critically endangered species with a case study of the Sumatran rhinoceros, evaluating its current status using probability of extinction. Our estimates of pE are subjective, but represent a synthesis of opinion from rhino biologists and managers. We then will analyze management interventions that might be used to improve the species' status, with a consideration of random events that could influence the outcome of those management strategies. Finally, we will use two criteria for choosing among alternatives: probability of extinction and financial cost. The purpose of the analysis is to identify management plans with the best combination of low probability of extinction and low cost.

Current status

The Sumatran rhino persists in small, isolated subpopulations in increasingly fragmented habitat (Van Strien, 1974; Mittermeier and Konstant, 1982) (Figure 8.1). Unprotected habitat is threatened by timber harvest, human resettlement, and hydroelectric development.

Figure 8.1. (a) Current range of the Sumatran rhinoceros. Numbers indicate areas where one or more rhinos are presumed to persist. Boldfaced numbers indicate populations probably preservable in the wild if actively managed and adequately protected.

a

Sabah

1 Silabukan/Lumerau
2 Around Silabukan
3 S./SE. Forest Res.

Sumatra

17 Gunung Leuser
18 Kerinci/Seblat
19 Torgamba
20 Sumatera Selatan
21 Siak River Area

Kalimantin

22 Banumuda

Thailand

23 Phu Khio Reserve
24 Tenasserim Range
25 Koo Soi Doo Res.

West Malaysia

4 Endau Rompin
5 Taman Negara
6 Sungai Dusun
7 Gunung Belumut
8 Mersing Coast
9 Ulu Lepar
10 Sungai Depak
11 Kuala Balah
12 Bukit Gebok
13 Krau Reserve
14 Ulu Selama
15 Ulu Belam
16 Thai Border

Burma

26 Schwe U Daung
27 Elsewhere

Java

28 Udjung Kulan
(Javan Rhino)

Figure 8.1 *continued* **(b) Detailed map of West Malaysia. Locality 4 is a 1000 km² reserve, proposed as a national park. Locality 5 is a national park, but under pressure. See text for further details. (c) Detailed map of Sabah.**

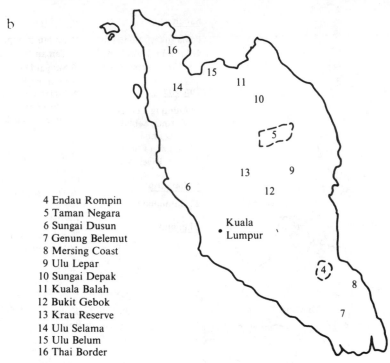

b

16
15
14   11
        10
        5
13   9
6   12

4 Endau Rompin
5 Taman Negara
6 Sungai Dusun
7 Genung Belemut
8 Mersing Coast
9 Ulu Lepar
10 Sungai Depak
11 Kuala Balah
12 Bukit Gebok
13 Krau Reserve
14 Ulu Selama
15 Ulu Belum
16 Thai Border

Kuala
• Lumpur

4
8
7

c

1 Silabukan Reserve
2 Kretam/Dent Peninsula
3 Other Areas

Kota Kinabalu
Sandakan
2
1
3

There are only a few designated reserves, and even these are subject to exploitation. Poaching takes a heavy toll, and this pressure can only increase as the human populations rise. Disease, such as the recent epidemic in the Javan rhino population, or a catastrophic storm could wipe out most of the remaining wild populations. Only two Sumatran rhinos are currently held in captivity. The rapidity of both ecological and political change in Southeast Asia argues for quick action if any is to be effective.

Known wild populations of Sumatran rhinos fall under three political jurisdictions: Sabah (East Malaysia), Indonesia, and West Malaysia; small remnant populations also may persist in Thailand and Burma. We evaluated pE over a period of 30 years, which is about two generations for this species. With current management practices, and in the absence of an epidemic, we estimate pE for rhinos in Sabah to be very close to unity (say 0.99). For the Indonesian population the probability of extinction within 30 years is probably about 0.95, only because some isolated subpopulations are in remote and inaccessible terrain. The West Malaysian population is the smallest but best protected, with a pE of about 0.9. Combining these estimates gives the species as a whole a pE of $(0.99)(0.95)(0.9) = 0.85$ within the next three decades. The choice between *status quo* management and intervention is shown on the decision tree in Figure 8.2 as two branches emerging from a square (a convention in decision analysis indicating a decision point).

Many unpredictable or random processes also influence pE and the outcome of management actions. These include natural events, such as disease, unusual weather, and unpredictable human actions, such as changes in government attitudes toward habitat protection and control of poaching. To weigh the impact of these random events on pE, one must estimate their probabilities of occurrence. For some events, objective probabilities expressed as theoretical expectations or long-term frequencies are available; for example, weather records help predict the expected frequency of severe typhoons in rhino habitat. For other factors, subjectively estimated probabilities are the only option.

Under *status quo* management perhaps the random event with the greatest potential impact on pE for the Sumatran rhino over the next 30 years is epidemic disease. We estimate the probability of this event to be at least 0.1. The events 'epidemic' or 'no epidemic' appear in Figure 8.2 as branches emerging from a circle, indicating a random process that rhino management cannot influence. The probability of each event appears on the corresponding branch. We estimate that an epidemic would increase the pE to at least 0.95. (The pE for each outcome is shown at the end of its corresponding branch in Figure 8.2.) Following equation (1), we use the probability of each random event (epidemic disease or not) to weight pE for each action/event combination, to get E(pE) for current management: $(0.1)(0.95) + (0.9)(0.85) = 0.86$, which we list under the column headed E(pE) in Figure 8.2. Since maintaining *status quo* management involves no increase in cost over what is currently being expended, we list this as \$0 under the dollar cost criterion.

Management interventions

If an E(pE) of 0.86 for the Sumatran rhino under current management conditions is judged to be unacceptably high, what might be done to reduce it? Table 8.1 lists examples of intensive management strategies for endangered animal populations, both wild and captive. Several of these have been proposed for recovering the Sumatran rhino. They are shown in Figure 8.2 and include: (1) increasing control of poaching in existing reserves; (2) doubling the size of one national park;

Figure 8.2. Decision tree for management of the Sumatran rhino. Squares indicate decision points; circles indicate random events. Probabilities of random events are estimated for a 30-year period; pE = probability of species extinction within 30 years; E(pE) = expected value of pE for each alternative. Costs are present values of 30-year costs discounted at 4% per year; M = million.

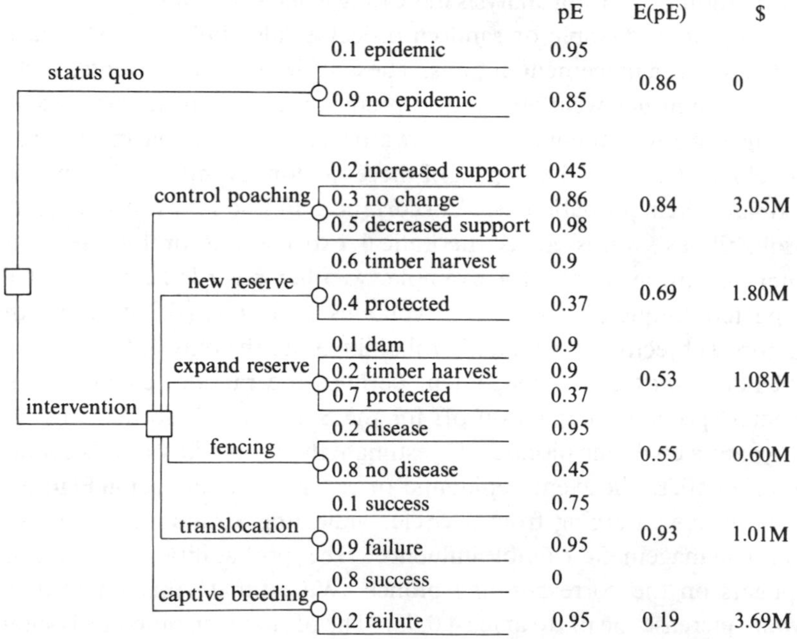

		pE	E(pE)	\$
status quo	0.1 epidemic	0.95		
	0.9 no epidemic	0.85	0.86	0
control poaching	0.2 increased support	0.45		
	0.3 no change	0.86	0.84	3.05M
	0.5 decreased support	0.98		
new reserve	0.6 timber harvest	0.9		
	0.4 protected	0.37	0.69	1.80M
expand reserve	0.1 dam	0.9		
	0.2 timber harvest	0.9	0.53	1.08M
	0.7 protected	0.37		
fencing	0.2 disease	0.95		
	0.8 no disease	0.45	0.55	0.60M
translocation	0.1 success	0.75		
	0.9 failure	0.95	0.93	1.01M
captive breeding	0.8 success	0		
	0.2 failure	0.95	0.19	3.69M

Table 8.1. *Examples of management interventions for critically endangered animal species*

Wild populations and habitat only
Translocating individuals or genetic material
Raising carrying capacity (e.g., artificial feeding)
Restricting dispersal (e.g., fencing)
Fostering and cross-fostering young
Reducing mortality (e.g., vaccination; parasite, predator, poaching control)
Culling
Preserving habitat
Restoring habitat

Captive populations only
Maintaining captive breeding populations for reintroduction and/or perpetual
   captivity
Genetic and demographic management
Maintaining gametes or embryos in 'miniature zoos' (i.e., freezers)

Captive and wild populations
Reintroduction of captive-reared individuals or genetic material to occupied or
   unoccupied habitat
Continued capture of wild individuals or genetic material for captive propagation

---

(3) creating a new national park; (4) fencing a large area of prime habitat, managing the enclosed population with supplemental feeding and veterinary care, and translocating isolated rhinos into the enclosure; (5) translocating rhinos among wild subpopulations to restock depleted habitats and to maintain gene flow among subpopulations; and (6) capturing wild rhinos to form captive breeding populations in at least four separate institutions in four countries. The captive populations would serve both as a reservoir of genetic material and as a source of animals to bolster populations in currently or previously occupied habitat.

To choose among management alternatives, assessments of each option must include both their respective expected improvements in the species' status and their costs. We now will examine each strategy for recovery of the Sumatran rhino (Figure 8.2), including uncertainties affecting the expected probability of extinction for each plan and an estimate of its financial cost.

The effectiveness of efforts to control poaching is critically dependent on government support for conservation. If protection against poaching is increased by four additional rangers in Sabah and six in Indonesia, with a vehicle for every two rangers, pE might be reduced to roughly 0.45 over the next 30 years. This additional effort would cost about $3.05 million (in this analysis all annual costs were discounted at 4% per year). However, the probability that government support for conservation would both be uninterrupted and high enough to permit this level of success is only about 0.2. If the *status quo* is maintained (probability about 0.3), we expect pE to remain at about 0.86. If government support for rhino conservation is seriously eroded, especially in Sabah and Indonesia (probability about 0.5), control efforts would be wasted; and pE could increase to at least 0.98. The expected value of pE for control of poaching is thus $(0.2)(0.45) + (0.3)(0.86) + (0.5)(0.98) = 0.84$.

Designating a new national park for rhino protection would support approximately 25 animals; this action would reduce pE to about 0.37. The cost of acquiring and maintaining the new national park would be about $1.8 million, not counting loss of revenue from timber harvest or agricultural use. However, even if the area is designated as a park, pressure to exploit timber within it will be extreme, with perhaps a 0.6 probability of timber harvest in the reserve within the next 30 years. We estimate that pE would rise to about 0.9 in that case because of habitat loss and poaching by loggers.

The third alternative is to double the size of an existing park, which also would support about 25 additional animals. The same site has been suggested for a hydroelectric dam. If installed, this project would eliminate a large proportion of prime rhino habitat. Although the hydroelectric project has been deferred for the next five years, it has not been permanently abandoned. We estimate the probability of the dam being built within the next 30 years to be about 0.1. Even if the dam is not built, timber interests threaten the integrity of the expanded reserve, with perhaps a 0.2 chance of harvest. If the reserve were maintained intact, pE for the species as a whole might drop from 0.86 to about 0.37; if either dam-building or timber harvest occurs, pE would rise to about 0.90. The combined probabilities of these events result in an E(pE) of 0.53. The cost of acquiring and maintaining the expanded reserve over the next 30 years is estimated at about $1.08 million, not counting income lost from reserving the timber and not building the dam.

Another option is to fence an area in an existing or new reserve, managing the resulting high density of rhinos with supplemental feeding and veterinary care, as in the successful South African rhino ranches (Martin, 1984). Most problems, such as food shortage or nutrient imbalance, probably can be detected and remedied quickly enough to avoid heavy mortality.

Disease is a major risk associated with this plan. We estimate the probability of such a disease outbreak to be about 0.2. If an epizootic occurs, pE for the population as a whole would rise to about 0.95. This increase from the *status quo* level of 0.86 is due to the transfer of animals from isolated subpopulations to the fenced area; isolation, *per se*, provides some assurance of escape from exposure to the pathogen. On the other hand, if the fenced population can be maintained successfully, pE would decline to about 0.45. Together, these alternatives result in an E(pE) of 0.55. The fenced area would cost about $60 000 to establish and about $18 000 per year to maintain, for a total 30-year cost of about $0.60 million.

The fifth management intervention illustrated in Figure 8.2 is the translocation of rhinos among isolated subpopulations. Many remaining rhinos exist in groups of two or three individuals, and random mortality and reproductive failure (demographic stochasticity) are big threats to the viability of such small groups. Subdivided populations that are as small and as isolated as these easily slip below the level for long-term viability (see Goodman, Chapter 2). In addition, habitat fragmentation reduces the chance that subpopulations which go extinct will be recol onized by migrants from other areas.

Deliberately moving rhinos among subpopulations to compensate for mortality and lack of natural recolonization is one way to assure survival of these populations, but there are hazards at each phase of the operation. Capture and transport have a high probability of death or injury. Furthermore, the chances are rather high that translocated animals will disperse from the new site or not be accepted into the social hierarchy and, hence, will fail to reproduce. An intensive effort to adapt rhinos to their new locations could cost $100 000 per rhino. A translocation program with no follow-up after release might have about a 0.1 chance of success and would cost about $20 000 per animal. If animals were translocated among subpopulations at the rate of seven per year for the first three years of the program and two per year for the remaining 27 years, the program might reduce pE over the next 30 years to about 0.75. On the other hand, if translocation results in death or injury to several rhinos, the pE for the species as a whole may increase to 0.95. These alternatives result in an E(pE) of 0.93 and a total cost of $1.01 million.

The last management alternative for the Sumatran rhino is the establishment of a captive breeding program. Success or failure depends on a series of random factors, including capture of wild animals, shipping, behavioral adaptation to captivity, breeding success, disease, and cooper ation among institutions. Animals captured for captive propagation would come from small isolates under heavy pressure from poaching and timber harvest and, therefore, with little potential to contribute to long-term population growth. Nevertheless, loss of these long-lived animals from the wild population might increase pE to about 0.95 if the captive breeding program fails. However, if the captive program is successful, and breeding populations are established at several facilities in Malaysia, Indonesia, the United States, and Great Britain, the pE for the species would be reduced to zero over the next 30 years.

To estimate the probability that the proposed captive breeding program will be successful, we can draw on previous experience with capturing and breeding white *Ceratotherium simum*, black *Diceros bicornis*, and Indian *Rhinoceros unicornis* rhinos with judgements about differences between these species and the Sumatran rhino. We can also use subjective information. For example, the likelihood of successful breeding by the existing captive Sumatran rhino female has been assessed by biologists familiar with other rhinocerus species. Those who have observed her unusually calm and 'friendly' behavior and obvious adjustment to captivity feel confident that breeding will be no problem, provided an appropriate mate can be found. Based on previous experience with captive breeding of other rhino species and on the current levels of political support for the program, we believe the chances of success to be about 0.8, resulting in an E(pE) of 0.19.

The costs of a captive breeding operation will be high. Development of facilities and propagation techniques in Malaysia and Indonesia will cost about $1.25 million for the first three years plus $30 000 per year for maintenance, or $2.06 million over 30 years. Costs of maintaining captive rhinos in the United States and Great Britain are about $3000 per animal per year. The original populations of about eight animals in the US and eight in Great Britain are expected to quadruple in the 30-year period. The total cost for captive populations in these two countries, not counting expansion of physical facilities, is at least $1.63 million, bringing the total to $3.69 million.

Evaluating management alternatives

For each of the six proposed management interventions, and for the *status quo*, we have estimated the expected probability of extinction and financial costs, listed on the right in Figure 8.2. Given that the purpose of rhino management is to minimize the probability of extinction, preferably also with minimum cost, which alternative is best?

Translocating animals among wild subpopulations is far too risky to be recommended. Its E(pE) is even higher (0.93) than for the status quo (0.86). The chances of success and attendant benefits to the populations are not high enough to outweigh the loss of translocated animals if the program fails.

Captive breeding is the most promising option in terms of minimizing the expected probability of extinction for the species, with an E(pE) of 0.19. Even if removal of rhinos to captivity raises pE for the wild population, the chances of successful captive breeding are high enough to justify this option. However, many conservationists are wary of emphasizing captive programs, feeling that survival of the species in captivity is a poor second to survival in the wild and fearing that captive programs will divert attention and resources from the conservation of wild populations. These concerns could be incorporated into this analysis by assigning lower values to survival in captivity than to survival in the wild, as described by Maguire (1986). However, in cases like the Sumatran rhino, where extinction in the wild seems likely even with strong conservation efforts, we feel that the most pressing issue should be survival of the species in any form.

Beyond identifying the obviously best and worst management strategies (i.e., captive breeding and translocation for our rhino example), is it possible to evaluate objectively the remaining options within the middle range of E(pE)? These options can be treated more formally by constructing a utility function for pE (Figure 8.3), which

Figure 8.3. Utility function illustrating current social assessment of probabilities of extinction, where the most desirable pE has a utility of 1.0, and the least desirable has a utility of 0. The straight dashed line is the linear utility function U(pE) = 1 − pE.

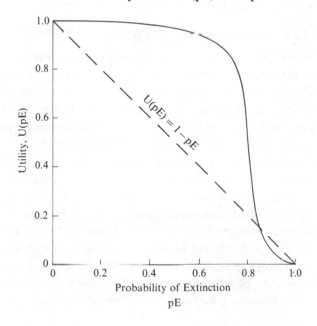

reflects relative preferences for different values of pE. The best pE (0.0) is assigned a utility value of 1 and the least acceptable pE (1.0) a utility value of 0. We note that in the current social and political climate, intervention is often delayed until extinction seems imminent. Thus, the utility function we have drawn in Figure 8.3 (solid line) reflects our observation that society evidently considers high pE quite acceptable until it is very close to 1. For comparison, we include in Figure 8.3 a linear utility function (dashed line) where incremental improvements in pE are viewed equally enthusiastically over the entire range of pE.

When using utility to choose among alternatives, the best choice is the one that maximizes expected utility, rather than the one that minimizes pE. The curved utility function in Figure 8.3 (solid line) is used to assign utility values corresponding to each pE in Figure 8.2. For example, the utility of pE = 0.45 is about 0.98. Then expected utility, E(U), for each option is calculated using the probabilities of random events just as in calculating E(pE). The resulting E(U) values are compared to see which is highest.

Utility functions reflect individual preferences and are influenced by a person's current circumstances, including wealth, education, religious views, and so on. Decision analysts elicit an individual's utility function for an attribute such as pE by asking a series of questions about preferences (Keeney and Raiffa, 1976). Utility functions elicited at different times from the same individual tend to be similar, but they do change when the person's wealth, education, or other circumstances change (Officer and Halter, 1968).

Conservation education may be one means of altering a person's utility function for pE. Because utility functions reflect individual preferences, it may be difficult to develop utility functions for public decisions, where no single person is responsible for making the choice and where special interest groups may have divergent opinions. Keeney and Raiffa (1976) and Keeney (1977) have outlined a method for combining utility functions of different groups to form a composite useful for public decisions.

Because the utility curve in Figure 8.3 is only hypothetical, we will not calculate and compare E(U) for the rhino example, but will instead use E(pE) to evaluate management options. Our criteria for choosing among management alternatives include minimizing cost as well as minimizing pE. Which options are most cost-effective? Our estimates of costs are admittedly crude, and we have chosen to neglect the fact that random events will sometimes change the actual costs of a management activity. For example, reductions in government support for poaching control probably will result in reductions in the success of those efforts. Likewise, our cost estimates for the establishment and expansion of reserves neglect potential revenues from timber harvest or other commercial exploitation.

Both the captive breeding and poaching control programs are very expensive, but captive breeding is clearly the preferred option because of its greater expected benefit to the species' security. Of the several management choices for wild populations with $E(pE)$s between 0.5 and 0.7, fencing looks most cost-effective, but we suspect that the costs of establishing and maintaining a fenced population have been underestimated. Methods for assessing the trade-offs between conflicting criteria, such as financial cost and species recovery, are described by Maguire (1986).

In many cases several options may be pursued at once, and the problem is to choose the mix of activities with the best impact on species recovery for the available budget. Multiobjective programming (Cohon, 1978) is a method of achieving this integration of population and cost criteria, but a detailed analysis of this is beyond the scope of this chapter. We simply point out that a number of the proposed interventions, including fencing and captive breeding, involve collecting animals from some of the remaining wild subpopulations and, therefore, compete for limited biological, as well as financial, resources. In addition, the impacts of the proposed interventions on population status may not be independent, and their interdependence must be expressed in any programming analysis.

As is common in endangered species management, the probability estimates in this analysis are themselves uncertain quantities, although they represent the best we can do with the information available. We need to assess how sensitive our ranking of management alternatives is to changes in the probability values used. If the selection of alternatives changes with small alterations in one of the probability estimates, we can focus research efforts on reducing uncertainty in that parameter.

What changes in probability estimates could change our ranking of the proposed interventions? Even if the probability of success of the captive breeding program were as low as 0.5, its $E(pE)$ would still be lower (0.48) than any other alternative, although its cost might then be too high for the expected benefit. For the $E(pE)$ of the translocation program to be lower than the value for the *status quo* (0.86), the probability of success for translocation would have to be at least 0.5. However, providing the follow-up care to ensure this level of success would be extremely costly. Note that the fencing and the captive breeding options differ only in pE for success (0.45 versus 0) and in cost ($0.60 million versus $3.69 million). If pE for a successful fencing option were as low as 0.2 or 0.3, it would become a more attractive option than captive breeding in zoos because of its lower cost. The sensitivity analysis shows that only large changes in probability estimates would alter our conclusions.

Implementation

A formal process for implementing an international conservation program for the Sumatran rhino was initiated by the Species Survival Commission (SSC) of the IUCN. A meeting in Singapore in October 1984 was attended by representatives of Indonesia, West Malaysia, Sabah, captive breeding groups from the UK and USA, the SSC, and researchers familiar with the status of the species in the wild.

An important feature of the meeting was the general agreement that the Sumatran rhino is a greatly endangered species, that its extinction will be a great loss, and that it is necessary to intervene if the species is to be saved. A basic set of goals was formulated, and tentative agreements for their implementation were drafted. The fundamental tenets of the agreements were that: (1) primary support would be given to conserving the Sumatran rhino as viable populations in sufficiently large areas of protected native habitat; (2) an educational program to enhance public awareness and support for the Sumatran rhino would be developed; and (3) a captive breeding program for preserving genetic diversity in the species would be developed in the countries of origin and elsewhere (USA and Europe), using animals with no hope of long-term survival in the wild.

Translating these agreements into working documents, budgets, a program, schedules, and a management and policy structure, required six months' activity after the meeting with numerous consultations among the parties. The entire exercise has been an important activity by the SSC/IUCN and will provide a working model for collaborative international intervention.

Conclusions

It is critical to identify species in imminent danger of extinction in order to focus conservation efforts on them. Methods for estimating the probabilities of extinction (pE) range from sophisticated analytical or simulation models to informed judgements. How high pE must be to be unacceptable is likely to depend on the species' position in the taxonomic hierarchy, its aesthetic or economic value, and the region of the world in which it is found. An extinction probability of unity for a small species of brown moth inhabiting the Falkland Islands is not likely to arouse much concern, while a pE of 0.25 or so for a large, well-known predator usually galvanizes considerable action.

Once a species has been designated as critically endangered, a number of management options must be considered, including no intervention. Decision analysis provides a framework for evaluating the efficacy of these options. In addition to facilitating identification of the best management alternatives, decision analysis helps pinpoint potential sources of uncertainty, provides a way of comparing costs and benefits, and permits a sensitivity analysis to assess the robustness of its conclusions.

While decision analysis provides a useful framework for discriminating among management alternatives, political processes play a large part in the implementation of any conservation program. Some elements of the political process can be included in a decision analysis *via* utility functions. However, political winds are notoriously shifty, and conservation biologists must be prepared to accept the fact that today's worst option may be tomorrow's first or only choice.

References

Behn, R. D. and Vaupel, J. W. 1982. *Quick Analysis for Busy Decision Makers*. Basic Books, New York.

Brussard, P. F. 1985. Minimum viable populations: How many are too few? *Rest. and Mgmt. Notes* **3**: 21–5.

Cohon, J. L. 1978. *Multiobjective Programming and Planning*. Academic Press, New York.

Geo. 1985. World's biggest fire was ignored by news media. *Geo* **7** (February): 105.

Keeney, R. L. 1977. A utility function for examining policy affecting salmon on the Skeena River. *J. Fish. Res. Board Can.* **34**: 49–63.

Keeney, R. L. and Raiffa, H. 1976. *Decisions with Multiple Objectives: Preferences and Value Trade-offs*. John Wiley and Sons, New York.

Leigh, E. G., Jr. 1981. The average lifetime of a population in a varying environment. *J. Theor. Biol.* **90**: 213–39.

MacArthur, R. H. 1984. *Geographical Ecology*. Harper and Row, New York.

MacArthur, R. H. and Wilson, E. O. 1967. *The Theory of Island Biogeography*. Princeton University Press, Princeton, New Jersey.

Maguire, L. A. 1986. Using decision analysis to manage endangered species populations. *J. Env. Mgmt.* **22**: 345–60.

Martin, E. B. 1984. They're killing off the rhino. *National Geographic* **165**: 404–22.

Mittermeier, R. A. and Konstant, W. R. (eds.) 1982. Species conservation priorities in the tropical forests of Southeast Asia. IUCN Occasional Papers, No. 1. Gland, Switzerland.

Officer, R. R. and Halter, A. N. 1968. Utility analysis in a practical setting. *Am. J. Agric. Econ.* **50**: 257–78.

Oryx. 1982. Notes and news: Javan rhino deaths. *Oryx* **16**: 298–9.

Raiffa, H. 1968. *Decision Analysis*. Addison-Wesley, Reading, Mass.

Richter-Dyn, N. and Goel, N. S. 1972. On the extinction of a colonizing species. *Theor. Pop. Biol.* **12**: 406–33.

Shaffer, M. L. and Samson, F. B. 1985. Population size and extinction: a note on determining critical population sizes. *Am. Nat.* **125**: 144–52.

Soulé, M. E. 1985. What is conservation biology? *Bioscience* **35**: 727–34.
Spetzler, C. S. and Stael von Holstein, C.-A. S. 1975. Probability encoding in decision analysis. *Management Science* **22**: 340–58.
Van Strien, N. J. 1974. *Dicerorhinus sumatrensis* (Fischer). The Sumatran or two-horned Asiatic rhinoceros. A study of the literature. *Meded. Landbouwhogeschool Wageningen* 74-16.
Wilcox, B. A. 1980. Insular ecology and conservation. Pp. 95–117 in M. E. Soulé and B. A. Wilcox (eds.) *Conservation Biology: an Evolutionary-Ecological Perspective*. Sinauer Associates, Sunderland, Mass.

9

The role of interagency cooperation in managing for viable populations

HAL SALWASSER
USDA Forest Service, P.O. Box 2417, Washington, DC 20013

CHRISTINE SCHONEWALD-COX
AND RICHARD BAKER
Department of Environmental Studies, Wickson Hall, University of California at Davis, Davis, CA 95616

The challenge of managing lands, resources, and people to sustain viable populations of large vertebrates and other taxa is enormous. Conservation biologists (e.g., Soulé, 1980; Frankel, 1983; 1984) have emphasized that few existing protected areas can provide this service for all desired species found within their bounds. However, most analyses of the ability of reserves to sustain viable populations (e.g., Soulé, 1980; Frankel and Soulé, 1981; Schonewald-Cox, 1983) consider each jurisdictional unit as a separate entity. This reflects a frequent lack of cooperation and the conflicting priorities and management practices that can exist in adjacent areas (Schonewald-Cox and Bayless, in press; Harris, 1984). The future of many species would not be nearly as bleak if managers who share species of concern would cooperate to minimize conflicts and reach mutual conservation goals.

The effectiveness of cooperation in attaining conservation goals has been demonstrated by The Nature Conservancy since its inception in 1951 (Jenkins, 1984). More recently, the value of cooperation was recognized in the first recommendation of the Terrestrial Animal Species Panel at the US Strategy Conference on Biological Diversity (US Dept. of State, 1982): '. . . identify, establish, and manage a worldwide system of national parks and other conservation areas to insure the perpetuation of all major ecosystem types and the diversity of organisms and processes they contain . . . in a way which promotes local economic development compatible with long-term ecosystem integrity and the sustained use of natural resources.' Current public interest in an 'ecosystem approach' to

National Park protection also reflects a growing recognition of the value of cooperation in conservation efforts (Newmark, 1985).

However, attempts to orchestrate cooperative agreements among land and resource management agencies can be frustrating, if not futile. Discord among persons responsible for management policies and activities can arise from differences in training, orientation, and priorities. Personal and political views as well as conflicting agency mandates on how conservation should proceed can interfere with the most urgent or well-intentioned conservation effort. The cumbersome logistics of creating agreements between agencies, private concerns, and even governments can also be discouraging. Still, the prognosis for the long-term survival of many species is poor if adequate conservation areas are not provided for the protection of self-sustaining populations (Frankel and Soulé, 1981).

Large tracts of land are generally not available for increasing the size of protected areas. The prudent alternative is to improve the quality of protection in whatever kinds of areas offer a suitable environment. For the continued existence of many species in the wild, especially those with large home ranges or migratory life styles, this will often necessitate a multi-agency (or multi-institutional) effort. Rarely will a single agency or landowner possess a large enough tract of the right kinds of habitats to support a self-sustaining population of animals such as large cats (*Felis* spp.), wolves (*Canis* spp.), bears (*Ursus* spp.), large cervids (*Cervidae*), anadromous fish (*Salmonidae*), or eagles (*Haliaeetus* spp.). Often the home ranges of such animals will encompass lands that are under widely different management goals, ranging from full protection to intensive agriculture and minerals extraction.

Even where governmental agencies are the land stewards, there are differences in missions and legal mandates. For example, all Federal agencies of the United States operate under the same laws and regulations regarding the conservation of listed endangered and threatened species (the Endangered Species Act of 1973, as amended). But the day-to-day operations of those agencies vary from the protection and management of parks where hunting and logging are prohibited (the USDI National Park Service) to the management of forests and rangelands for sustained production of timber, minerals, livestock grazing, wildlife, fish, and recreation (the USDA Forest Service). Yaffee (1982) has recognized the limitations of organizational arrangements in the management of endangered and threatened species.

Conflicting mandates as well as complexities of land use and ownership characterize the species conservation milieu in most developed countries.

A diverse mix of people and organizations often interact to effect species conservation programs. Consequently, there are two levels of cooperation necessary for effective conservation – among government agencies and between agencies and private (non-governmental) groups. Implementation of the Endangered Species Act exemplifies the cooperative approach, as seen in the management of the grizzly bear populations in the United States south of the Canadian border.

The grizzly bear (*Ursus arctos*) population in the contiguous United States currently occupies less than 1% of its historic range. This population, estimated to be 700 to 900 individuals, is divided among six areas (Servheen, 1984). Two of the areas, Yellowstone and Selway–Bitterroot, are considered to be isolated by human development from other grizzly bear populations. There are approximately 200 bears in the Yellowstone population. This number may produce viability over the short run (several decades) based on demographic and environmental considerations (Shaffer and Samson, 1985), but appears to be well below the numbers deemed necessary for long-term (centuries or more) survival and adaptability of most vertebrates (Soulé, 1980; Salwasser *et al.*, 1984; Goodman, Chapter 2; Belovsky, Chapter 3; Lande and Barrowclough, Chapter 6). There is no estimate for the Selway–Bitterroot population. The four remaining areas are adjacent to Canadian parks supporting grizzly bears, but populations in the North Cascades, Cabinet–Yaak, and Selkirk areas each probably number far less than 100 individiuals. Only the Northern Continental Divide area approaches a 'safe' level (Frankel and Soulé, 1981; Salwasser *et al.*, 1984; Lande and Barrowclough, Chapter 6) at 440 plus bears (Servheen, 1984).

Grizzly bears in the lower 48 states are protected by a species recovery plan under the Endangered Species Act of 1973, as amended. This plan formalizes population recovery goals and the responsibilities of agencies for habitat, resources, and recreation management in areas occupied by grizzlies. Grizzly bear habitat is largely under federal management, although some state and private lands are involved. The development and implementation of the grizzly bear recovery plan has been facilitated by an 'organic' organizational structure (Kanter, 1983) initially called the Interagency Grizzly Bear Task Force and resulting in the establishment of the Interagency Grizzly Bear Committee in 1983 (Servheen, 1984). Members of the committee include the National Park Service, the US Fish and Wildlife Service, the Bureau of Land Management, the US Forest Service, four state wildlife agencies, two Indian tribes, the US Bureau of Indian Affairs, and forestry and wildlife management branches of the British Columbia and Alberta provincial governments in Canada.

Several private conservation organizations are also deeply involved in the political and economic aspects of bear recovery. Many scientists from universities, management agencies, and private conservation groups contribute their expertise.

The combination of low population numbers, isolated populations, sensitivity to human activities (grizzlies, like many other large, aggressive vertebrates, are frequent targets for persons whose interests conflict with the needs of the bears), and administrative and political complexity makes the grizzly situation a classic example of how difficult managing for viable populations can be.

By themselves, government agencies cannot and do not chart and negotiate the course of species conservation. They must rely on outside individuals and groups for much of the scientific and monitoring aspects of management plans. In addition, non-governmental organizations and foundations such as The Nature Conservancy often provide funding for the acquisition of lands and the implementation of conservation programs. The means of coordinating the goals and strategies among diverse groups are as important to the survival of many species as is knowledge of their biology and habitat needs.

There is no substitute for a multi-institutional approach to conservation of animal diversity. It may provide our only hope for creating the huge conservation areas necessary to preserve most large vertebrates in the wild.

Mechanisms for multi-institutional cooperation

Cooperation can be achieved through carefully designed agreements involving federal, state, and private agencies with land management responsibilities. Such efforts can take a wide variety of forms. Management practices can be coordinated to reduce conflicting goals, researchers can collaborate to share data and expertise, and resources can be exchanged. This cooperative approach to conservation has been used by the Programme on Man and the Biosphere in setting up its biosphere reserves around the world during the past decade (MAB, 1973; 1974; Risser and Cornelison, 1979).

It would be naive to assume that cooperation among units *within* a land management agency (let alone among individuals within units) is so easily established as to be unworthy of discussion. However, the problems associated with creating cooperation *among* agencies are often so much greater that they deserve the majority of our attention in this discussion.

Formal organizational arrangements are probably most effective in dealing with the complexities of managing for viable populations (Clark,

1985), and there are three general approaches to establishing such cooperation among land management agencies. While neither discrete nor exclusive, each has strengths and weaknesses in terms of (1) the time and effort required for its creation, (2) its breadth of impact and effectiveness in achieving an intended goal, and (3) its ability to endure through time. The first approach, locally arranged, informal cooperation, may be the most easily attained, but is also likely to have only a small impact and be the least stable through time. The second, agreement requiring the signatures or endorsement of top-level administrators (e.g., department heads or agency directors), is more difficult to obtain, but is more likely to survive and affect management activities. Finally, a legislative act mandating cooperation among federal (national) land management agencies is likely to produce long-lasting and broad results, but usually requires equally strong financial backing, public interest, and political support.

The simplest route by which to establish cooperation is through mutual agreement at the local level. A local cooperative agreement may result, for example, when the range of a population of a species of concern crosses over the jurisdictional boundaries between two or more management units (e.g., a national park and a forest reserve). If the park superintendent and the forest supervisor decide to cooperate in managing habitat for this population, they may agree to alter their land use practices to provide the population with optimal habitat conditions. Unfortunately, a change in directives or administrators for either unit may nullify existing arrangements without providing any replacement. At worst, new management practices could produce conditions detrimental to the protection of the population. It might then be necessary to undertake an entirely new sequence of discussions and negotiations in order to re-establish cooperation, perhaps without success. Thus, highly localized agreements, while easiest to obtain, are vulnerable to the frequent changes that can occur in personnel, directives, and budgets.

If, for example, Schonewald-Cox and Salwasser wished to cooperate on a project, they would simply do so, as long as it didn't conflict with their work assignments. No formalized agreement would be necessary unless they desired one. If one of them needed funds from the other in order to accomplish the work, or if the project took one of them away from their existing responsibilities for a substantial period, they would have to start exchanges of signatures, contracts, and product requirements. This exchange of papers would have to be repeated each new fiscal year. Thus, the potentially demanding logistics and administration of local cooperation may at times overwhelm its benefits in convenience. In addition, the local approach may initially cost less, both financially and in time spent developing public and agency support, but opposition by almost anyone with greater authority or influence can interfere with the effort. On the other hand, the agreement may persist long enough to establish the changes in tradition, practice, or public attitude necessary to preserve a species.

The next level of formalization, memoranda of agreement that result from endorsements by organization heads (e.g., agency or regional director, federal department secretary, society executive), have a high chance of persistence beyond a single individual's tenure. However, a great deal of preparation and negotiation among all entities must be accomplished prior to obtaining the signatures of top-level adminis-trators. In addition to public interest, public lobbying, and within-agency appeals and support, the recognition of a need by the administrator or an associate can not only accelerate, but may be critical in obtaining, a recommendation to cooperate. This form of agreement most frequently develops when substantial support exists on the individual level within the cooperating organizations, and may evolve from existing local-level agreements. The resulting interagency agreement or memorandum of agreement tends to be long-lasting, although it usually contains provisions for cancelation by mutual consent within a defined period of notification.

The Interagency Grizzly Bear Task Force (and resulting Committee) is an example of a cooperative agreement with top-level administrative endorsement. Preparation for the creation of the task force took about two years of concentrated effort, not including time spent in obtaining public and administrative support. The signature process was initiated around 1972, but it was not until 1974 that the interagency task force began to function. During the next nine years, the task force remained intact, and shifted its emphasis from research to planning in response to change in political administrations, public attitudes, and public con-troversy. With the creation in 1982 of a memorandum of agreement signed by four state governors and three assistant secretaries in the Departments of Interior and Agriculture, the Interagency Grizzly Bear Committee was then formed. The Committee took charge in 1983, after a year of reorganisation. Its role has continued to evolve, and the committee now participates in coordinating research needs of managers, public education, law enforcement and protection, and habitat manage-ment and planning.

Mandates from the federal (national) level usually provide the greatest stability and effectiveness in the creation of a cooperative agreement.

There have been occasions in the United States, however, when Congress has passed an act or amendment that required organizations to cooperate but failed to provide the necessary appropriations. Participation was limited by inadequate funding to those few individuals available to carry out the work. Without adequate appropriations, such a large-scale arrangement can be reduced to the status of a political maneuver.

Congressional action requires far more planning and support than any other approach to cooperation. In the United States, for example, legislation such as the Endangered Species Act and the Migratory Bird Treaty Act can only result from lengthy planning, the availability of enormous financial resources, a substantial public lobbying effort, and the development of strong support among congresspersons.

One example in which Congressional action has been successful in bringing agencies together is in response to the decline of the tule elk (*Cervus elaphus nannodes*) (Phillips, 1976; Tule Elk Interagency Task Force, 1979; Bureau of Land Management, 1983). This subspecies was originally distributed throughout much of California. It now exists in thirteen isolated populations, the products of a series of extensive relocation efforts during the last 80 years. Only one of these locations is free-ranging, but this population (Owens Valley) occupies the most arid and southern extreme of the species' current range. The tule elk's previous habitat has largely been converted to croplands, grazelands, and developments.

Strong public interest in the tule elk stimulated similarly strong interest and support within the government at both the state and federal levels. In 1971, the California legislature mandated maintenance of the subspecies and its habitat. Since much potential tule elk habitat is under federal control, the US Congress passed a law in 1976 directing the Departments of Agriculture, Interior, and Defense to cooperate with the California Fish and Game Commission in preserving this species. The following year, the Tule Elk Interagency Task Force was established to facilitate this cooperative effort. The task force currently includes participants from six federal agencies, two state agencies, and nine private or local governmental organizations.

The California Department of Fish and Game has assumed the major role in this conservation effort. Despite inadequate lands, funding, or personnel within any one agency for achieving the protection of this subspecies, tule elk are increasing in numbers, due largely to the efforts generated by the Congressional order to cooperate. This cooperative effort has provided the special attention necessary to manage tule elk into an expanding population of multiple demes. Furthermore, the project has survived four presidential administrations, demonstrating the durability of this approach to cooperation.

The range of possible participants in cooperative agreements is great. Cooperation may include not only the national government, but also regional and local governments (as with the tule elk), universities, private organizations (e.g., The Nature Conservancy, corporations, etc.), ranchers, farmers, and any other entities or individuals that own and manage land. Zoos will have an increasingly important role in cooperative agreements as a source of captive-bred surplus animals for reintroduction. In some cases, countries with adjacent protected land or with the same species of concern may also become cooperators. The set of potential participants in a cooperative agreement will likely dictate the approach or combination of approaches that provides the optimal balance of convenience, speed, effectiveness, and durability.

Conservation networks for population viability

Most societies wish to conserve species diversity, but are not likely to set aside large enough tracts of land specifically dedicated to full protection. Many species, however, can survive on lands that are managed for the production of renewable resources such as timber, livestock forage, and wildlife for sport hunting. The task appears to be to take advantage of the full network of available lands in order to maintain viable populations.

The most ideal and effective cooperative arrangement for managing self-sustaining populations of species with large area requirements is a conservation network. The network might enlist the cooperation of all major land management agencies, including different governments in some cases, abutting an existing high-protection 'core.' This network approach is similar to the core/buffer concept utilized by the Program on Man and the Biosphere in establishing Biosphere Reserves (MAB, 1974).

The creation of a conservation network might require modification of certain activities such as clear-cutting, road-building, or high-density camping. Alternatively, cooperation may result in the shifting of some activities to less critical areas or areas isolated from the locations of sensitive species within the conservation network. The cumulative effects of all human-related activities such as forestry, fire suppression, minerals development, hunting, or livestock grazing must be considered in order to maintain the effectiveness of the entire network. Statements modifying these activities might be among the elements of an agreement leading to the creation of a network. The goal of such an agreement would be the creation of a combined area large enough and with a sufficient level of coordinated protection to sustain the focal species as well as the integrity of the entire ecological system.

In some cases (e.g., where contiguous lands are not available or necessary), the conservation network might involve management units which are not adjacent, but nonetheless share species of concern. In this case, cooperation might entail an agreement to transfer animals or plants as needed for gene flow or restoration, or to preserve seasonal habitat for a migratory species.

A conservation network would likely require actions of some participants which, performed outside the context of the network, might be counter-productive. For example, a participating management unit adjacent to the core unit could be encouraged to continue its timber-cutting practices in order to provide the focal species with a greater diversity of habitat types within the network. Elsewhere, however, in the absence of uncut adjacent lands, the same timber-cutting would be detrimental to the focal species. Thus, in a conservation effort, cooperation can produce a valuable and potentially synergistic effect.

To illustrate the effect of cooperation on the ability of conservation networks to protect populations, we show how 10 potential networks could be formed from existing adjacent national parks, national forests, and national wildlife refuges in the United States. In the US, the National Park Service is mandated to protect the resources contained within its lands (national parks, monuments, seashores, lakeshores, and riverways) in a 'virgin' state while also providing recreational opportunities to the public. This results in the maintenance of older successional stages in these lands. Conversely, the US Forest Service manages its lands (national forests) for 'multiple use' through the production of renewable resources such as timber and wildlife in addition to providing a wider variety of recreational opportunities than are available in national parks. Greater ecological diversity tends to result from this type of management. The third agency included in our examples is the US Fish and Wildlife Service, whose lands (national wildlife refuges) are managed to preserve native flora and fauna, especially threatened and endangered species, migratory birds, and game fish and wildlife. Many of these areas contain water or wetlands.

We have estimated the total contiguous area that might serve as an effective conservation network at each of 10 locations (Table 9.1). The outlines of these networks are shown in Figure 9.1. This demonstration is simplified; it ignores the conflicts that would inevitably result from attempting to coordinate lands with such a variety of mandates.

Table 9.1. *Ten potential conservation networks. Note that this is intended only as a demonstration of the network concept; actual application would require further refinement. Area estimates are grid-counts of contiguous lands as shown on USGS Public Lands Map (1 : 3 168 000). Since an up-to-date map was unavailable, these area estimates are subject to change. National parks (N.P.), national monuments (N.M.), national recreation areas (N.R.A.), national forests (N.F.), and national wildlife refuges (N.W.R.) were considered effectively contiguous if connection was greater than 10 miles in width. Corridors of effective size for most species may connect certain networks (e.g., South Cascades and Siskiyou, Selway–Bitterroot and Northern Continental Divide). Conversely, large rivers and other obstructions may reduce the effective size of some networks. Inclusion of potential cooperators in park area calculation (third column) is indicated by '*'.*

Conservation network	Approx. park area (hectares)	Potential cooperator(s)	Approx. network area (hectares)	Factor of increase
Selway–Bitterroot	N/A	Beaverhead N.F. Bitterroot N.F. Boise N.F. Challis N.F. Clearwater N.F. Coeur D'Alene N.F. Deerlodge N.F. Lolo N.F. Payette N.F. Nezperce N.F. Salmon N.F. Sawtooth N.F. St. Joe N.F.	7,535,000	N/A
Yellowstone	1,024,000	Beaverhead N.F. Bridger N.F. Caribou N.F. Custer N.F. Gallatin N.F. *Grand Teton N.P. National Elk Refuge Red Rock Lakes N.W.R. Shoshone N.F. Targhee N.F. Teton N.F. *Yellowstone N.P.	5,558,000	5.4
Sierra	700,000	Eldorado N.F. Inyo N.F. Lassen N.F. *Lassen Volcanic N.P. Plumas N.F. Sequoia N.F. *Sequoia/Kings Canyon N.P. Sierra N.F. Stanislaus N.F. Tahoe N.F. Toiyabe N.F. *Yosemite N.P.	4,972,000	7.1

Conservation network	Approx. park area (hectares)	Potential cooperator(s)	Approx. network area (hectares)	Factor of increase
South Cascades	77,000	Clear Lake N.W.R. *Crater Lake N.P. Deschutes N.F. Fremont N.F. Klamath N.F. Klamath Forest N.W.R. *Lava Beds N.M. Lower Klamath N.W.R. Modoc N.F. Mt. Hood N.F. Rogue River N.F. Shasta N.F. Tule Lake N.W.R. Umpqua N.F. Upper Klamath N.W.R. Willamette N.F. Winema N.F.	4,859,000	63.1
North Cascades	299,000	Gifford Pinchot N.F. Lake Chelan N.R.A. Mt. Baker/Snoqualmie N.F. *Mt. Rainier N.P. *North Cascades N.P. Okanogan N.F. Ross Lake N.R.A. Wenatchee N.F.	3,239,000	10.8
Northern Continental Divide	410,000	Flathead N.F. *Glacier N.P. Helena N.F. Kaniksu N.F. Kootenai N.F. Lewis and Clark N.F. Lolo N.F.	2,987,000	7.3
Siskiyou	61,000	Klamath N.F. Mendocino N.F. Oregon Caves N.M. *Redwood N.P. Rogue River N.F. Shasta N.F. Siskiyou N.F. Six Rivers N.F. Trinity N.F.	2,914,000	47.8
Southern Appalachian Highlands	208,000	Chattahoochee N.F. Cherokee N.F. *Great Smokies N.P. Jefferson N.F. Nantahala N.F. Pisgah N.F.	2,399,000	11.5
Olympic	370,500	Olympic N.F. *Olympic N.P.	609,000	1.6
Black Hills	12,000	Black Hills N.F. *Jewel Cave N.M. *Wind Cave N.P.	565,000	47.1

Figure 9.1. Outlines of 10 potential conservation networks. National Parks used in park area calculations are shown in shading. Private inholdings are shown in black. See Table 9.1 for information on areas included in each network.

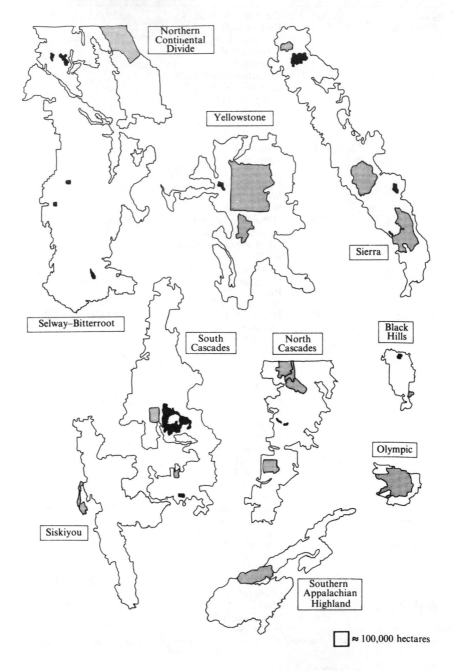

Furthermore, the network areas do not include all conceivable participants. They could be expanded by including Canadian parks as well as a
variety of additional protected and managed wildlands under federal
Bureau of Land Management, Department of Defense, state, county,
local, and private ownership. Finally, the 'core' areas we identify consist
of only National Park Service lands. This is deceptive since substantial
areas within national forests included in these hypothetical networks are
under equal, if not greater, protection due to their inclusion in the
recently created National Wilderness Preservation System.

In Figure 9.2, we evaluate these hypothetical conservation networks in
terms of their increased ability to protect wildlife populations.
Schonewald-Cox (1983) published regressions of census population size
against park area for three trophic levels of vertebrates. We use the
regression for large carnivorous mammals, which is based on estimates of
census (not effective) population sizes for 21 populations of seven species.
Several of these are averages of multiple year estimates. Because of the
variety of sources for these data, the regression should be interpreted as
providing only a rough estimate of area required for a population.

Figure 9.2 shows that these conservation networks would be far more

Figure 9.2. The effect of ideal cooperation on the potential of 10
conservation networks for protecting populations of large carnivores. See
text for information on data used.

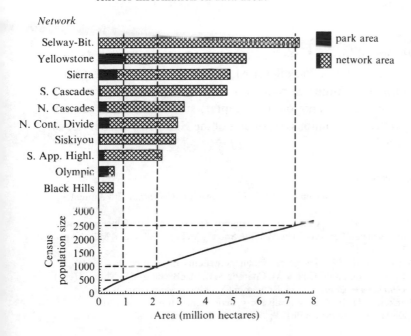

likely to protect a population of, say, 500 individuals of a large-bodied carnivore than would the 'core' area alone. A census size of 500 would likely translate to a relatively small effective population size. On the other hand, we might consider a census size on the order of 2500 individuals, which would be equivalent to a more substantial effective size. In only one case might maintenance of this size population be possible (recall the grizzly bear in Yellowstone).

Populations of vertebrates and other taxa that require large amounts of space will have a better chance for long-term survival in habitats without limits defined by jurisdictional borders. Perhaps most importantly, we will begin to view networks of lands under different ownerships and management policies as being able to sustain the structural and functional diversity of entire ecosystems while providing a steady flow of resources to local and regional economies.

The future for wildlife will be more secure if cooperating organizations can deemphasize the contrasts between their land use practices and draw on each other's special talents and facilities. Cooperation among land management organizations will be most easily achieved when there is a mutual accountability for the cooperative organization (as is the case with the Interagency Grizzly Bear Committee) and the cooperation is undertaken with a recognition that what is accomplished through this process can contribute to the ability of each organization to attain its own goals and objectives.

Acknowledgements

We wish to thank J. Bayless (National Park Service), J. Dennis (IGBC member, National Park Service), and C. Servheen (IGBC Chairman, US Fish and Wildlife Service) for their assistance. We are solely responsible for the contents of this chapter; statements made do not necessarily reflect the opinions or policies of the National Park Service or the US Forest Service.

References

Bureau of Land Management. 1983. *The Tule Elk in California*. 7th Annual Report to Congress.

Clark, T. W. 1985. Organizing for endangered species recovery. Paper presented at Northwest Section of The Wildlife Society Meeting, Missoula, MT. 4 April 1985. 14 pp.

Frankel, O. H. 1983. The place of management in conservation. Pp. 1–14 *in* C. M. Schonewald-Cox, S. M. Chambers, B. MacBryde, and L. Thomas (eds) *Genetics and Conservation*. Benjamin Cummings, Menlo Park, Calif.

Frankel, O. H. 1984. Genetic diversity, ecosystem conservation, and evolutionary responsibility. Pp. 414–27 *in* F. di Castri, F. W. G. Baker, and

M. Hadley, (eds.) *Ecology in Practice. Part I: Ecosystem Management.* Tycooly Int., Dublin and UNESCO, Paris.

Frankel, O. H. and Soulé, M. E. 1981. *Conservation and Evolution.* Cambridge University Press, Cambridge.

Harris, L. D. 1984. *The Fragmented Forest: Island Biogeography Theory and the Preservation of Biotic Diversity.* University of Chicago Press, Chicago.

Jenkins, R. E. 1984. Our partners in conservation. *Nature Conserv. News.* **34**(4): 4–7.

Kanter, R. 1983. *The Change Masters.* Simon and Schuster, New York.

MAB. 1973. Program on Man and the Biosphere (MAB). Expert Panel on Project 8: Conservation of natural areas and of the genetic material they contain. MAB Report Series No. 12, UNESCO.

MAB. 1974. Program on Man and the Biosphere (MAB). Task Force on Project 8: Criteria and guidelines for the choice and establishment of biosphere reserves. MAB Report Series No. 22, UNESCO and UNEP.

Newmark, W. D. 1985. Legal and biotic boundaries of western North American national parks: A problem of congruence. *Biol. Conserv.* **33**: 197–208.

Phillips, W. E. 1976. *The Conservation of the California Tule Elk.* University of Alberta Press, Edmonton.

Risser, P. G. and Cornelison, K. D. 1979. *Man and the Biosphere.* University of Oklahoma Press, Norman.

Salwasser, H., Mealey, S. P., and Johnson, K. 1984. Wildlife population viability – a question of risk. *Trans. N. Amer. Wildl. and Natural Resour. Conf.* **49**: 421–39.

Schonewald-Cox, C. M. 1983. Guidelines to management: A beginning attempt. Pp. 414–45 *in* C. M. Schonewald-Cox, S. M. Chambers, B. MacBryde, and L. Thomas (eds) *Genetics and Conservation.* Benjamin Cummings, Menlo Park, Calif.

Schonewald-Cox, C. M. and Bayless, J. W. in press. The boundary approach: A geographic analysis of design and conservation of nature reserves. *Biol. Cons.*

Servheen, C. 1984. The status of the grizzly bear and the interagency grizzly bear recovery effort. *Proc. Western Assoc. Fish and Game Commissioners.* Victoria, BC, Canada.

Shaffer, M. L. and F. B. Samson. 1985. Population size and extinction: A note on determining critical population sizes. *Am. Nat.* **125**(1): 144–52.

Soulé, M. E. 1980. Thresholds for survival: maintaining fitness and evolutionary potential. Pp. 151–70 *in M. E. Soulé and B. A. Wilcox (eds) Conservation Biology: An Evolutionary-Ecological Perspective.* Sinauer Associates, Sunderland, Mass.

Tule Elk Interagency Task Force 1979. A Management Plan for the Conservation of Tule Elk.

US Dept. of State 1982. Proceedings of the US Strategy Conference on Biological Diversity. Dept. State Pub. 9262.

Yaffee, S. L. 1982. *Prohibitive Policy: Implementing the Endangered Species Act.* MIT Press, Cambridge, Mass.

10

Where do we go from here?

MICHAEL E. SOULÉ
School of Natural Resources, University of Michigan, Ann Arbor, MI 48109-1115

The bottom line

Administrators, policy makers, and managers have a right to ask for the bottom line – in this context, the bottom line is the MVP for a 'typical' vertebrate. And biologists have the right and sometimes the obligation not to give an oversimplified, misleading answer to such a question (Soulé, 1986). Nevertheless, I think that scientists owe it to the rest of society to provide rules of thumb, even when they know that sometimes the rules will be misunderstood and misused.

Let's rephrase the question: When taking into account all of the relevant factors mentioned by the authors of this book, what is the lowest MVP that one might expect for a vertebrate? Here, I am assuming a 95% expectation of persistence, without loss of fitness, for several centuries.* My guess is that it would be in the low thousands. The bases for this order of magnitude number are theory and observation (empirical biogeography). Regarding observation, there isn't a lot of data, but it appears that populations with carrying capacities much smaller than this don't persist for very long, except, perhaps, in very constant environments, and even then will lose most of their variation.

Newmark (1986) has shown that the most consistent predictor of persistence of mammalian species in western US national parks is estimated population size at the time of establishment of the parks (averaging about 75 years ago). He has also compared the estimated, initial population sizes of surviving populations with those populations of the same species that have gone extinct. Some of his data are summarized in

---

* This is equivalent to a low level of risk, appropriate perhaps for the last population of an endangered species. Higher levels of risk are acceptable for individual subpopulations.

Table 10.1. *Comparison of estimated, initial, median sizes for extinct populations of lagomorphs, artiodactyls, large carnivores, and small carnivores with the estimated, initial median sizes for surviving populations in 24 western North American national parks and park assemblages. From Newmark (1986)*

Group	Extinct populations			Extant populations		
	Median population size	95% confidence interval	N	Median population size	95% confidence interval	N
Lagomorphs	3276	702–56 952	9	70 889	34 720–173 150	60
Artiodactyls	241	3–1273	7	792	429–1504	88
Large carnivores	24	14–68	16	108	70–146	153
Small carnivores	256	122–880	26	1203	908–1704	127

Table 10.1. The numbers vary over several orders of magnitude, depending on the taxon and trophic level. Nevertheless, the median initial sizes for most surviving populations fall within a range of one hundred to a few thousand. Surviving lagomorph populations are about two orders of magnitude higher, a probable effect of the legendary outbreak-crash population cycles in rabbits and hares. These figures are all minimum estimates because the extinctions have occurred in a relatively short time interval. Persistence for longer periods would probably require larger numbers.

Second, arguing from theory, several lines of analysis produce estimates of several thousand or larger (e.g., Leigh, 1981; Goodman, Chapter 2; Belovsky, Chapter 3). From a genetical perspective, an effective size of about 500 (Lande and Barrowclough, Chapter 6) will usually translate into a census size of several times this number, when taking into account all of the determining factors including age structure, sex ratio, variance in family size, and fluctuations in population size over time.

It is reassuring, on the one hand, that estimates for minimum MVPs for single, unmanaged populations are in the same ball park. On the other hand, these numbers have not stood the test of time. In any case, it is necessary to stress that MVPs will likely span a range of two or three orders of magnitude, and that anyone who applies the 'few thousand' estimate to a given species, citing this author as an authority, deserves all of the contempt that will be heaped on him or her. A viability analysis must be performed for each case, because each case is different. 'Few thousand' is not a rule-of-thumb. Rather, it is a possible, order of magnitude lower boundary (assuming the 95%, several centuries criterion). Estimates below this range should be an automatic signal for scrutiny.

There will be unusual situations where populations will persist for centuries, perhaps millennia, with numbers in the hundreds. For example, species for which reproduction is highly density dependent and that live in a very constant environment will be expected to persist a long time, even if most of their genetic variation is eroded (e.g., fish inhabiting desert springs in geologically stable areas). At the other extreme, species that are subject to wide swings in population size, such as lagomorphs, will have MVPs that are larger, by orders of magnitude.

At this point, two things bear repeating. First, in most cases, MVP estimates assume the absence of management, although they may contain corrections for certain, potential kinds of human disturbance such as poaching. Second, most MVPs will be so large that it will be impossible to contain this many individuals of a large animal in reserves and sanctuaries of modest size (up to thousands of km^2). This only serves to emphasize the importance in these cases of alternatives such as captive breeding (Chapter 8) and of the necessity of interagency cooperation (Chapter 9).

If asked what has been the most important result of viability analysis to date, I think that many would agree that it is contained in the preceding paragraph: MVPs are large, so large in fact that the only recourse in most situations will be to establish the species in several sites, since there won't be enough space in any given site (Chapters 2, 3, 4, and 5). For reasons discussed below, it is most desirable if these sites have uncorrelated environments, so that major environmental perturbations do not occur simultaneously, or with the same severity in each site. Precautionary quarantine is also inherent in this obvious strategy.

One possible misinterpretation of the above is that a given jurisdiction might be tempted to avoid responsibility for a critical species by arguing that their jurisdiction could not possibly sustain a viable population, and therefore it should not be required to cooperate in its preservation. Such a proposition is fallacious on several points, but it is most effectively countered with (1) the 'fairness doctrine' of shared responsibility, with (2) the effective population size argument: a small group may contribute significantly to the overall effective size of the population, and with (3) the negative biological argument of 'gap prevention' mentioned by Gilpin (Chapter 7) and in Chapter 1: gaps in the distribution of a species increase its overall vulnerability by reducing immigration and colonization rates between groups or patches, and by lowering effective population size.

Bottleneck size versus MVP

But what about the golden hamster (*Mesocricetus auratus*) and the northern elephant seal (*Mirounga angustirostris*)? That is, some species have gone through bottlenecks of just a few individuals, and are still around. Isn't this proof that much smaller MVPs are sometimes justified? No; there are some logical and evidential flaws in this argument. First, for endangered species, bottleneck size is the smallest number ever recorded, whereas MVP is the upper limit or ceiling of some regime. That is, these numbers usually represent the opposite extremes of a population's size through time; they should not be confused. When we say that the MVP for species *S* in place *P* is *Y*, we are saying that we must provide enough habitat area so that at least *Y* healthy individuals of *S* can exist in *P*. At the other extreme, the bottleneck size, *X*, is the *smallest* number of individuals ever observed for species *S* in place *P*, where *X* is usually much smaller than *Y*. (From demographic theory alone (Goodman, Chapter 2; Shaffer, Chapter 5), we know that populations cannot persist long at small size. Inbreeding during the bottleneck will only exacerbate demographic stochasticity, as described by Lande and Barrowclough in Chapter 6.)

More formally, in arguing from 'Some bottlenecks do not lead to immediate extinctions' to 'Bottlenecks do not lead to extinctions' we are guilty of the fallacy called fallacy of the accident. It consists of going from a qualified statement ('Some bottlenecks') to an unqualified one ('Bottlenecks'). Less formally, the fallacy is arguing that the observable exception (some populations survive extreme bottlenecks) contradicts the invisible rule. The rule (most bottlenecks have deleterious consequences) is empirically invisible because the only bottlenecked populations that can be observed in nature at a given point in time are the exceptions, the rare survivors. It is like arguing that most humans die in infancy because the only funeral I ever attended was that of a child.

The hamster example has already been shown to be very misleading – hamsters are very sensitive to inbreeding; furthermore, a single bottleneck in a species with a high *r* does not necessarily lead to a serious loss of genetic variation (Ralls and Ballou, 1982; Lande and Barrowclough, Chapter 6).

Finally, where it has been studied, a severe loss of genetic variability, probably associated with one or more bottlenecks, often leads to a noticeable decline in fitness. Ledig (1986) reviews the evidence for *Pinus torreyana*, and O'Brien *et al.* (1985) review the evidence for the cheetah. Exceptions are expected, in part because of the random distribution of deleterious alleles in gametes, and the finite, if small, probability that founders will have very few deleterious genes. In addition, some species may normally carry little genetic load (the frequency of deleterious alleles) by virtue of a chronically low effective population size. Such species will have a higher tolerance to bottlenecks. Pinnipeds are good candidates for such a tolerance because of the highly skewed sex ratio of breeding adults and its probable impact on effective population size (Chapter 6).

Are the theories any good?

How 'good' are the models presented in this volume? Anyone knowing the history of mathematical population biology and community ecology has to be a sceptic. The ground of these disciplines is littered with broken stick models, with discarded alpha matrices, and other strange and wonderful debris. Mathematical models serve as useful vehicles for thought, but it is foolish to hitch a bandwagon to any particular one. 'A huge variety of models can be invented, so one should not place too much faith on the results deriving from one . . . Real world people should be very cautious in placing too much reliance on this or that theoretical model.' (Warren Ewens, pers. comm.) The point is that models are tools for thinkers, not crutches for the thoughtless.

The theories described in this volume contain many simplifying assumptions. While assumptions are necessary for analysis, the results can be sensitive to changes in them. In the genetic models, for example, one of the critical assumptions is the rate of mutation for new, selectable genetic variation. If rates are higher, then the effective number of individuals needed to maintain variability for quantitative traits (Lande and Barrowclough, Chapter 6) is less; if lower, it is more.

Some categories of genetic variation are known, *a priori*, to have lower rates of mutation than the rate employed by Lande and Barrowclough (Chapter 6) for quantitative variation. Say, for example, that we wished to preserve some specific alleles at histocompatibility loci that were assumed to be important for resistance to rare, but lethal epidemic diseases. Mutation rates for specific alleles will be two or three orders of magnitude lower than those for quantitative variation, so the effective population size would have to be two or three orders of magnitude higher to maintain levels of heterozygosity for these and similar 'marker' loci. Therefore, if we were to base the genetic components of MVP models on the objective of maintaining the current frequencies of electrophoretic or other visible alleles, our MVP estimates would be much higher (Chapter 6). Indeed, such stratospheric MVPs are probably unrealistic biologically. For one thing, they ignore the strong, if episodic, selection that may often favor such alleles (current models don't incorporate such selection).

Some of the models described in this volume make the assumption that all individuals in the population are experiencing the same environment at the same time (Goodman, Chapter 1; Ewens, *et al.*, Chapter 4). For example, Ewens, *et al.* (Chapter 4) suggest that the extinction rates are relatively insensitive to population size, when considering only catastrophes. But this result may lean heavily on the assumption of perfect spatial environmental correlation.

A conservative effect of this assumption is to inflate MVPs in some species (Gilpin, Chapter 7). Where spatial correlations are high, say for small or relatively sessile organisms living in a homogeneous environment, most disturbances will affect all of the individuals in more or less the same way. But if we are dealing with a population that is distributed rather widely (in two or more watersheds, for example), then many perturbations such as storms, floods, or fires will affect only part of the population. Larger animals are also better able to find and migrate to patches of good habitat during inclement conditions.

As a result, we might expect large mammals to persist longer than Goodman's model predicts, but Belovsky's projections (Chapter 3) indicate the opposite. There could be many explanations for this, but the one that springs immediately to mind is the genetic one – populations of large mammals, reptiles, and birds may persist long enough at low effective size to enter the vicious circles of inbreeding and loss of selectable genetic variation (Gilpin and Soulé, 1986). These vortices reduce r and N_e still further, increasing the rate of inbreeding, and so on.

It is clear that we are not yet at the point where we can plug in some species-specific parameters to a formula and come up with a reliable MVP estimate. Nonetheless, we can make order of magnitude estimates, and this is a vast improvement over the situation just 10 years ago.

The important point is that a mature viability analysis is one that integrates all of the factors in a biologically realistic way. It is misleading, therefore, to frame the issue in such terms as 'Which is more important, genetics or population dynamics?' These are not isolated, additive factors, though we may decide to treat them that way in the early stages of analysis, or for pedagogical reasons.

One possible direction for the integration of population dynamics and genetics is the study of the effects of inbreeding and the loss of genetic variation on r and its variance. r is a critical parameter in most viability analyses, so it may be possible to collapse many of the genetic factors affecting fitness into this parameter.

There is another challenge regarding the interaction between genetics and population dynamics – it is to increase our understanding of the consequences of age structure and overlapping generations on effective population size. Some effects of age structure increase effective size, while others may reduce it. The matter may be too complex for analytical solution, but it is ripe for simulation studies.

Hopeless cases

There are no hopeless cases, only people without hope and expensive cases. That is, given the resources, even a handful of individuals can constitute the basis of a successful effort to salvage a population or species. Recall that a short-term bottleneck, itself, does not reduce genetic variation nearly as much as most people's intuition suggests. The real danger is random demographic or environmental events or diseases that can easily wipe out a population while it is still small.

When genetic variation is lost by genetic drift or inbreeding, it can eventually be regenerated by mutation, assuming that the population can grow to a reasonably large size (Lande and Barrowclough, Chapter 6). In theory there should be no difficulty in saving endangered species like the black-footed ferret (*Mustela nigripes*) or the California condor (*Gymnogyps californianus*), assuming they can be bred successfully in captivity. Some will decry the loss of the 'wild culture' of such species that must be temporarily confined in unnatural surroundings. We must consider, however, that it is often the existing behavior patterns that brought them into conflict with humans in the first place, and that some alternative behaviors might serve them better in the future. Better captively bred dinosaurs, trained to roar at tourists in Disneyland, than the present alternative.

It would be cavalier to quickly dismiss the difficulties in saving a large, rare species. But the difficulties will usually be economic and institutional, not biological. For one thing, it is very expensive to care for one rhinoceros, let alone several hundred. In the future, perhaps, lay enthusiasts can be recruited to participate in the captive breeding of large creatures, keeping one or two on their farms, just as thoroughbred horses and parrots are kept and bred today by thousands of non-biologists. This would require some courageous legislation and leadership.

Research

Models and computers won't take us very far unless we have good data to check them against. We need several kinds: (1) retrospective studies examining the likelihood of extinction of isolated populations as a function of such variables as carrying capacity of the site and past climatic variability; (2) long-term studies of extant populations, with annual monitoring of demographic (N, r) and genetic parameters including N_e, heritabilities of quantitative traits, and gene frequencies at marker loci; (3) comparative genetic and demographic studies of very small and large populations of the same species in order to detect the effects of inbreeding; (4) studies of metapopulation dynamics, especially in species such as insects and annuals with a high rate of population turnover. In addition, we have reached the stage where laboratory studies of extinction could be informative.

The beauty of doing research on vulnerability is that it abolishes the distinction between pure and applied science, and it is thereby more satisfying than is either alone. The authors of this book hope that many other biologists are enticed by the opportunities offered by the viable population problem to contribute something of value to science as well as to the world.

Implementation

Some will be disappointed that this book contains no simple prescriptions for calculating MVPs. The principal reason for this is the complexity of the biological world. Simply put, species are too diverse in their life histories, ecological relations, and distributions.

The state of the art, then, is a case by case analysis, taking into account the existing body of theory (as described in this book) and the available information about each situation. As our information grows, and as the number of case histories accumulates, the situation will change. Probably within a decade or so, the experience of managers and field biologists, along with the continuing efforts of theoreticians and modelers, will facilitate the development of generalizable protocols for the estimation of MVPs. There are already some efforts in this direction (Salwasser *et al.*, 1983).

References

Gilpin, M. E. and Soulé, M. E. 1986. Minimum Viable Populations: the processes of species extinctions. Pp. 13–34 *in* M. E. Soulé (ed.) *Conservation Biology: Science of Scarcity and Diversity*. Sinauer Associates, Sunderland, Mass.

Ledig, F. T. 1986. Heterozygosity, heterosis, and fitness in outbreeding plants. Pp. 77–104 *in* M. E. Soulé (ed.) *Conservation Biology: Science of Scarcity and Diversity*. Sinauer Associates, Sunderland, Mass.

Leigh, E. G. 1981. The average lifetime of a population in a varying environment. *J. Theor. Biol.* **90**: 213–39.

Newmark, W. D. 1986. Mammalian richness, colonization, and extinction in Western North American National Parks. Ph.D. Dissertation, University of Michigan, Ann Arbor, Mich.

O'Brien, S. J., Roelke, M. E., Marker, L., Newman, A., Winkler, C. A., Meltzer, K. D., Colly, L., Evermann, J. F., Bush, M., and Wildt, D. E. 1985. Genetic basis for species vulnerability in the cheetah. *Science* **227**: 1428–34.

Ralls, K. and Ballou, J. 1982. Effects of inbreeding on juvenile mortality in some small mammal species. *Lab. Anim.* **16**: 159–66.

Salwasser, H., Mealey, S. P., and Johnson, K. 1983. Wildlife population viability – a question of risk. *Trans. N. Am. Wildl. Natur. Res. Conf.* **48**: 421–37.

Soulé, M. E. 1986. Conservation biology and the 'real world.' Pp. 1–12 *in* M. E. Soulé (ed.) *Conservation Biology: Science of Scarcity and Diversity*. Sinauer Associates, Sunderland, Mass.

Index